When Minoritized Languages Change Linguistic Theory

For decades, a small set of major world languages have formed the basis of the vast majority of linguistic theory. However, minoritized languages can also provide fascinating contributions to our understanding of the human language faculty. This pioneering book explores the transformative effect that minoritized languages have on mainstream linguistic theory. With their typologically unfamilar syntactic, morphological, and phonological properties, these languages challenge and question frameworks that were developed largely to account for more widely studied languages. The chapters address the four main pillars of linguistic theory – syntax, semantics, phonology, and morphology – and provide a broad range of case studies to show how minoritized language can disrupt assumptions and lead to modifications of the theory itself. It is illustrated with examples from a range of languages and is written in an engaging and accessible style, making it essential reading for both students and researchers of theoretical syntax, phonology and morphology, and language policy and politics.

ANDREW NEVINS is Professor of Language Sciences at University College London. He is the author of *Locality in Vowel Harmony* (MIT Press, 2010) and coauthor of *Morphotactics: The Structure of Spellout and Basque Auxiliaries* (Springer, 2012).

When Minoritized Languages Change Linguistic Theory

Andrew Nevins
University College London and Universidade Federal do Rio de Janeiro

Shaftesbury Road, Cambridge CB2 8EA, United Kingdom

One Liberty Plaza, 20th Floor, New York, NY 10006, USA

477 Williamstown Road, Port Melbourne, VIC 3207, Australia

314–321, 3rd Floor, Plot 3, Splendor Forum, Jasola District Centre, New Delhi – 110025, India

103 Penang Road, #05–06/07, Visioncrest Commercial, Singapore 238467

Cambridge University Press is part of Cambridge University Press & Assessment, a department of the University of Cambridge.

We share the University's mission to contribute to society through the pursuit of education, learning and research at the highest international levels of excellence.

www.cambridge.org
Information on this title: www.cambridge.org/9781009014892

DOI: 10.1017/9781009029889

© Andrew Nevins 2022

This publication is in copyright. Subject to statutory exception and to the provisions of relevant collective licensing agreements, no reproduction of any part may take place without the written permission of Cambridge University Press & Assessment.

First published 2022
First paperback edition 2025

A catalogue record for this publication is available from the British Library

Library of Congress Cataloging-in-Publication data
Names: Nevins, Andrew, author.
Title: When minoritized languages change linguistic theory / Andrew Nevins.
Description: Cambridge, United Kingdom ; New York, NY : Cambridge
  University Press, 2022. | Includes bibliographical references and index.
Identifiers: LCCN 2022031357 (print) | LCCN 2022031358 (ebook) |
  ISBN 9781316516379 (hardback) | ISBN 9781009014892 (paperback) |
  ISBN 9781009029889 (epub)
Subjects: LCSH: Linguistic minorities–Case studies. | Linguistics. |
  BISAC: LANGUAGE ARTS & DISCIPLINES / General
Classification: LCC P40.5.L56 N48 2022 (print) | LCC P40.5.L56 (ebook) |
  DDC 410–dc23/eng/20220917
LC record available at https://lccn.loc.gov/2022031357
LC ebook record available at https://lccn.loc.gov/2022031358

ISBN   978-1-316-51637-9   Hardback
ISBN   978-1-009-01489-2   Paperback

Cambridge University Press & Assessment has no responsibility for the persistence or accuracy of URLs for external or third-party internet websites referred to in this publication and does not guarantee that any content on such websites is, or will remain, accurate or appropriate.

CAMBRIDGE
UNIVERSITY PRESS

Shaftesbury Road, Cambridge CB2 8EA, United Kingdom

One Liberty Plaza, 20th Floor, New York, NY 10006, USA

477 Williamstown Road, Port Melbourne, VIC 3207, Australia

314–321, 3rd Floor, Plot 3, Splendor Forum, Jasola District Centre, New Delhi – 110025, India

103 Penang Road, #05–06/07, Visioncrest Commercial, Singapore 238467

Cambridge University Press is part of Cambridge University Press & Assessment, a department of the University of Cambridge.

We share the University's mission to contribute to society through the pursuit of education, learning and research at the highest international levels of excellence.

www.cambridge.org
Information on this title: www.cambridge.org/9781009014892

DOI: 10.1017/9781009029889

© Andrew Nevins 2022

This publication is in copyright. Subject to statutory exception and to the provisions of relevant collective licensing agreements, no reproduction of any part may take place without the written permission of Cambridge University Press & Assessment.

First published 2022
First paperback edition 2025

A catalogue record for this publication is available from the British Library

Library of Congress Cataloging-in-Publication data
Names: Nevins, Andrew, author.
Title: When minoritized languages change linguistic theory / Andrew Nevins.
Description: Cambridge, United Kingdom ; New York, NY : Cambridge
  University Press, 2022. | Includes bibliographical references and index.
Identifiers: LCCN 2022031357 (print) | LCCN 2022031358 (ebook) |
  ISBN 9781316516379 (hardback) | ISBN 9781009014892 (paperback) |
  ISBN 9781009029889 (epub)
Subjects: LCSH: Linguistic minorities–Case studies. | Linguistics. |
  BISAC: LANGUAGE ARTS & DISCIPLINES / General
Classification: LCC P40.5.L56 N48 2022 (print) | LCC P40.5.L56 (ebook) |
  DDC 410–dc23/eng/20220917
LC record available at https://lccn.loc.gov/2022031357
LC ebook record available at https://lccn.loc.gov/2022031358

ISBN   978-1-316-51637-9   Hardback
ISBN   978-1-009-01489-2   Paperback

Cambridge University Press & Assessment has no responsibility for the persistence or accuracy of URLs for external or third-party internet websites referred to in this publication and does not guarantee that any content on such websites is, or will remain, accurate or appropriate.

When Minoritized Languages Change Linguistic Theory

Andrew Nevins
University College London and Universidade Federal do Rio de Janeiro

Dedicated to Julio Magaña-Saludado, whose intellectual impact on me has finally resulted in this project.

There is only one language, called human – with many dialects.
— Victor Manfredi.

Contents

List of Figures		*page* ix
Acknowledgements		xi
List of Abbreviations		xii
Map		xiv
1	Expanding the Canon: Minoritization in the World and in Linguistic Theory	1
2	Indexical Shift in Zazaki and Uyghur	10
	2.1 With an Eye and an Ear towards Zazaki	10
	2.2 Indexical Shifting in Zazaki	12
	2.3 The Consequences of an Overwriting Operator	16
	2.4 Two Kinds of Embedding in Uyghur	20
	2.5 Towards an Implicational Hierarchy of Shifting Patterns	23
3	Why Ergative Case Requires Structure in Basque and Ch'ol	26
	3.1 A Sole Survivor	26
	3.2 'A' Is for Agent	27
	3.3 When Ergative Can Be Removed or Imposed	32
	3.4 Splitting Hairs: The Progressive Aspect	35
	3.5 How the Mayan Language Ch'ol Thickened the Plot	38
4	Closest Conjunct Agreement in Slovenian and Xhosa	42
	4.1 *Has the woman who coffee is happy?	42
	4.2 Data Is Not the Plural of Anecdote	46
	4.3 So Where Can Linearity Prevail over Hierarchy?	51
	4.4 A Two-Step Theory of Agreement	55
	4.5 Southern Bantu: Nonbinary Gender to the Seventh Power	56
5	Configurationality of Objects in Chichewa and Warlpiri	61
	5.1 Rethinking Direct Objects	61
	5.2 Symmetries within Bantu Applicatives	66
	5.3 Transfer-of-Possession Is a Low Matter	71
	5.4 Warlpiri: A 'Nonconfigurational' Language with Asymmetric Objects	74
	5.5 Be Wary of Flatland	81

viii   Contents

6   Partial Nasality in Maxakalí and Kaingang   84
    6.1   What My DoktorGroßVater Proposed, and What He Didn't
          Have a Chance to See   84
    6.2   The Trouble with /b/   87
    6.3   Enhancement Theory and Hypervoicing   90
    6.4   Nasal Shielding   91
    6.5   On the Timing of Contoured Consonants   93

7   Symmetric Hands in Sign Language Phonologies   99
    7.1   Sociohistorical Variation as a Window onto Sign
          Language Structure   99
    7.2   From Cheremes to the Asymmetry of the Two Hands   103
    7.3   A Paucity of Unmarked Shapes of the Base Hand   109
    7.4   The Feature [+bimanual] in Minimal Pairs and Allophony   116
    7.5   Empirical Contributions of Black ASL Phonology to the Model   122
    7.6   Modeling the Restricted Status of H_2: Features vs. Prosody   128
    7.7   Conclusion   134

8   Number-Encoding on Verbs in Hiaki and Chechen   137
    8.1   Roots and Suppletion: How Marginal?   137
    8.2   The Subset Principle: Back to Warlpiri   138
    8.3   Speech Errors to the Rescue   140
    8.4   Going and Wending in Hiaki   143
    8.5   When Suppletion Is Based on Morphosyntactic Features   149
    8.6   Suppletion beyond Uto-Aztecan Verbs   153
    8.7   Uncountable Mass Events in Chechen   156
    8.8   Mass and Count in Dëne Sųłiné   159

9   Conclusion: Towards Healthy Futures in the Language Sciences   163
    9.1   The Argument So Far   163
    9.2   On Unattested Chapters in This Version of This Book   165
    9.3   The Value of Inclusivity, and Rethinking Aspects
          of Our Discipline   168
    9.4   When Minoritized Languages Change Linguists' Daily Work   171

Bibliography   175
Index   193

Figures

1.1	The Müller-Lyer illusion, in which the right line appears longer to some populations	4
2.1	A sequence of events in Zazaki doubly reported speech	18
3.1	Schematic of ergative vs. nominative alignment	28
4.1	Alexander Calder's spinning mobiles: hierarchically structured with no fixed linear order	45
4.2	Rates of highest conjunct agreement vs. closest conjunct agreement in South Slavic	49
4.3	Predictions of distal conjunct agreement given flat vs. hierarchical structures for &P	50
4.4	Results of asymmetries in distal conjunct agreement for SV and VS configurations	50
4.5	Principal Component Analysis showing clusters of morphosyntactic relatedness	52
6.1	Nasalance track of prenasalization in Maxakalí voiced stop loanwords: Solid line is nasal intensity; dotted line is oral intensity	89
6.2	Earbud methodology for nasalance	89
7.1	Minimal pairs based on handshape, place of articulation, and movement (Klima & Bellugi, 1979, figure 2.2, p. 42)	106
7.2	Peripheralization of ALIVIO by the signer on the right (Xavier, 2014)	107
7.3	The two-handed BSL alphabet	110
7.4	Battison's proposed seven unmarked NDH base handshapes	111
7.5	NDH classifier for airplane in NGT (Crasborn, 2011)	113
7.6	Diachronic change towards base hand symmetry in ASL 'DEPEND' (Klima & Bellugi, 1979, figure 3.7, p. 78)	115
7.7	Minimal pair for [+bimanual]: ASL 'SAME' vs. 'MEASURE' (Klima & Bellugi, 1979, figure 2.11, p. 50)	116
7.8	Reciprocalized semantics in 'LOOK-AT' by derivational [+bimanual] (Klima & Bellugi, 1979, figure 12.4, p. 280)	117
7.9	Alternating [+bimanual] signs start with DH: ASL 'TO MILK' (Padden & Perlmutter, 1987)	117

7.10 Weak Drop in ASL 'INTERESTING' yields neutralization with 'LIKE' — 118
7.11 Two-Handed vs. one-handed versions of 'DON'T KNOW' in BASL (McCaskill et al., 2011) — 124
7.12 Deletion of [+facial] in BASL 'TEACHER' (McCaskill et al., 2011) — 126
7.13 Two-handed signs with [contact] or [alternating] resist Weak Drop in ASL (Brentari, 1998) — 129
7.14 Assimilation of [+bimanual] in connected discourse (Xavier, 2014) — 130
7.15 Slip of the hand: Anticipation of [+bimanual] (Klima & Bellugi, 1979, figure 5.7, p. 135) — 131
7.16 Assimilation of [+bimanual] in compounding (Gu, 2018) — 131
7.17 Slip of the hand involving metathesis of nonmoving identical H_2 specification (Klima & Bellugi, 1979, figure 5.4, p. 132) — 132

Acknowledgements

My profoundest thanks to John Bailyn and the participants at the 2018 NYI during a lovely summer in St. Petersburg, who provided the opportunity to first assemble this material for a course I offered – specifically in response to the thoughts stirred in me during an installment of the same school. Over a decade earlier, a few students had earnestly asked me whether it was true when they had been told that "Generative Grammar was designed only to work for English." These chapters develop and provide my most detailed attempts to answer their question as broadly as possible.

Thanks to Yasutada Sudo, Maria Kouneli, Matt Coler, Travis Major, Amy Rose Deal, Camelia Muldermans, Livia Camargo Souza, Peter Msaka, Andrew Bevis, Jessica Coon, Karlos Arregi, Jenneke van der Wal, Hazel Mitchley, Eviana Hartman, Andre Xavier, Adam Singerman, Diane Stoianov, Jill Morford, Josh Birchall, Gabrielle Hodge, and Jeffrey Parrott for extremely valuable feedback on earlier versions of these chapters.

Cover Art: Sabrina Pintos

Abbreviations

SUBJ	subject
OBJ	object
AGR	agreement
FV	final vowel
SR	switch reference marker
ASP	aspect
PERF	perfect
IMPF	imperfect
PRFV	perfective
IMPFV	imperfective
PROG	progressive
PRES	present
NONPST	nonpast
FUT	future
EVID	evidential
CNTF	counterfactual
NONFACT	nonfactive
PLURACT	pluractional
AUX	auxiliary
PTCP	participle
INF	infinitive
FEM, F	feminine
MASC, M	masculine
NEUT, N	neuter
PL	plural
SG	singular
DL	dual
DFLT	default
ERG	ergative
ACC	accusative
DAT	dative

List of Abbreviations

ALLAT	allative
ABS	absolutive
NOM	nominative
GEN	genitive
OBL	oblique
1	first person
2	second person
3	third person
I,II,III,...X,...	noun classes (in Bantu)
AUTH	author
ADDR	addressee
LOC	locative
BEN	beneficiary
INST	instrumental
NMLZ	nominalizer
REL	relativizer
DEF	definite
t	trace (of syntactic movement)
C	complementizer node
T	tense node
Top	topic
Foc	focus
$\forall$	for all
CCA	Closest Conjunct Agreement
HCA	Highest Conjunct Agreement

Map

Map Locations

1. Diyarbakır, Turkey
2. Ürümqi, China
3. Ladainha, Brazil
4. Nonoai, Brazil
5. Gernika, Spain
6. Tila, Mexico
7. Solkan, Slovenia
8. Makhanda, South Africa
9. Zomba, Malawi
10. Alice Springs, Australia
11. Great Plains, USA
12. Black ASL, USA
13. Tucson, USA
14. Great Slave Lake, Canada

Map locations generated using maps.google.com

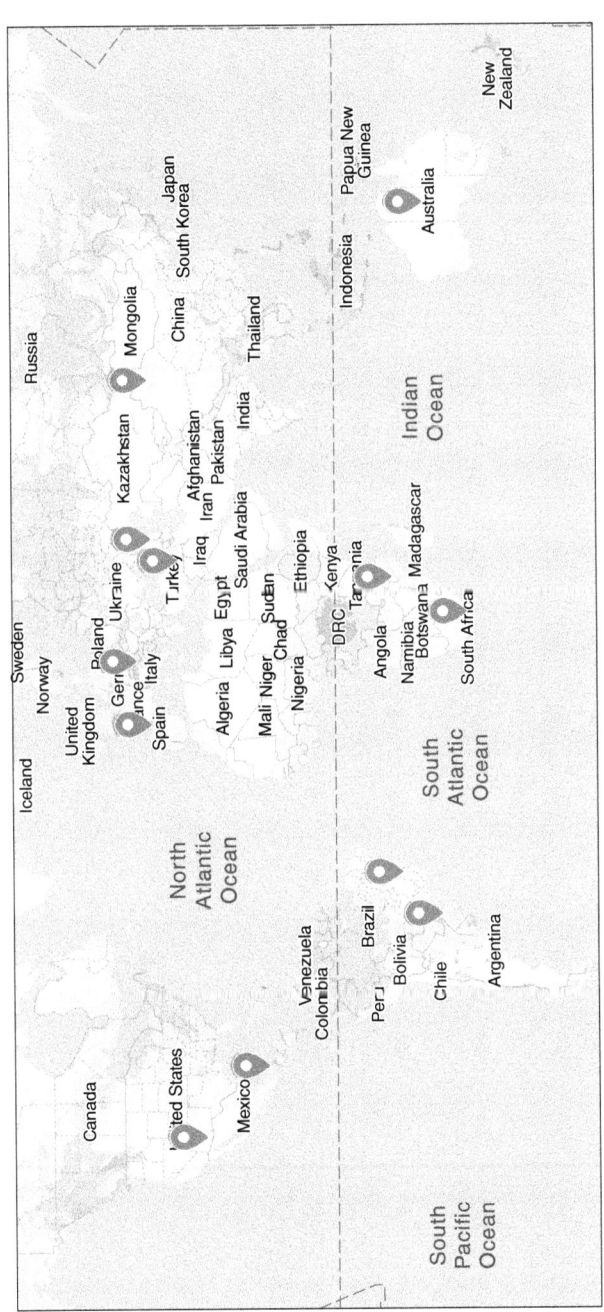

1   Expanding the Canon
Minoritization in the World and in Linguistic Theory

> Narrowness in observation protects narrowness in theory.
>   – Wolfgang Köhler

You are about to begin reading a new book with a less evocative title than *If on a Winter's Night, a Traveler*. But as that book's author Calvino would tell you: Just the same, Relax. Concentrate. Dispel every other thought. Let the world around you fade. Best to close the door; it's been said before, the TV is always on in the next room. Tell the others right away, "No, I don't want to watch TV!" Raise your voice – they won't hear you otherwise – "I'm reading! I don't want to be disturbed!" Maybe they haven't heard you, with all that racket. Speak louder, yell: "I'm beginning to read about minoritized languages and linguistic theory!" Or if you prefer, don't say anything. Make sure the page isn't in shadow.

    What follows is written with the starting viewpoint that the field of linguistics is closely related to the science of psychology. As such, to understand the human mind, we must understand language. And to understand language, we must adopt the same methodology successfully applied to other faculties of the human mind. The title of this book reflects the fact that, far beyond the well-studied set including English, German, Dutch, Russian, Japanese, Italian, and Spanish that formed the original basis for linguistic theory, minoritized languages (see below on this term and how it differs from 'minority' languages) – languages spoken by smaller populations, or languages that are not even official national languages – nonetheless have transformative effects on our understanding of the human language faculty. Instead of merely demonstrating that contemporary syntactic, semantic, phonological, and morphological theory can 'handle' phenomena found in lesser-studied languages, this book brings forth cases in which data from such languages actually change linguistic theory, creating discomfort and a reshuffling of assumptions that eventually leads to modifications of the theory itself. The twin goals of this book, aimed at a broad readership, are to showcase specific developments in linguistic theory based on minoritized languages that are of inherent interest to researchers across domains, as well as to establish the overarching argument that just because a given language is not an official national language does not make it any less interesting in terms of its potential contributions to science – and often quite the contrary.

Why have I written such a book? In many corners of the world one can hear uttered the lament that "generative grammar was invented only for English" (given that Chomsky's [1957] *Syntactic Structures* did focus almost exclusively on English). Even so, in the following four decades, languages such as Russian, Spanish, Italian, German, Dutch, and Japanese contributed greatly to the development of syntactic theory, and even early developments within generative grammar, such as Matthews (1965) and Postal (1963), were based on indigenous North American languages. Hale (1967) evaluated these works as providing "indication of the extent to which a linguist working in the generative transformational framework can succeed in making interesting and significant statements about the grammatical structure of a language not his own" (p. 332). Nonetheless, the supposition persists that when generative linguistic theory is 'applied' to understudied minoritized languages, researchers might simply be paying lip-service to such languages or attempting to shoehorn them into existing molds so as to preserve the outlines of the theory. To choose just one citation, Foley and Valin (1984) assert, "We do not regard the structure of one language type as prototypical and other types as deviations from this prototype, a position often associated with current alternative models of grammatical description such as Government and Binding Theory," and that "much current and recent theorizing has depended too heavily on English and familiar European languages, with the result that this theorizing has been biased in favor of languages of essentially one grammatical type" (p. xii).[1] The aim of this book is to thoroughly debunk this conception and to showcase over a dozen well-entrenched moments in the recent history of the field in which generative linguistic theory has actively reformulated the notion of possible and representative linguistic structure based on compelling findings from non-familiar, and indeed minoritized, languages.

Right from the first case study presented in the book, Zazaki Kurdish, it is shown that a type of reported-speech structure so unfamiliar to philosophers of language that David Kaplan called it a 'monster' is nonetheless robustly attested and requires serious modifications to our notions of what a possible language is and how languages syntactically achieve clausal embedding of attitude reports. Reported speech in Zazaki Kurdish represents the kind of 'monstrous' construction in natural language that has not gone ignored but rather has spurred a wealth of further research in a range of typologically diverse languages to understand the limits of and variation in such kinds of reported speech constructions. This is truly a case in which a minoritized language has

---

[1] I have selected this citation as one proposition that can be clearly evaluated, chosen among a wide spectrum of claims with similar sentiment, from the meek questions by students in St. Petersburg (whom I thank in the acknowledgements) to hyperbolistic affirmations such as Olson (1977) who claims that "Chomsky's theory is not a theory of language generally ... It is a model for the structure of autonomous written prose" (p. 272).

completely reshaped our theory of the way that speech reports are mentally represented, which would not have occurred without taking the contribution of minoritized languages seriously. This book showcases seven chapters of such case studies, drawn from around the globe and contributing to all subareas of linguistic theory.

These choices very much reflect my own attempts to answer the question of when minoritized languages have wrought the most compelling changes in linguistic theory. These chapters can be read in essentially any order. They may be taken like one of those lists of great films that your friends might recommend for you, which usually come in no prescribed sequence but resonate with aspects of their own biographies. (After all, the reason I was born in Santa Fe was because my parents had just moved to New Mexico to work with the Navajo.) I harbor no doubt that somebody else, were they to attempt to answer the same question of when minoritized languages steered linguistic theory in wholly new directions, might come up with an entirely different and equally valid set of case studies. (At least, this is what I take away from the answer to the question posed about "Life, the Universe, and Everything" in *The Hitchhiker's Guide to the Galaxy* – where "42" was one of many equally valid possible answers.) Like all such answers, they reflect in part my own biases, expertise, and familiarity. As for me, I have often found myself more fulfilled in thatched dwellings than ivory towers. My greatest moments of connection with language enthusiasts have not necessarily been the ones at All Souls' College, the Institut Jean Nicod, Johns Hopkins University, or Goethe University Frankfurt but rather the ones with a group of whistling shepherds in a darkened local mayors' office on a Greek isle, an isolated group of deaf homesigners in the desert backlands of northeast Brazil, or an audience of all-African academics in Mozambique struggling to cast off a still-colonial tongue. Some of the case studies in this book reflect my personal experiences in attempting to highlight the scientific relevance of minoritized languages to the speakers of these languages, valorizing the pertinence of their linguistic identities even when the details may sit uncomfortably with existing theories and require dialogue and revision. Other case studies involve what might be considered by-now canonical, 'greatest hits' of successful marriages between minoritized languages and linguistic theory. The goal is to provide a representative smattering of what has been done, more than anything else, as a means of continuing to invite and point towards what I consider to be healthy futures for continued linguistic work.

We must acknowledge that it is cavalier to pose and respond to questions of human nature on the basis of data drawn from thin and rather unusual slices of humanity (Henrich et al., 2010) as they are not really representative of how the numerical majority of humans do, have, or will live, and they may have been influenced – or I daresay corrupted – by systems that don't apply

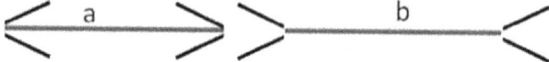

Figure 1.1 The Müller-Lyer illusion, in which the right line appears longer to some populations

to everyone. As comparative and typological work has always suggested, the number of similarities across all languages of all peoples, past and present, is quite large. But there has been a continued extension of theoretical findings outward, on the implicit assumption that work on a handful of languages that contingently have greater institutional access, support, and convenience to researchers will generalize broadly. In research, the very set of questions or assumptions to be posed often originates from the implicit linguistic biases of the researchers themselves. To cite a well-known example of this phenomenon from outside linguistics, Segall et al. (1966) found that the famous Müller-Lyer visual illusion, in which two lines of equal length have inward and outward-facing arrows and the latter usually appears longer, was not an illusion at all for San foragers of the Kalahari (nor for a variety of other worldwide populations) (Figure 1.1).

Why did the San foragers not perceive the illusion the same way as the humans who were tested in North America and Europe? The explanation is a matter of interest in itself. As Henrich et al. (2010) discuss, one interpretation of these results is that "carpentered corners of modern environments favor optical calibrations and visual habits that create and perpetuate this illusion" (p. 4). But the broader finding, regardless of the explanation, is that one cannot use the Müller-Lyer illusion to make broad claims about the way the human visual system works based on the assumption that the illusory results for European populations represent the default and the others a deviation from the baseline. Perhaps quite the contrary is true; across psychology, and our subsequent understanding of many social sciences as well, the results observed with people who do experiments in Europe might be *un*representative of many aspects of human nature if we wish to make claims about human tendencies, past, present, and future.

In much more subtle ways, the same may be true for the very formulation of indexical shift in pronouns, as found in Zazaki Kurdish, as a 'deviation' from the expected maintenance of references in indirect discourse – particular versions of written texts and written registers are products of particular cultural trajectories in Western, educated, industrialized, rich, and/or democratic (WEIRD) societies and not part of most environments for most of human history. Kiparsky (1995) suggests that the particular syntactic structures for finite embedding in what we might call European WEIRD languages (and which have determined the baseline for syntactic theories about the complementizer layer in syntax) may reflect one particular historical outcome of the lottery – and this outcome happened to be spoken in and around the same country as where the printing press originated. As but one more potential example of how it may be that Western European languages are 'weird' compared to others, consider Dahl's (1990) observation that "inversion as a device for marking yes–no questions seems to be rather infrequent outside Europe" (p. 4). I should stress that I do not necessarily subscribe to Henrich et al.'s (2010) classification of what they call WEIRD cultures or languages as holding a typological cluster of common properties – in fact, linguistic structure has so many distinct levels that I would consider it impossible to cluster any large group of languages in terms of similarity metrics (do we privilege morphosyntax and ignore the stark differences between, say, the vowel systems of French and Spanish?). But I fully embrace Henrich et al.'s (2010) *methodological* point that we cannot rely on the convenience of samples of students and languages in our university classrooms as broadly representative of humanity and must be aware that an all-too-easy "lack of epistemic vigilance underscores the prevalent, though implicit, assumption that the findings one derives from a particular sample will generalize broadly" (p. 3).

It's still an empirical question and one that requires not only stronger empirical foundations of the language sciences but stronger connections betweeen observations and theory – including theories of social dynamics and interaction, where relevant. Lupyan and Dale (2010), based on a statistical analysis of more than 2,000 languages, suggest that the overall traits of individual languages, such as their level of morphological complexity, may be related to demographic and sociohistorical factors: Languages spoken by large groups have morphological structures with fewer case distinctions and less verbal inflection for grammatical categories such as negation, evidentiality, and aspect, than languages spoken by smaller groups. Why should this be? Languages spoken by large groups (often ones that minoritize others) are more likely to include adult learners of the language (this has certainly been historically true for English, Spanish, French, German, and so on), and as a result, features of language structure that are harder for adults to learn are more likely to disappear over generations of language use. Similarly, Wray and Grace (2007) suggest that certain types of compositionality in the structures of many of the more familiar languages today are the gradual result of the 'exoteric' nature (larger speaker populations, greater geographical coverage, and greater degree of contact with other languages) of most modern languages, rather than being a defining characteristic of human language per se. They liken making conclusions about the human language faculty disproportionally on the basis of the languages most easily and most often studied today to trying to work out how humans jump over horizontal obstacles on the sole basis of watching the high jump event at the Olympic Games.[2]

Let's take one more example from cognitive psychology. Classic studies on construals of others' dispositions and cognitive strategies, originally based on Western participants, argued that 'people' (i.e., humans in general) tend to make strong attributions about the core dispositions of an individual and ignore compelling situational constraints specific to certain moments. This led to a cognitive theory called the fundamental attribution error (Ross et al., 1977), whereby, say if Alice, a driver, is cut off in traffic by Bob, she attributes Bob's behavior to his fundamental personality (e.g., he thinks only of himself, he is selfish, he is a jerk, or he is an unskilled driver), instead of considering it as situational (e.g., he is going to miss his flight, his wife is giving birth at the hospital, and so on). This became enshrined as a cornerstone of psychology, until, in subsequent comparative ethnography (e.g., Choi et al., [1999]), it was discovered that non-Western populations found contextual beliefs more strongly endorsed than personality in experimental scenarios. This work changed the theory according to which the fundamental attribution error was such a fundamental and constant aspect of the model of what people tend to think – in essence, the status of this claim about pan-human psychology was an artifact of having done the experiments with North Americans first. Could the semantic formalization of contextual parameters governing indexical expressions like *I, now* in embedded speech reports have started on the foot it did because of having started with English? Where might we be by now if philosophers had started writing things down with Zazaki's linguistic patterns at hand in 1977?

To take one more instructive case from the behavioral sciences, Nowak et al. (2000) construct an evolutionary-theoretic analysis for the 'Ultimatum Game' in decision and game theory. In the Ultimatum Game, two players are offered a chance to win a certain sum of money. All they must do is divide it. The proposer suggests how to split the sum. The responder can accept or reject the deal. If the deal is rejected, neither player gets anything. Obviously, rational responders should accept even the smallest positive offer, since the alternative is getting nothing. Nonetheless, in experiments, the observed bias is towards cooperation only in fair splits of the sum. Nowak et al. (2000) ultimately argue that a mathematical model of the results will show change over time, mimicking evolution and moving away from this 'rational' solution and towards a pattern of fairness, if the proposer can obtain some information on what deals the responder has accepted in the past. In other words, they

---

[2] In a similar vein, Ladefoged (1975) suggests that the alphabet now "standard" on all keyboards – which went viral after the Phoenicians and through the Romans and their descendents – is a kind of linguistic aberration that happened to originate in a particularly influential slice of geohistorical time.

needed to add a mathematical coefficient based on 'reputation knowledge' of the collaborator in the game in order to account for deviations from the expected model. This coefficient became a necessary cornerstone in their theory of the evolution of universal cognitive biases in social interaction and decision-making. Nonetheless, in replications with 23 societies of foragers, horticulturalists, pastoralists, and subsistence farmers, Henrich et al. (2010) report that most of these small-scale societies, such as the Tsimane of Bolivia, show patterns that involve no need at all for this reputation coefficient as a basic part of the model. What's the takeaway message? If the mathematical research had been done first with participants who were Tsimane foragers instead of mid-Atlantic undergraduates, the unadorned original mathematical model would have been taken as more representative of humanity at large. The same concerns of generalizability would have been there – and perhaps even more sharply, in the opposite direction – but such vigilance about generalizability should actually be there when going in any direction, no matter which population one starts out with. Thus, could it have been the case that if the fervent syntactic theorizing of North America that happened in the 1970s had instead taken place within institutions with speakers of Kamaiurá – which embeds only nominalized clauses (Seki & Nevins, 2018) – that the theory of the complementizers may have started on a different foot? Of course, starting with Kamaiurá and later getting to English, as opposed to starting with English and turning to Kamaiurá later, it may (and ideally will!) still end up as the same complete theory when all is said and done – if Kamaiurá is still around then, that is. Minoritized languages may not always be there to work on later, as we know.

I contend that it is appropriate to use the verbal participle 'minoritized' (or marginalized) as opposed to the adjective 'minority' (which is simply inaccurate for languages such as Xhosa or Zulu in South Africa, which have never been numerically minority but have indeed been minoritized). Moreover, the term 'minority languages' potentially suggests an inherent quality as opposed to what is actually the case: Languages become minoritized as the contingent result of active choices and resultant actions carried out by agents ranging from political leaders to members of the scientific community, with intentions that may range from sinister to negligent. As England (2007) points out, the Mayan languages have an unparalleled number of speaker-linguists and academic research output among all indigenous languages within the Americas, even though "the current state of linguistics in Guatemala must be understood against the background of a country that has been profoundly racist at every level" (p. 3). She adds that "programs in linguistics in Guatemala have been tacitly understood as programs in the linguistics of indigenous languages and as such have been difficult to establish, in spite of the fact that 50% or more of the national population is Maya." Reconsideration and subsequent replacement of the term 'minority' by 'minoritized' has been forcefully argued for not only in linguistics (e.g., Kasbarian [1997] but in disciplines ranging from education (Stewart, 2013) to medicine (Sotto-Santiago, 2019), where the latter observes, "Minoritization recognizes that systemic inequalities, oppression, and marginalization place individuals into 'minority' status rather than their own characteristics" (p. 73). The term minoritized language (or its equivalents in Romance languages, such as French *minorisation*) has been firmly established for at least 30 years within linguistics (Py & Jeanneret, 1989); it has a full entry in Wikipedia, where it is succinctly reported that "Minoritized languages are typically restricted to a smaller range of domains than dominant languages, and frequently one-way bilingualism develops when speakers of minoritized languages learn the dominant language, but not vice versa." This sociolinguistic minoritization is a process (hence its verbal aspect, as opposed to static 'minority'), with dynamics that change for a range of reasons in communities of different types throughout the world (see, for example, Léglise & Alby [2006]), resulting from the ideologies or policies of nation-states to establish a single language as part of a national culture (as in Franco's Spain, as in nineteenth-century Bretagne, as in Vargas' dictatorship in Brazil, as in the Stolen Generation in Australia, and innumerable examples beyond). A minoritized language is a language that, as a result of purely social constructs, has less power than other languages (e.g., dominant languages, official languages, written languages, or language of schooling, as backed by regulating and prescriptive norms) and less overall representation in the scientific and cultural landscape. As my ten year-old son Arturo observed at the time of writing this paragraph, "A minoritized language must be one that you don't see many street signs written in." This constant state of diglossia (and one-way bilingualism) with dominant languages mean that, while signers of Black ASL must learn two other dominant languages within a larger sociolinguistic interactional scene (white ASL and American English), the reverse does not hold. Minoritized languages, when historically excluded from use in government and in formal education, sometimes end up being used only at home and in social situations. An immediate consequence is that they aren't spoken in class at universities, exactly where academics are doing their work.

Actions of minoritization of languages through violence, criminalization, or imposition have been countless over the centuries, with the imperial juggernauts and their descendants (e.g., Brazil, Australia, South Africa, North America) as some of the worst perpetrators. Even on a smaller scale within educational sectors, minoritization continues. Speakers of minoritized languages in many parts of the world have grown up hearing that their languages have no grammar. As England (2007) points out, Mayan languages are not called 'languages' in Guatemala but instead "tongues" (*lenguas*, with a pejorative connotation) or 'dialects'. I have heard pejorative equivalents around the globe, often uttered by 'innocent' and even seemingly well-meaning people. If there is one broad message this book can translate towards a greater sector of the public, it is that not only are minoritized languages, as a matter of fact, languages that have grammars, but their grammars show complex and challenging phenomena, the understanding of which bears the potential to transform our understanding of the manifestations of the human mind.

2 Indexical Shift in Zazaki and Uyghur

In this chapter, the contributions of the minoritized Zazaki and Uyghur shore up a theoretical battle for philosophical 'monsters', specifically introducing radical revisions to semantic models of reported speech and attitude reports.

2.1 With an Eye and an Ear towards Zazaki

When it comes to minoritization of their language, the Kurdish people of the near-east, and in particular of eastern Turkey, have been some of the hardest hit. Up until 2003, the Turkish constitution prohibited the teaching of any language other than Turkish as a mother tongue and stayed away from signing the Framework Convention for the Protection of National Minorities, a multilateral treaty of the Council of Europe aiming to respect the rights of national minorities and preserving and developing the cultural and linguistic identity of such communities. To make matters somewhat more complex, there isn't one single Kurdish language. The predominant language spoken by the ethnic Kurds of Turkey, Syria, Iran, and Iraq is called Kurmanji. The Zaza people of Eastern Turkey, while identifying with the Kurds, speak a distinct language, Zazaki, whose very name derives from a pejorative approximation of "za-za-za," similar to the origins of the linguistically pejorative word barbarian (approximating "those who go 'bar bar bar' when they talk").

The Zazaki language has faced discrimination and minoritization for years, and for reasons that have nothing to do with the language itself but with the fact that the people who speak it have found themselves caught in the middle of massive ideological and nationalist policies that have suppressed Kurdish identity. The language itself is within the same Indo-European family that broadly includes English, French, Hindi, Romani, and Farsi, specifically within the Indo-Iranian branch of languages. Publications and electronic media in Zazaki have flourished since the 1990s, originally with Zaza intellectual émigrés in Europe, and have led to a wide variety of broadcast media. In 2002, during the doctoral class entitled 'Topics in the grammar of a less familiar language," originally started at MIT by the polyglot and champion of minoritized language rights, Ken Hale, our language consultant that semester was a Zazaki-speaking journalist, Gulcem Aktas, who provided my first contact with Zazaki.

The aim of this semester-long class was to develop methods of 'urban fieldwork', bringing forth unknown results, alongside our other courses that were based on already canonized or crystallized results in linguistic theory. Typically, each week a different student would begin elicitation of grammatical structures within a pre-planned domain (e.g., possessive structures, wh- questions, or evidential constructions; see Kenstowicz [2004]), and that would inevitably open up further descriptive surprises. As a journalist working with Kurdish political issues, Gulcem had originally made contact with MIT through Noam Chomsky, and indeed many of our language consultants for his course were articulate intellectuals who lived in the Boston area and had, in addition to a strong commitment to the study of their language, highly ambitious personal goals in their lives as émigrés. Gulcem, in fact, wanted to make a movie documenting the very process of a semester-long inquiry culminating in individual grammatical sketches about Zazaki, and as she and I wrote the script and shot a documentary, I also recruited the film editor Alex Karpovsky (who later became a well-known acting star in a popular television series), and the movie, *With an Eye and an Ear towards Zazaki*, can still be found online today.

My own interest in the course had originally begun with ergativity (about which we will hear more in Chapter 3), but in the process of eliciting sentences involving reported speech (e.g., "Rojda said that she went shopping"), I discovered what at first seemed to be an error in communication that led to a far-reaching discovery. At first, as I said, it seemed to be a lost-in-translation episode about what I was asking about, akin to the probably aprocryphal anecdotes about linguists who, doing their first day of fieldwork in Amazonia, point to a tree and ask "What is this?" and when the consultant replies "yawanga," they note it down and proceed to point at a cloud and ask "What is this?" and the consultant replies "yawanga," and then points to an apple and the consultant replies "yawanga." How could tree, cloud, and apple be homophonous, one wonders? The linguist later discovers that "yawanga" means "your finger." With this homily, spurious or not, in mind, I was careful in making any conclusions on the basis of the first set of elicitations that day, but after a coffee break I returned and tried again, in wholly different contexts, to essentially ask the same kind of question. How does one say, in Zazaki, "Rojda$_r$ said that she$_r$ is a hero," where the subscripts r indicate coreference between Rojda and she? The answer I kept getting about hero-hood or any other predicate, whether the sentence was about Rojda or about anyone else as a reported-speech author, was that in Zazaki, one would say "Rojda$_r$ said that I$_r$ am a hero." In English, if we say "Rojda said that I am a hero," the pronoun *I* refers to me, the author of the current speech event, and not to Rojda, the author of the reported speech event. Words like

I are called indexicals because they have this property of not changing their reference during the course of a speech event.

I had a friend in graduate school, Pranav Anand, who was working on these topics from the standpoint of the philosophy-linguistics interface, and he pointed me to Kaplan's (1977) classic philosophical paper 'Demonstratives.' In this paper, Kaplan develops a 'direct reference' theory of indexical expressions such as *I* and claims that a semantic operator that could allow *I* to refer to the author of the context of utterance (such as Rojda above), outside of environments of direct quotation (i.e., Rojda said, "I am a hero"), would be what he called monsters, a term that was no doubt playful at the time but indeed designed to capture his intuition that operators of this sort would be not only impossible but perverse to find in a language. But Zazaki seemed to have them, and as we would discover, while it allowed these so-called *shifted indexicals*, it placed important constraints on when they could be found. Our first job, however, was to establish that this was not direct quotation and then to probe more complex environments, such as expressions with two indexicals, or with double embedding. Let us roll up our sleeves and turn to the patterns.

2.2   Indexical Shifting in Zazaki

We begin with the indexicals *ɛz* and *ti* in Zazaki, which are similar to English *I* and *you* but show different patterns: In contexts of reported speech, they can refer either to the utterance author (myself, Andrew, in this case) or to the reported-speech author (Hesen in (1a) below), and to the utterance addressee (yourself, the reader in this case), or to the reported-speech addressee (Ali, in example (1b) below). This 'shifting' of the reference of these indexical pronouns to the context of the reported speech event is optional.

(1)   *Optional Shift of Zazaki Indexical Pronouns to Context of Reported Speech:*

    a.   Hɛseni$_j$ (mi$_k$-ra)   va   kɛ   **ɛz**$_{j/k}$ dɛwletia
        Hesen.OBL (I.OBL-to) said that I   rich.be-PRES
        'Hesen said that {I am, Hesen is} rich.'
    b.   Hɛseni$_j$ (Ali$_k$-ra)   va   kɛ   **ti**$_{j/k}$ dɛwletia
        Hesen.OBL (Ali.OBL-to) said that you rich.be-PRES
        'Hesen said that {Ali is, you are} rich.'

In semantic models of reported speech, a reported speech event is not necessarily a literal quotation but rather involves a quantificational statement, one that states that *in all contexts consistent with the content of what Hesen said*, he is rich. What Kaplan and others had taken to be a universal of indexical expressions like *I* and *you* is that they escape this quantification and still refer to the author of the utterance. This is done by a kind of bookkeeping of variables, keeping track of who is who during a speech event, and the idea is that in every utterance, we keep track of the fact that the indexicals *I, you, now* refer to – in this case, Andrew, the reader, and the moment of reading, respectively. These variables are formally called *context parameters*. What's interesting about the examples in (1a–b) above is that the Zazaki indexicals *ɛz* and *ti* can either track these context parameters or they can *shift* and refer to the people in the reported speech event themselves (Hesen and Ali).

But it's important to make sure that this optionality isn't akin to the kind of optionality one might find by simply adding or removing quotation marks around the embedded material. (In English, it would be more complex than this, as the complementizer *that* can never be used in direct quotation, and the complementizer *ke* is found in (1a–b) whether shifting occurs or not). Let us illustrate two clear sources of evidence for this. The first comes from *negative polarity items*, like the English words *ever* or *anyone*. These items cannot occur freely, and are typically restricted to sentences involving negation (or other polarity-generating environments), and thus the sentences **I have ever been to Hawaii* and **I saw anyone this morning* are ungrammatical (indicated by the asterisks in front of them). Zazaki also has negative polarity items, and the word *kes* is akin to English *anyone*. Thus, in the sentence below, if negation is present, the negative polarity item (NPI) is licensed, but if negation is absent (indicated by the asterisk outside the parenthetical), the sentence is ungrammatical.[1]

(2)   **Mi**   kes   paci *(ne) kɛrd
        I.ERG anyone kiss *(not) did
        'I did *(not) kiss anyone.'

We can use this test to look at whether a purported instance of quotation interacts with other aspects of the sentence. In fact, *kes* can be licensed in an embedded clause, and in one that includes shifted indexicals, by a negation present in the upper ('matrix') clause:

(3)   Rojda ne va kɛ **mi** kes   paci kɛrd
        Rojda not said that I   anyone kiss did
        'Rojda didn't say that she kissed anyone.'

This clearly indicates we aren't dealing with a quote; if it were, the fragment *mi kes paci kɛrd* would be an ungrammatical string that we reported on. Since we know that the Zazaki equivalent of *I kissed anyone* is ungrammatical but that the Zazaki equivalent of *Rojda didn't say that she/I kissed anyone* is grammatical,

---

[1] You may have noticed that the first-person singular pronoun is *mi* in (2), instead of *ɛz*; this is due to the property of ergativity found in Zazaki, whereby subjects of transitive verbs may show a different pronominal case form than those of intransitive verbs.

the interaction of matrix negation with the embedded NPI, specifically in a shifting reported speech context, demonstrates that the shifting is not the result of direct quotation.

The second diagnostic of grammatical interaction with the embedded clause comes from relative clause formation. Relative clause formation, found in noun phrases like *The girl [who Hesen said he kissed]* show an absent object of the verb 'to kiss'. This object is absent because of an interaction with the noun phrase 'the girl', which is linked to the clause by a relative pronoun *who*. The relation between relativization and wh- question formation in grammatical dependencies was made explicit in Chomsky's (1977) paper on the topic. Whenever we find a noun phrase such as 'the girl' linked to a missing object slot via a relative clause (this missing object indicated by an italic *t* below), we are dealing with a grammatical interaction that requires integration of the two that would be impossible under quotation, as quotation is opaque to grammatical interactions from outside the quote into it:

(4)   *The girl that Hesen said,"I kissed *t*." is pretty.

Notably, relativization out of reported speech complements that include shifted indexicals is possible in Zazaki, again indicating that these are not instances of direct quotation:

(5)   čɛnɛkɛ   [kɛ   Hɛseni va   **mɨ**   *t* paci kɛrda]   rindɛka
      girl   that Hesen said I   *t* kiss did   pretty.be-PRES
      'The girl that Hesen said {Hesen, I} kissed is pretty.'

We've focused only on first- and second-person indexicals so far. Although in the examples above, shifted first- and second-person indexicals have been employed to refer to the author of the reported speech event, in Zazaki ordinary third-person pronouns can be used as well (in a strategy akin to their English equivalents, such as "Rojda told me that **she** is rich." Of relevance to the current discussion is the fact that these third-person pronouns can be used alongside shifting indexicals with *temporal* or *locative* reference, akin to *now* or *here*. Consider the sentence below, which reports on a speech event that took place a week earlier. In the reported speech, the indexical *vizeri* 'yesterday' is employed, and in this case *must* have a shifted interpretation, as one cannot have reported a week ago about something that happened yesterday (in the absence of a time machine) – the # below indicates a semantically anomalous interpretation. The interpretation of *vizeri* 'yesterday' in this case is thus squarely eight days ago, demonstrating shifting behavior as well – although this time alongside a third-person pronoun and hence not a direct quote (having established independently that Hesen does not talk about himself in the third person).

(6) Hefte nayeraraver, Hɛseni   mɪ-ra va kɛ o **vizeri**   Rojda paci
    week ago,   Hesen.obl me-at said that he yesterday Rojda kiss
    kɛrd.
    did
        'A week ago, Hesen told me that he kissed Rojda the day before
        {=eight days ago, #yesterday}.'

We can similarly demonstrate that locative indexicals shift. Suppose you and I are in London and I'm telling you about my trip last month to Diyarbakır (a city on the banks of the Tigris, considered the capital of Turkish Kurdistan) with Hesen.

(7) Waxto kɛ ma Diyarbakır-de bime, Hseni   mɪ-ra va kɛ o **ita**
    When that we Diyarbakır-at were, Hesen.obl me-at said that he here
    ame dina
    came world
        'When we were in Diyarbakır, Hesen told me he was born {here, in Diyarbakır}'.

In (7), the indexical *ita* can refer either to London (the location of the context of utterance) or to Diyarbakır (the location of the reported speech). We've thus observed shifting is possible for the indexicals corresponding to first person, second person, temporals, and locatives, suggesting that the phenomenon cuts across different kinds of referential items.

So Kaplan's monsters, thought never to exist, were found in Zazaki. Indications that elements of this sort might exist in other languages had been explored for Amharic by Schlenker (1999) – though these were limited to first-person examples. Given the opportunity to work with Zazaki further, I began meeting other speakers in the Washington, DC area, and in parallel Pranav and I began developing a new theory of how indexical shift happens in languages that allow it.

Since sentences like (1–2) show that indexical shift is apparently optional – meaning that there is no apparent difference in the phonological string between cases with a shifted and an unshifted indexical, although the meaning differences were significant – we posited a silent semantic operator that had the ability to perform *overwriting* of the context parameters normally kept track of throughout utterances that were used to maintain otherwise rigid indexicality of personal, temporal, and locative pronouns. Specifically, let us assume that the context parameter c is ordinarily a bundle of variables, which we can designate by subscripts for our example (7) above, used to keep track of the referent of expressions such as *I, you, here*, and *now*.

There is likewise an index parameter i that is maintained for the evaluation of the reported speech event and that reflects the participants and spatiotemporal coordinates of the speech event. These two sets of parameters are shown below:

(8) a. *Utterance parameters.* Context variables: c_{auth} = Andrew, c_{addr} = the reader, c_{loc} = London, c_{time} = today
b. *Reported speech parameters.* Index variables: i_{auth} = Hesen, i_{addr} = Andrew, i_{loc} = Diyarbakır, i_{time} = last month

What Zazaki teaches us is that, contrary to Kaplan's assertions, natural languages can possess an operator that, when present in a reported speech context, can completely overwrite the context parameters with those of the index parameters, thereby wiping out any access of expressions like *ɛz, ti, vızeri,* or *ita* to the utterance context. In Zazaki, these parameters are all simultaneously overwritten en masse, hence the notation $OP_\forall$ (for all) below:

(9) Zazaki: $[[OP_\forall [\alpha]^{c,i}]] = [[\alpha^{i,i}]]$

What the $OP_\forall$ notation is intended to encode is the fact that although indexical shift is optional for an embedded clause (this optionality due to the presence or absence of the operator), once it takes place, *all indexicals within the scope of that clause* must shift. That is, there is no "optionality within the optionality" – if the option of indexical shift *is* chosen, then all indexicals must obligatorily shift.

At the time, we grappled with various ways of shifting the reference of indexicals like *ɛz* to the reported speech author. The theoretical consequences of this particular implementation matter in important ways, not just for Zazaki but for potentially every language with indexical shifting, and we turn to these consequences anon.

2.3   The Consequences of an Overwriting Operator

There are two immediate consequences of this kind of operator. One is that, for sentences with *more than one indexical,* the optionality in shifting is now limited. These two indexicals must either both shift, or neither may shift.

(10) SHIFT-TOGETHER CONSTRAINT
All indexicals within a *speech-context domain* pick up their reference from the same context.

That is to say, of four logical possibilities, only two are actually attested – ones in which the indexicals refer to Rojda and Bill, respectively, or ones where they refer to the utterance author and utterance addressee, respectively. But there is no mixing and matching across these two pairings:

(11) Vizeri   Rojda Bill-ra va kɛ **ɛz to**-ra miradiša
Yesterday Rojda Bill-to said that I you-to angry.be-PRES
'Yesterday Rojda said to Bill, "I am angry at you."'
'Yesterday Rojda said to Bill, "AUTH(U) is angry at ADDR(U)."'
'*Yesterday Rojda said to Bill, "AUTH(U) am angry at you."'
'*Yesterday Rojda said to Bill, "I am angry at ADDR(U)."'

The reason for this is that, if the operator is present, all context parameters are overwritten, and if it is absent, none are. Similar patterns can be found with locatives, where given the right verbs (e.g., verbs of motion towards the utterance author), only a shifted interpretation is possible. Thus, if Hesen says to me that he is coming here now, this must be reported as *I am coming there now*.[2]

(12) Hɛsen mi-ra   va kɛ **ɛz** nika {**uža**, *ita} ena
Hesen me.OBL-to said that I   now {there, *here} coming
'Hesen told me that he is coming here now.'

The discovery of a shift-together constraint in Zazaki subsequently led to its exploration in a wide range of typologically unrelated languages. We found an Athabaskan language of Canada, Slave (pronounced [slevi]), studied by Rice (1986), where it can be found that only first-person indexicals shift, not second-person ones. This can be modeled in terms of an operator that overwrites *only* the author parameter:

(13)   Slave: $[[OP_{auth}[\alpha]^{<A_c,...>,i}]] = [[\alpha^{<A_i,...>,i}]]$

In this language, subject and object agreement are both indicated on the morphology of the embedded verb, which precedes the matrix verb. The embedded verb's morphology corresponds to a clause like 'You hit me', but it means that you – the utterance addressee – hit him, the reported-speech author:

(14)   Simon [rásereyineht'u] hadi
Simon [2.sg-hit-1.sg]   3.sg-say
'Simon said that you (ADDR(U)) hit him.'

Despite this seemingly Janus-faced behavior in which one indexical shifts and the other does not, appearances are deceiving, as *all first-person pronouns within a speech domain shift together*. Thus, as indicated below, the third-person subject of *want*, wants of a "fourth-person" object (the fourth person being a less-topical third-person category found in many First Nations pronominal sys-

---

[2] In Zazaki, as in my own California dialect of English, verbs of motion like *come* and *bring* are not restricted to motion towards the speaker's location.

18   When Minoritized Languages Change Linguistic Theory

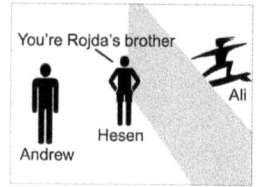

(a) Ali happens to overhear   (b) Ali confronts Andrew   (c) Andrew complains

Figure 2.1 A sequence of events in Zazaki doubly reported speech

tems with 'proximate/obviative' reference for third persons) that *my friend sews slippers for me*. Here we have two embedded indexicals, and they both shift.

(15)   [sehlégé   segha   goníhkie rárulu]   yudeli
       [**1.sg**-friend **1.sg**-for slippers 3.sg-will-sew] 3.sg-want-4.sg
       'She$_j$ wants her$_j$ friend to sew slippers for her$_j$.'

In this case, the pronominal reference of these embedded first-person pronouns cannot mix and match – both instances of these indexicals refer to x's friend sewing slippers for x, where x is the attitude-holder of the matrix clause's final verb.³

Thus, even when a language's 'monstrous' operator shifts only one category of context parameters, all such instances of it must obey shift together. Indexical shift cannot be viewed as an "every indexical for itself" affair, but is rather a property of an entire clause affected by an operator.

Perhaps one of the most compelling predictions of the particular overwriting implementation we adopted is that once the context parameter is overwritten in an embedded clause, one can never 'pop back up' to the matrix interpretation, even under a second level of embedding. To create the relevant scenarios, we employed the following background, enriched by a comic strip. Suppose that Andrew is the brother of the famous traitor Rojda. Understandably, he keeps this knowledge secret from his new friends, Hesen and Ali. One day, Hesen finds out Andrew's secret and confronts him.

Below is a comic strip of a series of conversations between Andrew and Hesen, Andrew and Ali, and Andrew and a third party. In Figure 2.1(a), Hesen confronts Andrew about his sister; Ali, flying by, happens to overhear Hesen's revelation. In Figure 2.1(b), Ali then proceeds to tell Andrew that he overheard what Hesen said to him (Andrew).

Given this setup, (16) is the crucial target sentence for the scenario, where Andrew describes to his neighbor what Ali said:

---

³ In the Slave example (15), the matrix verb is 'want'. Indexical shift has been documented across a range of languages with verbs spanning 'say' to 'know' to 'want' to 'dream', although crosslinguistically, as Deal (2020) states, building on work by Sundaresan (2011, 2012), "Verbs of speech are more likely to allow indexical shift in their complement than are verbs of thought, which in turn are more likely to allow indexical shift in their complement than are verbs of knowledge" (p. 58).

(16) (Andrew): Ali$_A$ mi-ra va kɛ Hɛseni$_H$ **to-ra** va ɛz$_{\{H,A,*U\}}$
Ali me-to said that Hesen you-to said I
braye Rojda-o
brother Rojda-GEN
'Ali said to Andrew that Hesen said to Andrew that {Hesen, Ali, *Andrew} is Rojda's brother.'

As indicated in the translation, (16) is not grammatical when Andrew is reporting to his neighbor what Ali said in Figure 2.1(b). This is precisely what our operator-theoretic account predicts, since the shifted indexical *to-ra* 'to you' (referring to Andrew as addressed by Hesen, not the neighbor) diagnoses the presence of OP$_∀$, which prevents the further embedded *ɛz* 'I' from referring to the utterance author. Thus, unshifting is impossible.

To recap, Kaplan (1977) and a host of subsequent work on the philosophy of language took operations that could shift indexicals to be so outlandish that they were literally considered 'monsters'. But Zazaki turns out to have such shifted indexicals and employs them by means of a context-shifting operator. What makes scientific theories distinct from descriptive overviews is that the specific implementation matters, and in this one, shift-together is obeyed (even in Slave), and unshifting is impossible.

This is because shifting operators overwrite contextual information and in Zazaki shift the first and second person parameters of context away from the original utterer and addressee. Thus, all first and second persons that depend on that operator for their choice of context will receive shifted readings, and information about the original context, once overwritten, is unrecoverable.

This kind of prediction, involving testing doubly-embedded clauses, involved careful methodological steps with a number of language consultants in order to verify the scenarios and the intended interpretations and ultimately provided confirmation for the operator-based view of shifting. Zazaki is a language that did not fit the theory of indexicals developed by Kaplan (1977). However, rather than radically rejecting all theories of indexicals, we proposed a new parameter of semantic variation: the presence of a context-shifting operator. The results turned out to lead to a surge of specific theoretical refinements about the syntax of such operators, the prosodic phrasing of indexical shifted clauses, and empirical extensions across languages spanning five continents. Since Anand and Nevins (2004), subsequent investigations of indexical shift have taken place with a host of underexplored languages, from Catalan Sign Language, to Magahi (Indo-Aryan), to Uyghur. Anand's (2006) dissertation went on to explore the intricate semantic consequences of so-called *de se* readings accompanying shifted indexicals (in a nutshell, whether the attitude holder knows that it is themselves they are talking about – a scenario that fails in contexts of amnesia or mistaken identity, for example). Work on signed languages (e.g., Quer [2013]) has gone to intricate depths in discussing whether the phenomenon of *role shift* (a kind of quotation device in which one 'embodies' the reported-speech author) is identical to indexical shift or not. Crucially, the burgeoning industry of work on shifted indexicals has taken place specifically within the overall goal of maintaining a close tie to existing linguistic theory. That is to say, when a minoritized language or underdescribed language presents empirical phenomena that do not fit the theory, rather than throwing out the theory altogether and attempting some homespun model unconnected to and unapplicable to any other language, the overall goal researchers in indexical shift have pursued is to modify in substantive ways, rather than wholly reject, existing linguistic theory.

When I was in graduate school, our semester-long semantics textbook, Heim and Kratzer (1998), was almost entirely composed of examples in English (one language I have never worked on!). But the field of semantic variation – often thought to be the domain of linguistic structure in which the least crosslinguistic variation is found – is now one of the most dynamic areas of research, and it has witnessed the growth of sophisticated elicitation methodologies as well. Works such as Lima (2018), Matthewson (2013), and Beck et al. (2009) represent a new generation of research on crosslinguistic semantic variation in the interpretation of count vs. mass interpretations of bare nouns, quantifiers, and comparatives, respectively, all of it informed by minoritized languages.

2.4 Two Kinds of Embedding in Uyghur

In 2009, around five years after I had completed my coursework for MIT's 'Topics in the Grammar of a Less Familiar Language' with Zazaki, the language under study in the course was now Uyghur, a language from the Turkic family spoken in Western China. The language consultant, Mettursun Bedulla, was again a political dissident who had resettled in Boston. As is well known, the Uyghur people are currently undergoing egregious and large-scale persecution in the Xinjiang province of China. Two students, Kirill Shklovsky and Yasu Sudo, began to investigate the syntax of operators such as the one we had posited for Zazaki. In our work on Zazaki, Anand and I had focused largely on the semantic consequences of such an operator and simply posited that it was somewhere directly within the complement of the embedding verb-of-saying, with scope above all of the indexical pronouns within the embedded clause but without a specific commitment to its structural position. Shklovsky and Sudo (2014) investigated the interaction of indexical shift with the fact that embedded clauses in Uyghur – as in many Turkic languages – show an alternation between two ways of expressing an embedded clause, either as a nominalization or as a finite clause:

(17) a. Ahmet [profesor-ning kit-ken-lik-i-ni] di-di.
Ahmet [professor-GEN leave-REL-NMLZ-3-ACC] say-PAST.3
'Ahmet said that the professor left.'

b. Ahmet [profesor ket-ti] di-di.
Ahmet [professor.NOM leave-PAST.3] say-PAST.3
'Ahmet said that the professor left.'

Of these two ways of performing embedding, only the (b) option above, the finite one, with a nominative embedded subject, allows the possibility of indexical shifting.

(18) a. Ahmet [mening kit-ken-lik-im-ni] di-di.
Ahmet [1SG.GEN leave-REL-NMLZ-3-ACC] say-PAST.3
(nonshifted) 'Ahmet said that I$_{auth}$ left.'
*(shifted) 'Ahmet$_i$ said that he$_i$ left.'
b. Ahmet [men ket-tim] di-di.
Ahmet [1SG leave-PAST.1SG] say-PAST.3
*(nonshifted) 'Ahmet said that I$_{auth}$speaker left.'
(shifted) 'Ahmet$_i$ said that he$_i$ left.'

Unlike Zazaki, when the subject is nominative, indexical shift is obligatory, not optional. Shklovsky and Sudo (2014) apply the aforementioned diagnostics to show this is not quotation. Now, it turns out that even in finite embedded clauses, there are two possibilities for case marking the subject. It can be either nominative or accusative, as indicated by the optional accusative suffix on the subject of the embedded intransitive verb:

(19) Ahmet [istakan(-ni) buz-ul-di] di-di.
Ahmet [cup(-ACC) break-PASS-PAST.3] say-PAST.3
'Ahmet said the cup broke.'

Interestingly enough, the accusative-marked ones can be shown to have a higher syntactic position than the nominative marked ones, based on their ability to appear in positions higher than the matrix subject itself, as shown in (20), where in the absence of accusative marking, this kind of 'scrambling' of the canonical SOV word order is ungrammatical:

(20) Istakan*(-ni) Ahmet [buz-ul-di] di-di.
cup*(-ACC) Ahmet [break-PASS-PAST.3] say-PAST.3
'Ahmet said the cup broke.'

What Shklovsky and Sudo found was that given these two options of case-marking on embedded finite clauses, only nominative-marked ones could undergo indexical shifting – a difference they attributed to distinct syntactic positions for the two and, more pertinently, to a dedicated syntactic position for the monstrous operator (indicated visually by a Pac-Man ghost in the tree below), according to which everything below it must shift:

(21) Position of Monstrous Operator in Uyghur:

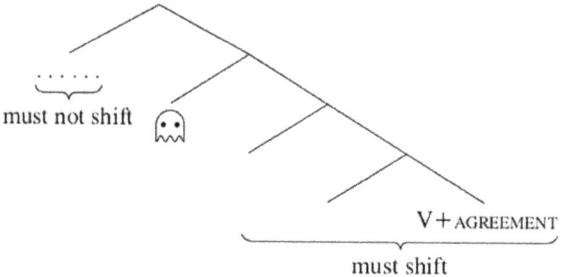

There are important consequences of this specific local position for the monstrous operator. In particular, shift-together will hold, but now it can be stated over a specifically delineated syntactic domain. When the embedded subject *the student of mine that you like* is nominative, both indexicals must shift, as by hypothesis this entire constituent is below the monstrous operator.

(22) Ahmet Aygül-ge [[sen yaxshi kör-idi-ghan oqughuchi-m]
 Ahmet Aygül-DAT [[2SG well see-IMPF-REL student-1SG]
 imtihan-din öt-ti] di-di.
 test-from PASS-PAST.3] say-PAST.3
 'Ahmet told Aygül that his student that Aygül likes passed the test.'
 *'Ahmet told Aygül that my student that you like passed the test.'
 *'Ahmet told Aygül that my student that Aygül likes passed the test.'
 *'Ahmet told Aygül that his student that you like passed the test.'

However, when it's accusative, they are all outside of the scope of the operator and must refer to the utterance author and utterance addressee:

(23) Ahmet Aygül-ge [[sen yaxshi kör-idi-ghan oqughuchi-m-ni]
 Ahmet Aygül-DAT [[2SG well see-IMPF-REL student-1SG-ACC]
 imtihan-din öt-ti] di-di.
 test-from pass-PAST.3] say-PAST.3
 'Ahmet told Aygül that my student that you like passed the test.'
 *'Ahmet told Aygül that his student that Aygül likes passed the test.'
 *'Ahmet told Aygül that my student that Aygül likes passed the test.'
 *'Ahmet told Aygül that his student that you like passed the test.'

Uyghur has added another refinement to our knowledge of how indexical shifting works: The operator can be syntactically localized. It has also suggested that indexical shift is restricted to finite complement clauses, perhaps because only these clauses have enough structure to support a context-shifting operator at their edge. Finally, Uyghur has suggested that the specific height of indexicals with respect to the context-shifting operator matters; an indexical's ability to shift correlates with its syntactic position inside the finite complement to the attitude verb.[4] Accusative elements, despite being linearly in the same apparent position in the embedded clause, may have actually undergone a kind of movement called scrambling leftward, and above the shifting operator.[5]

2.5 Towards an Implicational Hierarchy of Shifting Patterns

In Sudo's (2012) work on Uyghur, he shows that the locative indexical *bu jer* 'here' does not shift. Putting together the pieces from a range of typological work, including her own detailed fieldwork with the Nez Perce ('pierced nose' in French) Native American group of Idaho, Deal (2020) compiles a typological overview of universals and variation in indexical shift patterns similar to those in Zazaki across five continents and at least nine distinct language families. She finds a compelling implicational hierarchy: In no language can locatives shift if first person does not, although the opposite can easily hold. Deal contends that there is nothing within the definition of locative indexicals per se that would make this the case and instead proposes that if a range of different shifting operators (similar, in fact, to the variation already mentioned above between Zazaki and Slave) are posited as distinct functional items in the clausal spine of sentences, one can model these patterns.

Specifically, in the same way that if an embedded clause contains a complementizer, it will also contain lower tense and aspect projections, one can assume a rigid hierarchy of shifting operator projections:

(24) Hierarchy of Shifting Operators:

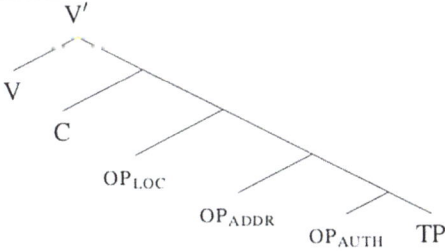

---

[4] Deal (2020) points out that Quer's (2013) investigation of indexical shift in Catalan Sign Language finds that temporal adverbs will shift depending on their syntactic position – specifically not when they are at the edge of the clause – in a way reminiscent of the clausal-height-based generalization from Uyghur.
[5] In fact, Major and Mayer (2019) present recent prosodic phrasing evidence on indexical shift in Uyghur, suggesting very high movement of the accusative embedded subjects that are immune to indexical shift and ushering in a wholly new dimension of research, namely the prosody-syntax-semantics interface with respect to diagnosing the position of the operator.

A language like Zazaki has all of these projections; Uyghur, which lacks locative shift, would lack the topmost operator projection. However, it would not be possible for attitude complements to include OP_{Loc} only, without any operators lower in the sequence. Given this 'stacking' view of operators, the variation between languages in their indexical shift possibilities boils down to the size of functional categories each attitude verb selects for within its clausal complement. This turns the variation into a familiar parameter of cross-linguistic (and even intra-linguistic) variation – a point that Sundaresan (2011, 2012) explicitly ties to different attitude verb types within shifting languages.

In summary, each case in Deal's (2020) typological overview of universals and variation in the "teratology" (the study of monsters) behind indexical shift initiates discussion, extension, and revision of the theory. Shifting indexicals presented a language type essentially ruled out by fiat in Kaplan's (1977) work, and the theory had to change in order to accommodate Zazaki. Once changed, however, it continues to evolve, with consequences for our models of the functional spine of clause structure and the order of shifting operators within the tree, and with consequences for understanding phenomena such as allocutives (agreement with the utterance addressee), which can be grammatically active in languages such as Magahi (Alok & Baker, 2018), The evolving theory also continues to develop diagnostics for phenomena that appear similar though distinct from indexical shift, such as free indirect discourse, as found in written forms of literature (Maier, 2014).

There is a great deal that can be further studied with indexical shift in other less WEIRD languages in years to come. For example, in Uyghur, the indexicals embedded by predicates of hearing refer to the matrix subject, not to the matrix speech-report author. Thus, in (25), the embedded first-person indexical refers to Ahmet as the subject of 'hear', even though Aygül is the agent of saying (Sudo, 2012):

(25)   Ahmet Aygül-din [qaysi imtihan-din öt-tim   dep]
       Ahmet Aygül-from [which test-from   PASS-PAST.1sg C]
       angla-di?
       hear-PAST.3
       'Which test did Ahmet hear from Aygül that he passed?'

This example – yet further evidence against a quotation analysis, as Aygül could not have referred to Ahmet with a first-person singular pronoun – suggests that the operator leading to indexical shift may be tied to the subject position of the matrix verb and not necessarily to the semantic source of the information that was linguistically conveyed. As this discussion shows, the relation between the argument structure of individual verbs and indexical shifting awaits much further study across a range of understudied languages, with the capacity to further refine our understanding of the syntactic and semantic encoding of reported speech as more diverse samples across the globe are made protagonists in linguistic theory.

Further Reading

Indexical shift is but one aspect of the phenomenon of reported speech. Clements's (1975) work on logophors in Ewe was one of the first formal studies of distinct morphological expression for the actual speaker of the discourse as opposed to someone else whose speech or thoughts are being reported, and eventually Sells (1987) developed a distinction between the source of a speech report, the self whose perspective is being reported, and the pivot from whose point of view the report is being made, with consequences for Binding Theory and the interpretation of pronouns. Speas (2000) contains an analysis of reported speech in Navajo in which some functional categories, such as agreement and complementizers, act as if they were part of direct discourse, while deictic and evaluative elements pattern as indirect discourse.

3 Why Ergative Case Requires Structure in Basque and Ch'ol

In this chapter, two languages spoken far apart from one another – Basque and Ch'ol – jointly show that once one considers sentences expressed in the progressive aspect, the entire theory of ergative case as lexically determined begins to unravel.

3.1 A Sole Survivor

The Basque Country (Euskal Herria), a region straddling the border of modern-day Spain and France, spans 8,218 square miles, which is slightly smaller than New Hampshire. Four provinces are in Spain and three are in France, leading to an old form of Basque nationalist graffiti: "4 + 3 = 1" (Kurlansky, 1999). One of the most well-known locales is Guernica, where one of the first modern horrific civilian aerial bombings took place during the Spanish Civil War in 1937, later becoming the subject of the famous anti-war painting by Picasso.

The Basque people have continuously inhabited this mountainous region, speaking their own indigenous European language, since before the Romans (who recorded the presence of Basques upon their arrival), and of course long before the French and the Spanish. However, once the Indo-European peoples began to maraud across Europe, few groups, no matter how isolated they may have been, were left untouched, although the Basque had conditions of relative autonomy under Roman rule. The Basque people remained unconquered and thus very likely speak the oldest living European language. While it is classified as an 'isolate' – a language unrelated to any other extant language or to any other language with written records – this may simply be because all of its relatives were wiped out. In fact, every language called an 'isolate' should perhaps instead be called a 'sole survivor'. The origins of the Basque people have been an enigmatic puzzle for European researchers for centuries, with nineteenth-century claims ranging from the lost thirteenth tribe of Israel to survivors of Atlantis, and continued in the twentieth century with biological studies showing that Basques have the highest incidence of Rh negative blood of any people in the world, attempts by scholars in the Republic of Georgia to connect Basque to

Georgian, and continued archeological findings at Paleolithic sites around the Pyrenees.

During the dictator Franco's rule in Spain, tombstone engravings in Basque were removed, and speaking Basque in public could get one arrested. Similarly, in France, from Napoleon onward, there was a move to quash any kind of regionalism, and a uniform school curriculum in France banned Basque and other regional languages, a policy that was only overturned after the election of François Mitterrand in 1981. In the last four decades, however, the Basque language has seen a great revival, including written literature (in the Latin script), language academies, teaching in schools, and the renaming of cities (such as Guernica > Gernika, Bilbao > Bilbo, San Sebastián > Donostia, Vitoria > Gasteiz, and Pamplona > Iruña), and now has nearly a million speakers.

Details about the Basque language still continue to elude everyone but specialists. My first encounter with it was through a fellow PhD student, Karlos Arregi, who I later found out had legally changed the spelling of his name so that it would start with a K – a letter not even a fully-fledged member of the Spanish alphabet, and thus a blazing emblem of Basque identity. It also dawned on me very late in life that my hometown of San Diego was named in 1602 by the sailor Sebastián Vizcaíno, whose surname reveals his origins in the Biscayan region of Euskal Herria. The Basque language is commented upon for its use of k and x, for its numerous postpositional suffixes, and for its extremely wide variety across dialects, and I teamed up with Mr. K, in Arregi and Nevins (2012) to coauthor a book-long tome about the microdialectal variation in hundreds of different forms of the two verbs *have* and *be*). Certainly, however, Basque's most famous property is being the only ergative language of Europe. As it turns out, it's also the language that has most changed the very theory of ergativity as a grammatical property.

Ergo, we turn to an in-depth discussion of this type of case alignment.

3.2 'A' Is for Agent

In Dixon's famous schematic (Dixon, 1979), shown with ovals in Figure 3.1, the key distinguishing propery of ergative languages is that they treat the *agent* role as different from the *subject* role. Thus, in Dyirbal, an Australian Aboriginal language, the intransitive verb 'return' has a subject with no overt case ending (the absence of a case ending, showing the noun in an 'absolute' form here, has come to be called 'absolutive' marking), as in (1a). But the agent of the verb 'see' (never mind, for the moment, that seeing is not the most agentive activity one can think of!) in (1b), has the case-marking suffix -ŋgu, which indicates that it is the agent of a transitive verb (Dixon, 1979):

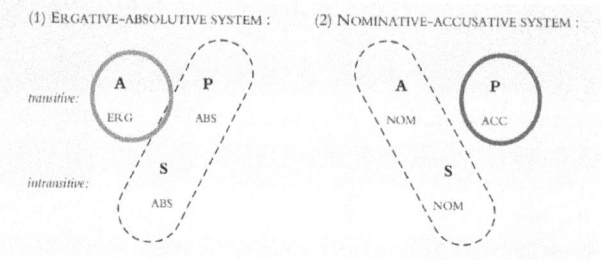

Figure 3.1 Schematic of ergative vs. nominative alignment

(1) a. yabu ŋuma-ŋgu bura-n
    mother father-ERG see-NONFUT
    'Father saw mother'
  b. ŋuma banaga-nʸu
    Father return-NONFUT
    'Father returned'

Unlike English, which would have nominative *We* as the case pattern for *We saw mother* or *We returned* in opposition to accusative marking in object position (*Mother saw us*), Dyirbal is well known for this ergative pattern. Thus, in Dyirbal, the subject of the intransitive verb 'return' is not case-marked with the suffix -*ŋgu*, while the agent of the transitive verb 'to see' (in an object-first word order, above) does bear this suffix, and due to Dixon's work on the topic, is one of the earliest-known cases to which the model distinguishing A, S, and V has been applied.[1] In this model, accusative languages like English group A with S to the exclusion of O (which is marked accusative, differently from the other two), whereas ergative languages like Dyirbal group S with O to the exclusion of A (which is marked ergative, differently from the other two).

Framed in the terms above, it seems that in accusative languages the O is set off as special, whereas in ergative languages the A is set off as special. But there's not really a language that sets S off as special, leaving A and O to be marked alike, to the exclusion of S. Instead, it looks like what distinguishes ergative languages from accusative ones is the direction that S itself 'leans'. If S leans towards A, it's an accusative language, and if S leans towards O (or perhaps, 'away from A'), it's an ergative language.

---

[1] Dyirbal is perhaps equally well known for its system of noun classes, which unlike masculine, feminine, and neuter, has four such classes, the second of which has groupings of nouns that do not seem at first blush to have a common semantic core, nonetheless leading to the provocatively titled book on cognitive metaphors, *Women, Fire, and Dangerous Things* (Lakoff, 1987), in which Dyirbal forms the eponymous case study—later revisited by Plaster and Polinsky (2007).

There are reasons to think that S itself is somehow special in this equation. Specifically, if there are contexts in which S itself sometimes seems to 'lean towards' A or not, with different marking on it, this would implicate S as a crucial player within the theory of ergativity. In a paper that I consider to be very important within the history of understanding ergativity typologically, Holisky (1987) points to crucial data from the minoritized language Tsova-Tush, a North-Central Caucasian language spoken in the mountains of Eastern Georgia, amplifying on an observation made earlier in Comrie (1973). Holisky shows that intransitive verbs like 'to fall' in Tsova-Tush may vary in their ergative case marking depending on how 'volitional' the event was on the part of the subject. If it was an intentional or fault-related fall, it is marked agentively, with ergative case, whereas if it is accidental and outside of the control of the subject, it is marked nominatively.

(2) a. as   wože
       1sg.ERG fell
       'I fell.' (It was my own fault that I fell down)
    b. so   wože
       1sg.NOM fell
       'I fell.' (No implication that it was my fault)

Holisky points out that languages with this kind of fluid marking of the S, depending on its degree of volitionality, are somewhat rare but establishes that this kind of variability is not marginal nor limited to few verbs but more systematic within the language. In a study of 303 intransitive verbs, Holisky groups them into those which only allow nominative marking, those which only allow ergative marking, and those which, like 'fall' above, allow variable marking. The conclusion for Tsova-Tush, and one that was subsequently adopted more generally, was that it must be listed lexically to indicate, almost verb-by-verb, which verbs require ergative marking, which verbs disallow it, and which verbs leave it underspecified, so that event-contingent factors like volitionality can come into play. Examples of optionality and variability with intransitive verbs of this sort were found with Hindi–Urdu verbs such as 'to bark', where the volitionality of the dogs involved could subtly condition ergative marking, but again, given that not all verbs were optional in this way, something lexical seemed to govern whether ergative was obligatory, impossible, or optional.

This lexically specific view of morphologically ergative languages (i.e., those diagnosed by case-marking or agreement patterns) grew in popularity, and in work such as Woolford (1997), ergative case on subjects came to be assimilated as similar in nature to the dative case on subjects that was by then the topic of much research on Icelandic and related Germanic languages. In particular, given that in Icelandic verbs like 'to capsize' have dative case on their subject in (3) as a lexically unpredictable fact of the language, the idea was to treat ergative as similar in nature.

(3) Bátnum hvolfi
 boat-DAT capsized
 'The boat capsized'

In Germanic, the dative marking on verbs whose subjects represent a kind of 'experiencer' is also variable, and in fact, the tendency of speakers, as an innovation, to impose more and more dative case marking on the subject of verbs that did not historically bear it is called 'dative sickness' (*Þágufallssýki*) in Icelandic grammars (see Smith [1997] for discussion). Thus, much like dative marking has been treated in terms of 'inherent' case, lexically assigned by specific verbs, the tendency within a great deal of ergativity literature, ranging from Hindi–Urdu to Basque, was to treat ergative case as an inherent case, especially given the existence of apparently idiosyncratic verbs like 'boil' in Basque, which are clearly intransitive in their usage below, but nonetheless take ergative marking, even on a nonanimate and nonvolitional subject:

(4) Ur-ak iraki-n du
 water-ERG boil-PFV has
 'The water has boiled'

In Basque, the auxiliary *du* 'have' is used in conjunction with ergative-assigning verbs. This kind of 'auxiliary selection', also known as the *have/be alternation* in many languages, such as French, is responsible for the fact that the past participle of verbs like 'arrive' in French are accompanied by finite forms of 'to be':

(5) Je suis arrivé
 I am arrived
 Literally: 'I am arrived ('I have arrived')

Many languages have versions of the *have/be alternation* – English used to, and retains relics of it in Christmas carol lyrics such as *Joy to the word! The Lord is come*. In Basque, the auxiliary verb used in sentences such as (4) also follows similar lines – when the verb assigns ergative case (and thus patterns 'transitively'), the auxiliary will be 'have', and otherwise will be 'be'.[2] This distinction will remain important in the glosses below. Thus, not only does Basque *boil* assign ergative case to its inanimate, intransitive subject, but also the presence of this ergative subject triggers the *have* version of the auxiliary.

---

[2] There are many other factors conditioning the form of the root in Basque varieties, including whether the verb is ditransitive as well. In Arregi and Nevins (2012), we present a fuller analysis of the *have/be* alternation in Basque.

Given the fact that there is no apparent synchronic reason for Basque's intransitive 'boil' to assign ergative case, many theorists ended up concluding that ergative case is simply something lexical, to be learned on a verb-by-verb basis (although with semantic regularities). Thus, in work on Hindi–Urdu, the fact that the verb *laanaa* 'to bring' is in fact transitive but does not assign ergative case is taken to be a lexical irregularity, adding more fuel to the fire that such things must be memorized on a case-by-case (no pun originally intended) basis. As such, ergative becomes parallel to Icelandic dative case, which is classified as inherent case. What does 'inherent' mean? Within case theory, it has come to mean that once a verb assigns an inherent, thematic-role-related case to a noun phrase, this case will follow the noun phrase around no matter what happens. Thus, famously, there is a difference between accusative case and dative case in Icelandic: The former can be tampered with, that is, it may not be assigned or may be overridden in passive constructions with the matrix verb 'to believe' (Sigurðsson, 1991), as in (6c–d). (note that participles like 'bought' agree in case with their arguments in Icelandic):

(6) a. Hún taldi   hafa   verið keypta   einhverja
       she believed.3sg to.have   been bought.PTCP.ACC several
       báta.
       boats.ACC
       'She believed to have been bought several boats'
    b. Hún taldi   einhverja báta   hafa   verið
       she believed.3sg several   boats.ACC to.have been
       keypta.   t.
       bought.PTCP.ACC t
       'She believed several boats to have been bought'
    c. Það voru   taldir   hafa   verið keyptir
       there were.3pl believed.PTCP.NOM   to.have been bought.PTCP.NOM
       einhverjir. bátar.
       several   boats.NOM
       'There were believed to have been bought several boats'
    d. Einhverjir bátar   voru   taldir   hafa   verið
       several   boats.Nom were.3pl believed.PTCP.NOM   to.have been
       keyptir.   t.
       bought.PTCP.NOM t
       'Several boats were believed to have been bought'

In (7c–d), once the verb is passivized, the noun phrase 'boats', whether it stays in object position, or moves to subject position, becomes nominative. For this reason, accusative is called a *structural* case, meaning precisely that, depending on the structure, it will or won't be assigned. For a case to be inherent, this means that it will be assigned regardless of the structure. Thus, the verb 'to rescue' in

Icelandic assigns inherent dative case to its object (in a similar way to the fact that you can't omit the preposition with a verb like *Sue spoke to me*), and this dative case remains on the object, even when the matrix verb is passivized, as in examples (7c–d) below (default agreement refers to the fact that dative objects aren't agreed with by verbs, even when they're plural):

(7) a. Hún taldi [hafa verið bjargað einhverjum bátum].
she believed to.have been rescued.DFLT several boats.DAT
'She believed to have been rescued several boats'
b. Hún taldi einhverjum bátum hafa verið bjargað *t*.
she believed several boats.DAT to.have been rescued.DFLT *t*
'She believed several boats to have been rescued'
c. Það var talið [hafa verið bjargað
there was.3s believed.DFLT to.have been rescued.DFLT
einhverjum bátum].
several boats.DAT
'There were believed to have been rescued several boats'
d. Einhverjum bátum var talið hafa verið
several boats.DAT was.3s believed.DFLT to.have been
bjargað *t*.
rescued.DFLT *t*
'Several boats were believed to have been rescued'

The contrast between (6) and (7) is what exemplifies inherent dative case in languages like Icelandic: Once a verb idiosyncratically (i.e. lexically) assigns it, it stays with the noun forever. On the other hand, structural case is assigned based on, well, the structure, and independent of the lexical properties of the verb that may be involved. Since ergative case, from Tsova-Tush to Hindi–Urdu to Basque, seems conditioned by lexical properties of the verb, it seems to be yet another instance of an inherent case. Now, surely learning the patterns of a language with morphological case involve memorization, but is that really all there is to ergative case?

3.3 When Ergative Can Be Removed or Imposed

Evidence as to whether Basque ergative case, or any ergative case, for that matter, was structural, had been elusive throughout over three decades of ergativity research. However, Rezac et al. (2014) point out the relevance of perception verbs in Basque, which, as in English, may take a complement clause that is a fully independent tensed clause, or one that is smaller than a fully tensed clause. Thus, in (8), the complement clause of the matrix verb 'see' (the verb is all the way at the end, as Basque is head-final) has a complementizer *la*, akin to 'that', and a fully-fledged complement clause with ergative marking on 'cat':

(8)   [Katu-ek   sagu-ak   harrapa-tzen dituzte   -la]
      cat-ERG.DEF.PL mouse-DEF.PL catch-ing   have.3PLABS.3PLERG -that
      ikusi dut.
      seen have.1SG.ERG
         'I saw that the cats were catching the mice.'

On the other hand, in a 'pruned' embedded complement to the perception verb (akin to the difference between *I saw the cat catch(ing) the mice*, with a nonfinite – either bare or gerundive form – and *I saw that the cat caught the mice*), the fact that there is less tense structure on the verb ends up meaning that the subject of 'catch' is no longer ergative:

(9)   [Katu-ak   sagu-ak   harrapa-tzen] ikusi ditut.
      [cat-DEF.PL mouse-DEF.PL catch-ing]   seen have.1SG.ERG
         'I saw the cats catching the mice.'

If ergative case were a purely lexical phenomenon, then 'catch' should assign ergative case, whether or not there is a higher tensed node above it. So matters can't be that simple. Instead, Rezac et al. (2014) suggest that there is a specific kind of tense node, a structural position above the verb phrase itself, that is responsible for enabling ergative case in examples such as (8). However, in gerundive examples such as (9), it is absent.

In order to make sure that the noun phrase 'cats' above is truly in an embedded clause (instead of, say, being the direct object of the verb 'to see'), we can consider idiomatic expressions, often a useful test for the constituency of phrases in syntactic diagnoses. In Basque, there is an idiomatic expression, literally 'water has made way', which means something like 'great strides have been taken', or more generally 'things have advanced'. In order to show that 'water' is within the embedded gerund, as opposed to being a direct argument of the perception verb, one can make sure that the resulting interpretation isn't one that involves perception of 'water' but rather perception of the fact that 'things have advanced'. Thus, both in (10a) and (10b), the noun phrase 'water' has the same idiomatic relation to the predicate 'made way', regardless of the fact that it loses ergative case marking in the gerundive structure in (10b).

(10) a.   Kontu horretan, ur-ak   bide egin du   azken
           matter that.in   water-ERG.DEF way made have.3sg.erg last
           urteotan.
           years.these.in
              'In this matter, things have advanced these last years.'

b. Kontu horretan, ur-a   bide egiten   ikusi dugu
    matter that.in water-DEF way mak-ing seen have.1pl.erg
    azken urteotan.
    last years.these.in
    'In this matter, we have seen things advance these last years.'

Rezac et al.'s conclusion is that these nonfinite complements lack T_{erg}, that is, they lack enough structure to assign ergative. They in fact make a strong parallel with nominative case, which in the nonfinite complement of English perception verbs (e.g., *I saw them leave*) does not have enough structure present to host the finite tense node needed for nominative case assignment to the embedded subject.

The broader conclusion is thus that ergativity is independent of the relations that these arguments have with the thematic system of their local verb, which is always present, whether or not the clause hosting them contains T_{erg}. This directly challenges prior models in which morphological ergativity is defined by the uniform assignment of inherent case to the subject.[3] The configurations with perception verbs we witnessed above demonstrate cases that the subject of an 'ergativey' verb can fail to have ergative case if there's not enough structure around it. The converse case, considered next, will show that a 'nonergativey' verb can *gain* ergative case if it moves to a place with enough structure around it.

This involves a phenomenon known as raising-to-ergative, in which ergative case emerges on the subject of an intransitive verb by means of raising to a higher position (and one in which there is no new thematic relation). Specifically, it involves movement of the subject from a lexical verb such as 'come', below, to above the position of a modal verb meaning 'must'. In (11b), the subject bears ergative case (and the auxiliary is 'have') not because of the intransitive verb, which is otherwise unable to assign ergative (cf. [11a]), but because of its derived position, having been raised to the subject position of the verb 'must':

(11)   a. Jon eta Miren etorr-iko dira.
           Jon and Miren come-FUT are-3PL
           'Jon and Miren will come.'
       b. Jon-ek eta Miren-ek   etorri behar du-te.
           Jon-ERG and Miren-ERG come must have-3PL.ERG
           'Jon and Miren must come.'

We can again employ certain noun phrases to make sure that the subject of the modal *behar* is not thematically related to it as an agent. For example, in the sentences below, one is saying that a stone must be there or that a stone must

---

[3] For example, the implementation for ergative case assignment proposed by Levin (1983) involved case assignment at D-structure before any higher nodes such as T_{erg} were even introduced.

Why Ergative Case Requires Structure in Basque and Ch'ol   35

break the window. But a stone does not experience this need – rather this 'must' refers to the state of the world (i.e., something like 'there must be that stone to break the window'). Rather, this is what is called a raising construction, and the raising verb, akin to 'needs to', although it has no thematic role to contribute directly to the raising noun phrase, confers ergativity on it.

(12)   Harri horr-ek {hor egon} / {leiho-a apurtu} behar du.
       stone that-ERG {there be} / {window-def break} must have.3sg.ERG
       'That stone must {be there} / {break the window}.'

The ergative case marking on the subject in (12) comes from the fact that this higher position is one where T_{erg} is found and shows once again that ergative case is dissociated from thematic relations. Again, an idiomatic expression may be used to diagnose constituency. Thus, the Basque expression 'seven feeble cows will come' means something like 'Hard times are ahead', and when placed within the complement of *behar*, the idiomatic expression is not lost (i.e., there is no sense in which seven cows are experiencing this need). Nonetheless, by virtue of the raising to the subject position of this higher modal, the noun phrase has gained ergative case (and still forms an idiomatic expression with the lower predicate, where it originated):

(13)   Zazpi behi makal-ek   etorri {behar dute}   oraindik.
       seven cow feeble-ERG come must   have.3pl.ERG still
       'Hard times must still be ahead.'

Raising-to-ergative of exactly this type was claimed not to exist in Marantz's (1991) influential case theory!

3.4   Splitting Hairs: The Progressive Aspect

Once we consider what are called *aspectual splits*, we find yet more evidence for structure as being crucial in ergative case assignment, above and beyond the lexical properties of certain verbs. Recall that, thus far, we've considered ergative as structurally assigned by a finite T_{erg}. In Basque perception verb complements, finite T_{erg} is lacking where the relevant nominal sits, and hence it cannot be assigned ergative, despite its agentivity and expected relations with the local verb. On the other hand, in raising-to-must, finite T_{erg} is landed upon and assigns ergative, even without agentivity in the originating verb.

Along similar lines, we now consider one of the broadest structural consequences: the loss of ergative case assignment in the progressive aspect. To anticipate what happens: In aspectual frames that are based on nominalizations or prepositional constructions, there is no finite T_{erg} at all. Thus, if in order to express the Basque equivalent of *Miren's a-dancin'*, the main verb is intransitive, it won't assign ergative. Precisely such an aspectual split, and its relevance for a structural theory of ergative case, was brought to the fore by Laka (2006), who pointed out that ergative case, otherwise found in the present tense for agentive verbs, is altogether lacking with progressive aspect:

(14) a. emakume-ak ogi-a jaten du.
woman-DEF.ERG bread-DEF eating has
'The woman eats (the) bread.'
b. emakume-a ogi-a jaten ari da.
woman-DEF bread-DEF eating PROG is
'The woman is eating (the) bread.'

What is the nature of the verb glossed as 'PROG' above? The English rendering with *Miren's a-dancin'*, which etymologically comes from the prepositional *at*, isn't far off. The element *ari*, meaning something like 'is engaged in', takes a locative complement, so that to express something like 'the woman is dancing' in (15), a postpositional element that makes 'dance' a locative is employed.

(15) emakume-a dantz-an ari da.
woman-DEF dance-LOC engaged is
'The woman is engaged in dance.'

The use of a locative postposition on 'dance' to express 'being engaged in' is similar to the way that the progressive is expressed in Mandarin Chinese, where *zài* is used either as a purely spatial locative (e.g., "Zhangshan is at the park") or as a means of temporally placing the subject in the midst of the event. As Laka herself puts it, "The syntactic structure of the various progressive forms in Basque is homomorphic with a locative structure. The homomorphism of spatial and temporal relations in human language is a pervasive and well known phenomenon, and the locative-like structure of the progressive is just one instance of this widespread homomorphism" (p. 187). The proposed structure, including a postposition introducing 'dance', is shown below:

(16)

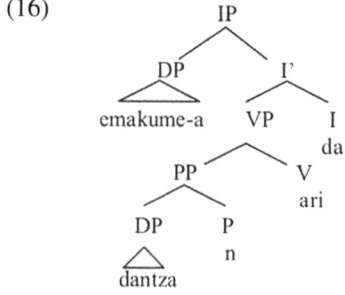

The main consequence of this kind of analysis is that the progressive marker *ari* is a main verb with its own auxiliary, and in examples such as (15b), takes a nominalized clause as its complement. As a result, progressive structures in Basque headed by *ari* are necessarily biclausal, and the higher clause has only a single argument. Therefore, in sentences such as (15b), there will be assignment of absolutive (nonergative) case to the main clause's subject, regardless of the nature of the verb embedded in the nominalized clause.

Furthermore, it can be shown that Basque *ari* is a verb (meaning 'to be engaged in') as it can be further nominalized itself:

(17) [[emakume-a lan-ean ari]   tze-a]   ona da.
      [[woman-DEF work-LOC engage] NMLZ-DEF]   good be.3sg
      'The woman's engaging in work is good.'

Now, aspectual splits (where ergative is found, say, only in the perfective) are widespread, as shown below for Hindi–Urdu. Sentences with perfective aspect have ergative subjects (18a) (as well as agreement with the object, as ergative case blocks agreement with the subject in Hindi–Urdu), while those in the imperfective have nominative subjects (18b).

(18) a. Raam-ne   roTii   khaayii   thii.
          Raam.MASC-ERG bread.FEM eaten-perf.fem AUX.FEM
          'Raam has eaten bread.'
      b. Raam   roTii   khaataa   thaa.
          Raam.MASC   bread.FEM eaten-impf.masc AUX.MASC
          'Raam was eating bread.'

Aspectual splits of this type are well known throughout the Indo-Aryan languages, as well as languages in the Polynesian and Pama-Nyungan families, and in Georgian. However, Basque makes the cut between progressive aspect, which is nonergative, and everything else – including imperfective:[4]

(19) emakume-ak   ogi-ak   ja-ten   ditu.
      woman-DET.ERG   bread-DET.PL   eat-IMPF has.3sg.ERG
      'The woman eats the breads.'

The analysis presented in Laka (2006) is thus that Basque progressives are formed of a biclausal structure, whereby the thematic verb that would ordinarily be responsible for assigning ergative does not do so because this verbal predicate is actually in a pruned locative+nominal structure. It is the complement to a

---

[4] Strictly speaking, therefore, Basque puts pause to Dixon's (1994) claim that in the tense- or aspect-based splits found in languages around the world, "the ergative making is always found either in past tense or in perfective aspect." (p. 99)

higher, semantically bleached predicate meaning 'engaged in' – and this higher predicate decides the case of its own subject argument. This analysis in many ways foreshadows another ergative split, witnessed in the progressive, where again ergative marking does not take place as expected, crucially because of the kind of structure involved.

3.5 How the Mayan Language Ch'ol Thickened the Plot

The syntactician Jessica Coon, who is also renowned for her work as a consultant on arguably the second most famous film about a linguist, *Arrival* (depending on whether the youth still cherish *My Fair Lady*), writes in Coon (2020) about her beginnings in fieldwork with the Mayan language Ch'ol (and how they indirectly tied to being a linguistic consultant for this film!). Ch'ol is spoken in the Chiapas highlands, and the Ch'ol people have struggled to maintain their sovereignty since the arrival of conquistadores in the sixteenth century, all the way through agrarian reforms in the twentieth century that took away their traditional corn cultivation practices and uprooted them from their fertile lands.

Mayan hieroglyphs carved in stone may represent an earlier form of the Ch'ol language. Although most nonspecialists assume that pyramids and archeology are all that is left of ancient Maya civilization, in fact by today's counts there are more than six million speakers of around thirty different Mayan languages, many of whom speak a Mayan language as their first language. The Mayan languages are all ergative, although Ch'ol itself exhibits an aspect-based split – one that at first blush seems the opposite of Basque under Laka's biclausal theory, but that in fact crucially vindicates the spirit of the model, albeit within a language that has different case-marking resources.

We can see ergative marking with transitive verbs versus intransitive verbs in the perfective aspect of Ch'ol below, in the examples from Coon (2010). Within these examples, the ergative pattern to be witnessed is not found through case-marking on the noun phrases themselves but rather in the system of cross-referencing affixes on the verb. In the glosses below, the affixes indicated by 'A' generally used for ergative agents (recalling the A for Agent above), while the 'B' markers are used for S and O.

(20) a. Tyi a-mek'-e-yoñ.
       PRFV A.2sg-hug-TV-B.1sg
       'You hugged me.'
    b. Tyi wäy-i-yoñ.
       PRFV sleep-ITV-B.1sg
       'I slept.'

However, in the progressives below, we find the 'A' marker used for the intransitive S as well. You'll recall that in Basque progressives, we found nonergative marking on the agent of transitive verbs because this agent was actually the subject of the verb 'engaged in'. In other words, in Basque progressives, we found a *reduction* of ergativity. However, in Ch'ol, we found that ergativity seems to *increase where it shouldn't*, precisely in the progressive:

(21) a. Choñkol a-mek'-oñ.
 PROG A.2sg-hug-B.1sg
 'You are hugging me.'
 b. Choñkol a-wäy-el.
 PROG A.2sg-sleep-NMLZ
 'You are sleeping.'

Earlier typological descriptions, such as Dixon (1979), called patterns like (21) 'extended ergativity' as these cases seem to put A-marking onto intransitive verbs like *sleep*. Crucially, however, this isn't like Tsova-Tush, where intransitives can be A-marked to enhance their volitionality, because in Ch'ol, there's no volitionality reading at all – it's simply obligatory to mark all intransitives this way in Ch'ol when they're in the progressive.

What's so special about the progressive construction in Ch'ol, such that it can manifest ergativity where it doesn't belong? The answer has two ingredients. According to Coon (2010), the forms *amek'oñ* and *awäyel* in (21b) are in fact not fully-fledged verbs but rather possessed nominals (in fact, they lack the verbal suffixes glossed as TV, ITV above). They actually are akin to English gerundive nominals like *my snoring* or *your hugging me*. Now, why should they show the A markers, which we said earlier were ergative? Because the A markers are not only used for ergative but also for genitive case (which is what's used for possessors – the English *my, your*, and *our* are genitive-case forms). In Ch'ol, ergative and genitive case are, of course, syntactically distinct: Ergative is assigned to the agent of a verb with a sufficient amount of tense structure above it, while genitive is assigned to the possessor of a nominal.

We can see this very clearly in environments with no gerund whatsoever, such as *Your mother's brother*. Note that there are two levels of possession here: first, a possessor-possessum relation between [you < r > mother] (where I have used <r> and <'s> to indicate the genitive case on the possessor). Then, a second possessor-possessum relation between that nominal and brother: [[you < r > mother] <'s> brother]. Interestingly, in Ch'ol, this is exactly what we witness, although in inverted linear order from the English:

(22) y-uskuñ a-mama
 GEN.3sg-older.brother GEN.2sg-mother
 '[[You r mother] 's older.brother]'

As a result, (21) should not be glossed with A, but rather with GEN. The entire sentence, as a result, is actually composed of two separate predicates. (This is starting to recall Basque *ari*, isn't it?) So what does the higher predicate mean in

Ch'ol? That's now the second ingredient to the answer begun above. The Ch'ol progressive marker *choñkol* can't really mean 'engaged in', because, unlike in Basque *ari* constructions, the subject of 'sleeping' and 'hugging' is confined as a possessor of the nominal. It turns out that the predicate *choñkol* found in (21) means something like 'what's happening is ...'. This is clear as it can directly take a noun as its complement:

(23) Choñkol k'iñijel tyi aw-otyoty.
      PROG   party   prep GEN.2sg-house
      'What's happening is a party at your house.'

Let's now return to a revised version of the glosses and translation of the progressive construction witnessed above. These are biclausal structures, whose higher predicate is intransitive and whose complement is a possessed nominal, the possessor of which is marked with genitive case. There's not actually any 'extended ergativity' going on at all here!

(24) a. Choñkol a-mek'-oñ.
          PROG   GEN.2sg-hug-ABS.1sg
          'What's happening is your hugging me.'
      b. Choñkol a-wäy-el.
          PROG   GEN.2sg-sleep-NMLZ
          'What's happening is your sleeping.'

Under this account, there is actually no split at all. All predicates in Ch'ol show ergative-absolutive agreement. It's just that *choñkol* is an intransitive predicate, and its complement is a nominal that involves a possessive structure, with a genitive-case possessor and a gerundive nominal (akin to *my snoring* in English).

What's happened across these last pages? We've seen two languages with progressive constructions that have split ergativity – but just calling it a split doesn't explain it. Instead, detailed analysis of the progressive particles in Basque and Ch'ol has shown that they are the main matrix predicates, whose meanings are akin to 'A is engaged in the location L' or 'What's happening is N'. In both instances, the verbal event of 'dancing' or 'hugging' isn't a verb at all. In Basque, it's treated as a location (in the same way that English and Mandarin express being 'within a spatiotemporal activity' in *Miren's at/a-swimming*), and we can see explicit locative morphology on it. In Ch'ol, it's treated as a gerundive nominal, and we see explicit genitive morphology on it. In neither case is ergative assigned because in neither case are these finite verbs.

What makes the progressive special is that it involves these predicates like 'A is engaged in the location L' or 'What's happening is N', and these form part of the way that progressive aspect comes to be syntactically expressed in many languages. No ergativity is expected on the location or the gerundive nominal, and any ergativity that is found will entirely depend on the matrix predicate. In Basque, a predicate like 'A is engaged in' will mark its subject with reduced ergativity, regardless of the thematic agentivity of the embedded predicate (expressed as a location). In Ch'ol, the extended ergativity is in fact illusory – it's just that the genitive cross-referencing affixes found on all kinds of nouns are morphologically identical to the ergative ones found on verbs.

The common thread that has run through all of these studies is that 'unexpected' patterns of ergative marking – namely its absence in the complement of perception verbs, its intrusion in raising-to-modal *must*, its disappearance in the Basque progressive, and its failure to be assigned at all in the Ch'ol progressive – are all consequences of structure. Ergative case cannot be chalked up to a semantic encoding of agentivity or volitionality of the predicates involved alone. It is the details of the structure wrought around such predicates that will predestine their arguments to be ergative or not.

Further Reading

The influence of minoritized languages on case theory has been steadily cumulative. For a classic discussion of ergativity and its relation to the passive, see Anderson (1977). Within Ch'ol specifically, there have been important contributions relating to the description of ergativity by native-speaker linguists, such as Gutiérrez Sánchez (2014). For additional linguistic evidence that locative predicates may be needed in order to express the progressive, see Salanova (2007) on Mẽbenkogre, where auxiliary predicates such as 'standing', 'sitting', or 'lying down' yield nominative, instead of ergative. An additional line of argumentation that ergative is not lexical comes in the overapplication of ergative marking in applicativized unaccusatives in Shipibo (Baker, 2014).

4 Closest Conjunct Agreement in Slovenian and Xhosa

In this chapter, the contributions of the teams working together on South Slavic and Southern Bantu languages, many of which began specifically as new research partnerships forged after the dissolution of the former Yugoslavia and the end of apartheid, provide compelling evidence that syntactic processes must include reference to linear order. Syntax may not be just a spinning Calderian mobile.

4.1 *Has the woman who coffee is happy?

Consider the sentences *Has he any idea?*, *Have you been feeling better?*, or *Is it raining?*, which show that when there is a main verb *have* or *is* in English polar questions (i.e., those with a yes-or-no answer), they are formed by moving this verb to the front of the sentence. Now consider *The woman who has coffee is happy*. The way that a question is formed is not by moving the *first* such verb to the front – if so, one would end up with the virtually unparseable gibberish in the section title above. Rather, it's *Is the woman who has coffee happy?*, and the lesson from this comparison is that when there is more than one such verb, it is not the leftmost (or linearly closest to the front of the sentence) that moves to the beginning, but rather the *main* verb, the matrix verb, the highest predicate, the hierarchically most local to the root of the tree that moves. Since Chomsky's (1975) discussion of such examples, the conclusion has been that syntactic locality – the determination of which of two lexical items is closer to a given target – is determined by hierarchical and not linear factors.[1]

In sentences like that one, the relative height of each of the verbs is clear: *is happy* is the main predicate, and *who has coffee* is a relative clause modifying the subject. Similarly, when there are two *wh-* phrases in a sentence, such as in *I know who read what*, the locality-violating **I know what who read* is unthinkable. Similarly, in American English, for two noun phrases in passivizations such as *John was told a lie* vs. **A lie was told John*.

---

[1] The force of such examples lent its title to Michel Gondry's 2013 animated documentary *Is the man who is tall happy?*

But not all cases of locality that involve comparison between two items are as clear cut. In particular, the structure of coordination (phrases like *pencils and erasers*) has long been discussed. In logic, and subsequently in model-theoretic semantics, a conjunction simply forms a larger set composed of the two conjuncts. But syntactically, is there a hierarchical difference between the first and second conjunct in *pencils and erasers*? A long tradition of syntactic research, with its crystallization in Kayne (1994), concludes that indeed such coordinations are not symmetric. Rather, the first conjunct asymmetrically sits higher than the second one.

The cases above have involved movement – be it movement of a verb to form polar questions, of a wh- word to form wh- questions, or of a noun phrase in passivization. From these clear-cut comparisons, the conclusion that all syntactic relations – which would include agreement morphology on verbs – involve hierarchically-based locality has been assumed by extension and largely seems to hold for cases of agreement involving coordinated noun phrases as well.

When I was a visiting PhD student at the University of Maryland in 2003, although (and perhaps because!) I didn't have an assigned desk in the graduate student lounge, I would walk in from time to time to ask students what they were working on. One of them, Usama Soltan (who had to temporarily introduce himself as "US" in the widespread paranoia following 9/11), was working on a creative solution to the problem of first-conjunct agreement in Arabic, whereby in a verb-initial sentence like "arrived$_F$ Marwan and Ali," the verb could show feminine agreement – not with the coordination as a whole but only with the feminine first conjunct, Marwan.

(1) ʒiʔ-na   hunna   wa ʔabaaʔ-u-hunna
     arrived-3pl.fem they.fem and fathers-NOM their
     'They (fem.) and their fathers arrived'

This problem was of interest because it supported the idea of a hierarchical structure for coordination phrases such as [Marwan and Ali], and the idea was that Marwan, the first conjunct, being hierarchically higher than the second (in other words, coordination not being a symmetric juxtaposition), would be closer to the verb and therefore have the potential to exert preferential influence on the verbal agreement. Usama had a very innovative solution for how the timing of these operations would take place, with the second conjunct being added to the structure after agreement was already computed (subsequently published as Soltan [2007]), and he sketched it out on a whiteboard, as we all used to do back then, with the unspoken proviso that nobody would ever erase someone else's diagrams on the board and that the person who drew it had the right to come back and copy it down later if it turned out worthwhile. The result was a continual multicolored palimpsest of fragments of different languages in different handwritings with different representational abbreviations. We stepped back from the board, and I nodded in concert with that outpouting lip gesture meaning 'Good for you, man – I'm happy to see you've come up with a novel solution', until he shrugged and said, "Although I have no idea what to do for Slovenian."

"Slovenian?" I asked, as I had been puzzled that Slovenian might have any property unique to its agreement system that I wouldn't have heard of in Russian, Polish, or Czech, and I admitted to trouble in keeping separate in my head that Slovenian was abbreviated as 'Sl' while Slovakian was 'Sk'. "Yeah, it's right here in Corbett's (1983) book," Usama pointed, "they have second conjunct agreement." Now this clearly didn't make sense under any theory of hierarchical structure in which the first conjunct was more prominent than the second, and we weren't ready to entertain the possibility that in Slovenian things were somehow backwards, with the second conjunct higher than the first. "But this data is from novels and newspapers," I frowned. "And the consequences for the theory are so drastic, I won't believe it until a real native speaker confirms this is possible." At that moment my memory transported me back to someone I had met at a European summer school a few years earlier. Lanko Marušič was known to all for being a spelunker with a disarming laugh, who made barrels of his own wine when he wasn't chasing after aquatic salamanders in karstic caves. Soon enough we were working together, having presented in 2006 at a Slavic conference in Toronto on a model whereby agreement with coordinations could wait until a very late stage of the sentential derivation, a point at which linear order had become more important than hierarchical order. Thus, sentences like the following have closest conjunct agreement (CCA) – as does Arabic above – but, crucially, with the coordinated NP subject in *preverbal* position.

(2)   Čolni   in ladje   so   se   gnetle   v pristanišču
      boats.M.PL and ships.F.PL AUX.PL REFL crowded. F.PL in port
      'Boats and ships were crowding the port.'

Examples like this showed that in Slovenian, when the subject contains two noun phrases (NPs) that are conjoined, the verb can sometimes agree with the linearly closest one (even if it is the second NP). This offered us the opportunity to examine whether agreement morphology may operate with its own principles, partially distinct from those of other syntactic relations. Linear order may become a relevant relation for syntactic operations specifically when it comes to coordinated phrases, given their different kind of structure from other syntactic phrases, as by hypothesis they are headed by neither one of the conjuncts. A tree-structural representation of the subject noun phrase from (2) would be as follows, where &P represents the fact that the coordinator, *in* in Slovenian, is the head of the entire &P.

(3) Asymmetric structure of &P:

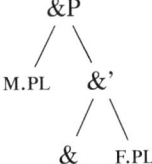

Given this structure, how could a verb that follows such a noun phrase ignore the hierarchical prevalence of the first conjunct and instead go for a linearly closer conjunct? And why only for gender? We proposed in Marušič et al. (2007) that gender agreement for inanimate nouns (i.e., with no semantic relevance), unlike other syntactic operations, might involve some computational operations carried out after the syntactic computation proper was already done, and at this point, if agreement computations were sufficiently delayed, linear order could be available. The idea was that during the syntax proper, there is no linear order at all – the entire set of hierarchical relations are spinning from a fixed point at the top like one of Alexander Calder's famous mobiles (Figure 4.1).

In order for such a structure to be externalized into the phonological system, these mobiles needed to be *linearized* – the equivalent of lying one of Calder's mobiles flat on the ground so that it could no longer spin. If gender agreement with coordinated NPs in Slovenian could wait this long, linear order would be accesible for the purposes of locality. The fact that agreement, however, could wait until after syntax proper was done, meant that something long cherished as syntactic might change our notions of the timing and interface of syntax and phonological linearization. All this on the basis of Slovenian?

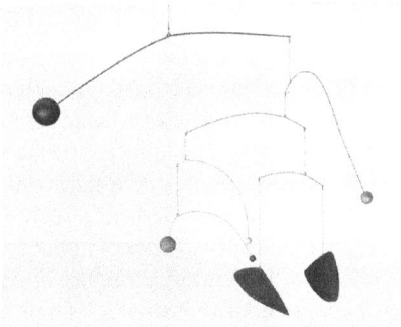

Figure 4.1 Alexander Calder's spinning mobiles: hierarchically structured with no fixed linear order

4.2 Data Is Not the Plural of Anecdote

Extraordinary claims require extraordinary evidence, however, and in 2007 I had a sabbatical in Trieste. The university at which Lanko worked was extremely close, and I ended up spending just as much time in Slovenia as I did in my host institution. We began distributing fill-in-the-blank questionnaires at local high schools to confirm that second conjunct agreement was alive and well but eventually wanted firm empirical proof. We teamed up with Bill Badecker, a psycholinguist who had been working on coordination of this sort in Greek, and the three of us developed an experimental paradigm called 'elicited production' to really establish, using randomized stimuli and real-time recordings, that second conjunct agreement was a robust phenomenon in Slovenian without making claims about any other South Slavic languages, no matter how closely related. In a way, publishing on second conjunct agreement and its theoretical significance for the theory of agreement based on Slovenian was a point of pride for Lanko, whose language is spoken by fewer people than live in Houston, Texas.

For a variety of reasons (the most dramatic being related to delays with the journal we sent it to), the paper only made it in print as Marušič et al. (2015). In the meantime, however, Željko Bošković, without using these time-consuming experimental methods and only his own judgements as a theoretician and native speaker, published a paper on similar phenomena on related South Slavic varieties.

As it turns out, the issue of what to call these related South Slavic varieties is a matter of great contention. For decades (in fact, starting with one of the Grimm Brothers), a language called 'Serbo-Croatian' was referred to as the tongue shared by Serbians (who are largely Eastern Orthodox Christians), Croatians (who are largely Roman Catholics), and Bosnians (who are largely Muslims). Now, you may have noticed that the label 'Serbo-Croatian' leaves out one of these three groups, and after the bloody wars of the 1990s, many of the speakers were not happy with this hyphenation at all. During these wars, the Bosnian population suffered numerous atrocities, including the four-year long Siege of Sarajevo (the capital of Bosnia and Herzegovina), and to this day, some linguists in Serbia still object to the use of 'Bosnian' to denote a language (somehow preferring 'Bosniak'). In most diplomatic circles, and indeed, by many criteria of grouping these varieties based on linguistic factors rather than contemporary national borders, the trinominal Bosnian/Croatian/Serbian – abbreviated as BCS – is what is used to refer to the continuum of varieties, without committing to the thorny question of whether they (or indeed any grouping of related and mutually intelligible varieties, anywhere on earth) constitute a 'single language' or not.

However, importantly for the current discussion, which pivots on the rarity of – and the dramatic grammatical implications of a language having – closest conjunct agreement, it was particularly relevant that Bošković (2009) described the facts of CCA as holding for "Serbo-Croatian," especially in 2009. Not only did this do him no favors with other linguists who strongly advocated for alternative names for their language varieties, but more importantly, it made it very hard to tell whether the scope of his claim was indeed intended for all of Bosnian/Croatian/Serbian or simply the specific variety that he may have spoken. Subsequently, it became all-too-frequent that every time we made passing reference to Bošković (2009) in our lectures on Slovenian, native speakers would often loudly proclaim their disagreement with one or more of Bošković's judgements (usually, in fact, regarding not CCA, but highest conjunct agreement [HCA]). Disagreements are not infrequent with linguistic data, but in this case we weren't sure of the source – was this true sociolinguistic variation, of the same type governing individual preferences in whether to say "There are / there's two detectives outside"? Or was it geographically based (say, with differences between Serbian, Croatian, and Bosnian varieties, not to mention their numerous historically entrenched varieties within each country)? Or might it simply reflect the fact that a theoretician might, innocently enough but implicitly, influence their own data judgements based on the theoretical consequences? There was only one way to find out, and this involved mobilizing a large-scale team.

In parallel, research such as Bhatt and Walkow (2013) and Bhatia et al. (2009) made clear that CCA of this type, potentially involving reference to linear order, was to be found in Hindi–Urdu and in Tsez, and this cross-linguistic interest in closest conjunct agreement made it possible to seize the moment. We assembled a team of two research partners in Croatia (in Zagreb and Zadar), two research partners in Serbia (in Novi Sad and Niš), and one in Bosnia (in Sarajevo) alongside the team in Slovenia, and the idea was to use literally the exact same stimuli (pending minor lexical differences, akin to *elevator* vs. *lift*), the exact same experimental setup, and the exact same number of participants (n = 30) across all six sites. With a total of 180 participants, we would be able to establish once and for all whether CCA was a robust phenomenon in these South Slavic languages.

The South Slavic languages have three genders – masculine, neuter, and feminine – which turns out to be very useful for diagnosing CCA. This is because, when one has only two genders in the plural (as in, say, French) or only one gender in the plural (as in Russian and German), one cannot tell CCA apart from what is called 'resolution' – the rule that in mixed gender combinations, one should use masculine as the default.[2]

---

[2] As for why masculine is the default in a given language (as is the case throughout numerous European languages), this seems to be an arbitrary fact, most likely an infelicitous holdover from archaic gender conventions already found as far back as the Old Testament.

Thus, if one observes masculine agreement in a [F&M] preverbal conjunct in South Slavic, one cannot tell if it is CCA or resolution. But in combinations such as [F&N] or [N&F], the presence of either of these non-masculine genders in the agreement morphology on the verb will diagnose either HCA or CCA.

We used an equal number of stimuli in all nine gender combinations, and in preverbal and postverbal position. This allowed us to compare postverbal position, in which agreement with the first conjunct would simultaneously converge in the case of HCA and CCA, with preverbal position, in which agreement with the second conjunct could only be CCA. We also compared coordination with cases of what is called 'agreement attraction', following Jespersen (1913/1961) and Bock and Miller (1991). This refers to cases of apparent performance errors, in which speakers say things like *The key to the cabinets are missing*, whereby the plural agreement on the verb tracks an NP buried inside the prepositional complement to a singular noun phrase.

The setup for elicited production was one in which participants first view what is called a 'model sentence', one with a simple NP subject such as (4a). Then, on the same computer screen, they see the 'replacement' noun phrase, (4b). Finally, their task is to *produce* a new version of (4a), replacing the subject with (4b) and adjusting the rest as necessary, as in (4c).

(4) a. Prevod je ovjeren pečatom.
      translation.M.SG AUX.SG authenticated.M.SG by.seal
      'The translation was authenticated by seal.'
   b. Molbe i rješenja
      requestsF.PL and decisionsN.PL
      'Requests and decisions'
   c. Molbe i rješenja su
      requestsF.PL and decisionsN.PL AUX.SG
      ovjeren-i/-a/-e pečatom.
      authenticated-M.PL/N.PL/F.PL by.seal
      'Requests and decisions were authenticated by seal.'

The findings of these elicited production experiments for F&N combinations in preverbal position (where CCA has the clearest ability to shine) across all six sites is shown in Figure 4.2, reproduced from Gold et al. (2018). We made sure participants were from a narrow age range (eighteen to twenty-two), not linguistics students, and native speakers who grew up in the region tested in order to ensure we were not dealing with heterogeneous groups but instead were making claims based on uniform sets of speakers who were representative of specific geographical variants.

These results demonstrate that CCA is chosen sometimes three times as much as HCA and that the preference for linear-based locality with respect to this kind of gender agreement holds across all the South Slavic varieties under study.

Closest Conjunct Agreement in Slovenian and Xhosa

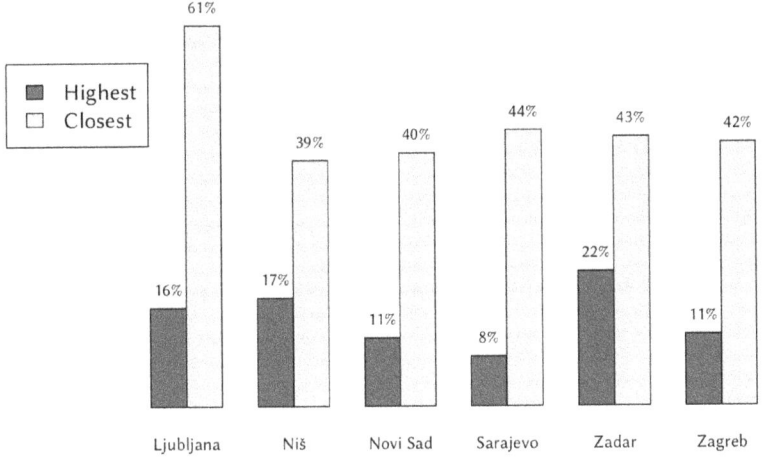

Figure 4.2 Rates of highest conjunct agreement vs. closest conjunct agreement in South Slavic

In fact, the rate of linear agreement obtained is much, much higher than that usually found in attraction studies, suggesting it is a distinct phenomenon – not a performance error at all, but a grammatical instance of linear order playing a role in agreement. What accounts for the optionality, however? Why is CCA not the *only* strategy available? We suggested that linearization, which turns an unordered Calderian mobile into a flattened structure, may be optional in its timing. When a speaker enacts linearization before gender features are copied, CCA results, but if gender features are copied before linearization, then HCA results. While there is a preference for earlier linearization, this preference isn't absolute, and the grammar leaves the options open either way – it's a bit like whether one mixes the dry ingredients before whisking the eggs to make a cake or vice versa.

By contrast, attraction rates were between 3% and 11% across all the sites. Why should CCA be so much more robust? We contend that the crucial factor is that unlike in attraction, the first conjunct in a &P is not the head of the &P and that hierarchy 'fails' given the details of the structure of the &P. Specifically, an &P has no way to compute its own gender, and between Conjunct 1 and Conjunct 2 (as neither is the head of the &P as a whole), Conjunct 1 can be ignored under certain circumstances. In attraction configurations, however, the first noun phrase *is* the head of the &P as a whole, and this makes ignoring it more difficult (hence the extremely low rate of attraction effects).

Of perhaps greatest interest was the finding that while CCA is preferred to HCA in preverbal contexts, these results don't mean that coordinations

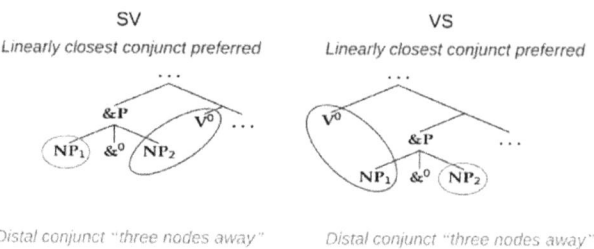

Figure 4.3 Predictions of distal conjunct agreement given flat vs. hierarchical structures for &P

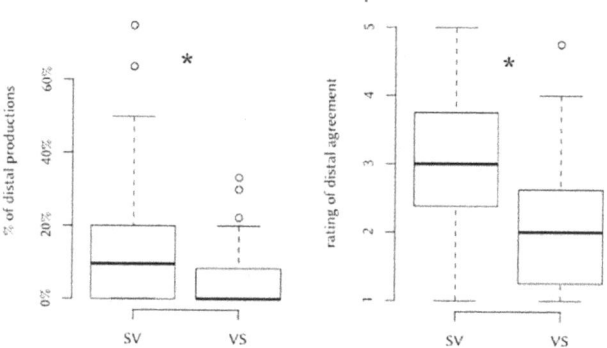

Figure 4.4 Results of asymmetries in distal conjunct agreement for SV and VS configurations

are flat. In a hierarchical model of the &P, even for the non-closest, that is, 'distal' conjunct, there is a difference between the first conjunct in preverbal cases and the second conjunct in postverbal cases. The first conjunct in SV (preverbal) configurations still enjoys a hierarchical advantage. On the other hand, the second conjunct in VS configurations is neither hierarchically highest nor linearly closest to the verb, and there should be little if any reason for it to be visible for agreement. However, what if &Ps were simply flat and symmetrical, as counterfactually shown in Figure 4.3?

In this case, one would predict symmetric results between the preverbal and postverbal distal conjunctions. But both in production (with the methodology described above) and in quantitative acceptability judgements, these were treated vastly differently, as shown in Figure 4.4 (the star * in the graph indicates statistically significant differences).

In the production data on the left, the rate of postverbal agreement with the second conjunct is hugging the floor. In the acceptability rating, it ranges between 1 and less than 3 on a scale of 1–5. These findings implicate an

Closest Conjunct Agreement in Slovenian and Xhosa   51

asymmetry in the two distal conjuncts, and such asymmetries are directly captured by the internal hierarchical structure of the &P. Far from proving that hierarchy doesn't exist in &Ps, the experimental syntax data based on these South Slavic languages crucially vindicates it.

4.3   So Where Can Linearity Prevail over Hierarchy?

It was a great success for us as a research team that we managed to design, run, and analyze the stimuli (coming up with the stimuli was one of the hardest parts of the project) and show that CCA is an inescapable fact for all six varieties across the research teams in the former Yugoslavia. I remember that, at a dinner we held for all of the partners in London, one of the research members from Niš, Serbia, and another from Zadar, Croatia, asked me, "We've been chatting about some parallels in the local varieties of our languages and would like to work together on something. Would you mind?" I nearly swooned. "Would I *mind*?" I chirped, "That would be my dream." I was thrilled by the idea that through this project, younger researchers, all now trained in similar research methods, could work together on highly similar language varieties and could do so across borders that had not seen the most active research collaborations (in some cases, literally because of arguments over what to call the language[s] – about which I always insisted that BCS was a convenient abbreviation never to be unpacked). Now that we had successfully established that linearity-based agreement in preverbal coordinations was a reality and provided a demonstration that hierarchical structure was still necessary as well to explain the results, it was time to turn to investigating some of the differences across these six South Slavic varieties.

There is, in fact, a long history of classifying the languages spoken in the former Yugoslavia as "štokavian, čakavian, kajkavian," based on their words for 'what'. While it might seem outlandish to classify languages based on the word for 'what', it is reminiscent of the classification of French languages in terms of their word for 'yes' into Langue d'Oui and Langue d'Oc (the latter eventually becoming known as the minoritized language Occitan). But while so much historical comparison of language distance, both in time and space, has been carried out based on individual lexical items – just words, words, words – it is definitely the case that adopting a new word is a lot easier in historical change than enacting an alteration to the internal, sometimes not even consciously accessible, mechanisms of one's grammar. For this reason, linguists such as Longobardi and Guardiano (2009) have made the argument, and even mathematically demonstrated, that grammatical parameters may be a better metric of seeing how far apart, say, the Celtic languages are from the Romance languages than individual words. Similarly, Emonds and Faarlund (2014) have contended that Middle English may reflect the influence of Viking invasions, largely based on syntactic properties (such as the ability to strand prepositions in sentences like *Who were you talking with?*, which did not come from Anglo-Saxon), providing evidence for being closer to a North Germanic language, as opposed to the lexical inheritance Middle English kept from West Germanic Old English.

Given that morphosyntactic comparisons may be reflective of linguistic distance in space in time, our idea was that the corpus of hundreds of responses in the experiment constituted a corpus we could analyze – granted, a corpus only with sentences that have conjoined subjects – but still, a corpus with enough data points to run a *Principal Component Analysis* comparing these six varieties. A Principal Component Analysis takes a pool of data that varies across many potential dimensions and attempts to compress it down to two factors that are most explanatory in mathematically accounting for the variation. These two dimensions become two axes of a graph (and in our case, roughly correspond to the height of the light and dark bars in Figure 4.2). These were, in fact, akin to the rates of HCA decreasing along the y-axis and of CCA decreasing on the x-axis, and please recall that these do not add up to 100% as the rate of default agreement is a third option, the value of which is computable based on these other two. We wanted to see how well the differences in conjunct agreement (the ratio of CCA vs. HCA vs. default agreement in all of the nine gender combinations) lined up with traditional classifications. These traditional classifications were "kajkavian, čakavian, štokavian" (as it would be along the x-axis), as well as the historical classification of a low front vowel, "jat," with different historical pronunciations in different regions (towards diphthongal realization along the y-axis) – perhaps akin to the pronunciations of English "bath" with [æ] vs. [a] – and finally with the geographic location of each dialect. The results are shown in Figure 4.5.

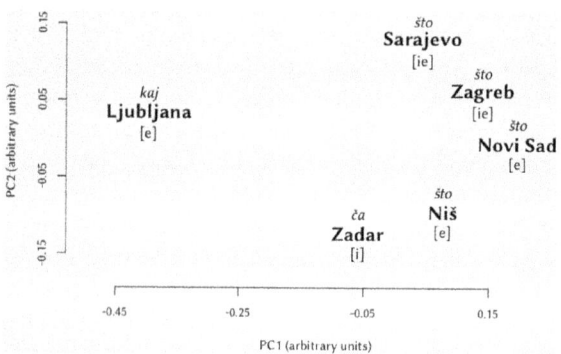

Figure 4.5 Principal Component Analysis showing clusters of morphosyntactic relatedness

It was not a huge surprise that Slovenian was morphosyntactically furthest away from the five languages within the BCS grouping, and it was also reassuring to see that the two axes of the graph largely mirrored the classifications based on words for 'what' and the low front vowel. But most surprising, perhaps, was the fact that the three varieties clustered most together in combined nearness along the dimensions of experimental morphosyntax – Sarajevo, Zagreb, and Novi Sad – are all spoken in what are today three different countries. Despite the efforts of national language academies to establish that certain badges of linguistic identity are decisive markers of being from one of these contemporary nations, factors like gender agreement with conjoined preverbal subjects are too far below the radar to be affected by these more recent-prescriptive influences. Languages seem to change more slowly than recently drawn national borders.

So where does linearity prevail over hierarchy? Only in a small corner of the grammar and in a small corner of the world. Even though these results could have been taken as evidence for a simplistic newsflash that "Chomsky (1975) was wrong," constructive efforts to build linguistic theory, on a community of findings that explain new results alongside an accountability towards preexisting results, do not throw out the baby with the bathwater. Rather, one must understand why linearity-based agreement shows up (a) only for gender, (b) only in coordinations, and (c) only in certain languages. Let's address each of these three in turn.

In a coordination, number features are predictable from what it means to coordinate two NPs. In fact, in Slovenian there is a special category of dual number, distinct from singular and plural – a category of inflectional endings used specifically for a group of two. This property is quite rare in contemporary European languages, although many classical languages, such as Ancient Greek and Sanskrit, used to have it. It's a whole category of agreement endings, not just within the noun phrase but on adjectives, verbs, and auxiliaries, specifically for when the subject is a set composed of exactly two members. (The linguist Tesnière apparently studied classified dating ads in the newspaper as one of the ideal corpora of a written genre with recurrent use of the dual). When a singular is coordinated with a singular in Slovenian, therefore, number agreement with the coordinated phrase will be dual, for exactly these compositional mathematical reasons (in fact, one might simply posit that the coordination head, &, is already 'born' with the feature [−singular]). Similarly, when a dual is coordinated with a dual, number agreement will be plural. On the other hand, for gender (and in particular, recall our experiments always involved inanimate nouns, on which gender is not interpretable in any biological sense), the set composed by a feminine noun and a neuter noun has no specific obvious automatic mathematical result. Gender is thus not the kind of feature that a coordination computes on its own in any semantically determined way.

Number information is highly relevant for semantics of nominals and can be deterministically computed in a conjunction. But grammatical gender has no semantic import, and therefore gender agreement can be delayed until a later stage of the agreement computation, where linear order becomes more predominant in representation and processing and where the features of an individual conjunct can be chosen from. The idea is that since a coordination is headed by &P, while &P can compute its own number, it cannot compute its own gender, and for that reason, agreement features are taken from one of the individual conjuncts. In other kinds of structures, unlike coordinations, the head of the entire phrase has its own gender features, and these will be the ones agreed with.

If being part of a coordination is all it takes, why hadn't similar patterns been found outside of Slovenian? Naturally, closest conjunct agreement is easier to observe in languages with more than two genders, so that one can diagnose it as distinct from default agreement. But we noticed another potentially highly relevant factor. Consider the verbal agreement endings for Slovenian, shown in the three-by-three table below for its three numbers (singular, dual, and plural) and three genders. You'll notice that the nine cells don't show nine distinct endings, but rather that quite a few of these endings are 'reused' across cells, in horizontal, vertical, and even diagonal patterns.

(5)

Number	Masculine	Feminine	Neuter
Singular	∅	-a	-o
Dual	-a	-i	-i
Plural	-i	-e	-a

This reuse of the same inflectional endings in distinct gender–number columns, called *syncretism* in morphological theory, leads to acute ambiguities of analysis for the child who may be learning Slovenian. After all, grammars are products of the children who build them as they witness the linguistic data around them. Suppose that, as a Slovenian child, you hear a coordination of Msg & Fsg and a verb with the ending -*a*. This could in fact be masculine dual, the result of default masculine agreement together with the dual ending computed by the conjunction of two singulars, but it could also be feminine singular – aka closest conjunct agreement. That is to say, without even wanting to 'teach their child' CCA, ambiguous endings in cases like this could be the trigger for the child themself to analyze the language as having CCA and build that into their grammar. Similarly for MPl and FDu, where a verb with the -*i* ending could be masculine default and plural or could be closest conjunct agreement with the FDu itself. Or to provide another example, conjoining NPl & MDu and hearing -*a* on the verb could be analyzed as the result of agreement with the first conjunct *or* agreement with the second conjunct – both would yield this same, syncretic verbal ending. The fact, therefore, that Slovenian has such a high degree of syncretism leading to ambiguous analyses of the surface result of combinations – some of it leading to CCA analyses – is arguably enough to trigger what may be an otherwise rare kind of grammatical pattern cross-linguistically. Put differently, CCA (modeled here as the result of a particular derivational timing between linearization and gender agreement) is a valid option in all grammars but one that requires sufficient evidence to be adopted within the grammar of specific individual languages.

4.4 A Two-Step Theory of Agreement

The facts of closest conjunct agreement in South Slavic became well known as the result of our investigations and put Slovenian on the map in terms of agreement theory. Not everyone, however, was willing to usher in such radical changes to the model as the one we proposed, in which agreement itself was partly post-syntactic – in other words, partly *non*-syntactic. A host of creative alternatives were developed, avoiding the kind of direct reference to linear order and instead privileging the second conjunct in other ways. One of those, by Murphy and Puškar (2017), proposed that CCA was the result of a computation that already took place *inside* the &P itself. In this highly interesting proposal, the &P head itself could agree 'downwards' first with the second conjunct and then keep those features as its own &P features, visible to agreement from the outside.

However, the theory of post-syntactic, linearity-based agreement is one in which each verb is searching for its own set of gender features to agree with, and doing so after linearization has already put the coordination and its contents in order. As a result, in what we called 'sandwiching' contexts in which there are *two* verbs, and in which each of these verbs is on a *different side* of the coordination, one would expect the verb on the left to agree with the conjunct on the left, and the verb on the right to agree with the conjunct on the right. This is in fact what happens in examples such as (6):

(6) Včeraj so bile [krave in teleta]
 yesterday AUX.PL been.FEM.PL COW.FEM.PL and calf.NEUT.PL
 prodana.
 sold.NEUT.PL
 'Yesterday cows and calves were sold.'

In Marušič and Nevins (2020), we demonstrated experimentally the acceptability of sandwiching configurations such as (6), which clinch the role of linear order, as each verb chooses from the conjunct linearly closest to it. These results provided further support for a theory in which the computation of agreement is cleft into two steps; let us call them Agree-Link and Agree-Copy. The first of these, Agree-Link, establishes that a grammatical dependency will take place between two elements, say a verb and the subject noun phrase. It is based on principles of hierarchy alone, and determined by the relative geometry of the subject noun phrase and the verb. The second operation, Agree-Copy, does the actual work of finding features within the subject noun phrase and copying them over to the verb. Now, if these two operations are separate, it actually means that, in principle, other linguistic operations or computations could be interleaved in between the execution of each. If linearization, the operation that flattens a Calderian mobile, takes place after Agree-Link but before Agree-Copy, then the latter operation will have access to linearized structure. This means, however, that if one has a coordination with three conjuncts (such as *the trains, the planes, and the automobiles*, the medial conjunct will never be agreed with as it will never be linearly closest (or hierarchically highest) with respect to any external source. Thus, even though the multiple 'grammars' allowed in Slovenian conjunct agreement allow more than one option, they are still restrictive – a property we experimentally confirmed (Marušič et al., 2015), to make sure that it wasn't the case that our experiments would reveal that 'anything is possible'.

4.5 Southern Bantu: Nonbinary Gender to the Seventh Power

Following the development of a multi-step theory of agreement featuring Agree-Link and Agree-Copy, with many consequences for the grammar and, in fact, all really made possible by studying Slovenian and other South Slavic languages in depth, I began a kind of 'lecture tour' in order to discuss the results, but more importantly, to hear feedback. For me, traveling through airports and living out of suitcases to give lectures is only as worthwhile as the questions or feedback that I receive makes it. At one such lecture at Rutgers University, New Jersey, where there would be ample interest in agreement from Mark Baker (about whom we will hear more in Chapter 5), upon concluding the lecture and the question period, I hung out in front of my laptop, taking extra long to unplug things, as I always do, in the hope that someone who might not have had the chance to ask a question in front of everyone would saunter up and say something. At that moment, a first-year student, somewhat shy in approaching me, introduced herself as Hazel Mitchley from South Africa (I later learned that she was baptized in the same Bloemfontein church as J. R. R. Tolkien) and told me that her MA thesis had shown highly similar patterns of closest conjunct agreement in three Southern Bantu languages.

I had read before about closest conjunct agreement in Southern Bantu and in fact read Moosally's (1998) dissertation, having noticed that a very similar kind of syncretism to the one in (5) may be at play. But Hazel's thesis brought up a number of striking parallels with the South Slavic cases. In particular, in Mitchley (2015), she found that in Xhosa (the mother tongue of Nelson

Mandela, Trevor Noah, and Miriam Makeba, who made it famous with the hit "Click Song"), closest conjunct agreement in gender was preferred. Thus, in the example below, 'men' and 'carrots' are conjoined, and the predicate agrees with 'carrots'.

(7)   Ama-doda nemi-nqathe   i-se   gadi-ni.
      VI-men   AND.IV-carrots SUBJ.AGR.IV-LOC garden-LOC
      'The men and the carrots are in the garden.'

Now, you may be wondering what those numbers like VI and IV are (I am using Roman numerals to distinguish these numbers from the 1, 2, 3 used for first, second, and third person in glosses). These are the so-called Meinhof noun classes of the Bantu languages, a way of understanding the different groups of nouns in the languages, and the agreement patterns they trigger, that has been around since Meinhof (1906). However, putting things in those terms makes these languages sound vastly unfamiliar and even incommensurate with other agreement patterns, and research beginning with Carstens (1991) and continuing to the present day with work such as Msaka (2019) has suggested that Meinhof's approach may have been on a misleading track. Instead, one can think of Bantu languages such as Xhosa as having a total of seven genders. (Similarly, for the three genders of Slavic – masculine, feminine, and neuter – which for inanimate nouns have no real-world relation to biological gender, we could have simply called them genders I, II, and III).

Seven genders? This definitely goes beyond binary. Then again, the word 'gender' itself may be misleading when used for describing the grammatical groupings of inanimate nouns. The system set up by Meinhof has all of the singulars with odd numbers, and their corresponding plurals with even numbers. But what Carstens (1991) suggests is that instead, these should be thought of as a series of genders – call them Gender A, Gender B, Gender C, and so forth – whose morphology can be described in terms of these gender–number pairings, as below for the subject-agreement morphemes for five genders in Xhosa:

(8) | Gender | Singular Version | Plural Version |
      |--------|------------------|----------------|
      | A | u | ba |
      | B | u | i |
      | C | li | a |
      | D | si | zi |
      | E | i | zi |

While it might be convenient for some (and inconvenient for others) to number the cells in the table above using "Class I, Class II, ... Class X," that essentially misses the point, which is that these genders have singular and plural forms and are used to classify nouns into groups. Why do languages have genders of this type at all? It seems to be a way to organize the lexicon. Having masculine, feminine, and neuter in Slavic inanimate nouns, or these five genders shown above for Bantu nouns, is a way that, like the conjugation classes of verbs in Romance, languages organize their vocabulary into groups. But just like the conjugation classes that one must learn in the morphology of Spanish verbs (e.g., *-ar, -er,* or *-ir*), these groupings don't necessarily correspond to specific semantic correlates – they are simply a way of partitioning the lexicon into sets that agree with similar types of morphology. This kind of morphological organization with nouns is, in general, more common in languages with free word order – if the subject can appear before or after the verb or in any position within the sentence, then there is still a reliable cue to what the subject is because it's the noun phrase that's controlling agreement on the verb.

Despite this formal cueing of the thematic and constituency relations between subject noun phrase and verb, much like gender agreement for inanimate nouns in South Slavic, the gender agreement found on Bantu verbs has no direct semantic interpretation. It is therefore a prime candidate for being 'delayed' until after linearization and thereby enabling a step of Agree-Copy that can refer to linear order. When a noun phrase is not conjoined at all, we actually cannot even tell whether linearization comes before Agree-Copy or not because there is only one noun phrase to copy agreement features from anyway. But when there is a conjoined noun phrase – and particularly within a system that, as you can see in (8), shows significant syncretisms, this ordering of linearization before Agree-Copy can lead to closest conjunct agreement, exactly as reported by Mitchley (2015) for Xhosa.

However, CCA isn't the only possibility for Xhosa – in fact, speakers may resort to default agreement in cases of conjunctions that combine two different genders. The very system of defaults is itself of great interest in the Bantu languages' gender systems as there is no 'masculine as default' to speak of but instead a very intricate set of patterns governing defaults for human-denoting noun phrases versus defaults for non-humans. In Carstens (2019), a set of preferences among the genders in Xhosa leads to different rates of CCA versus default agreement depending on the specific combinations, and this opens the way for rethinking the relative markedness of each gender with respect to another. In fact, very much like South Slavic, Carstens (2019) finds that both HCA and CCA are options in Xhosa:

(9) Imi-gewu   ne-z-anuse   zi/i-yacula.PL
     IV-criminals and-X-diviners   AGR.IV/AGR.X-sing
     'The criminals and the diviners are singing.'

It is worth mentioning that Xhosa, Sesotho, and Zulu are of interest specifically because of reports suggesting that they do hold the possibility for CCA with conjoined noun phrases, while for other Bantu languages (notably Chichewa, spoken in Malawi), it has been reported that only default agreement is an option. An experimental confirmation of the relative robustness of CCA with a wide range of balanced combinations of nonhuman noun classes in these languages is of the utmost priority.

Excitingly, in addition to having a specific slot on the verb for subject agreement, which is useful as a way of cross-referencing what the subject is, particularly when it is dislocated to a non-canonical position, the Bantu languages (including the Southern Bantu languages like Xhosa, Zulu, and Sesotho) have *object* agreement as well. Object agreement in Zulu is found when the object is dislocated from its canonical post-verbal position and serves as a way to track and cross-reference the object via dedicated gender agreement, with the object in a separate slot from that of the subject. Thus, the example below from Zulu (Zeller, 2012) shows that the verb has a subject-agreement prefix (accompanying a null first-person plural pronoun), followed by an object agreement prefix, and the latter agrees with the object 'students', which has been dislocated to the right past an adverb:

(10)   Si-zi-bon-e   kaningi izi-tshudeni
        1pl.OBJ.VIII-NC-PAST often   VIII students. PL
        'We see often the students'

What happens when the object itself is a coordinated noun phrase? It is fair to say that the gender agreement patterns with conjoined noun phrases in object position have not been widely studied within linguistics. Luckily, Riedel (2009) conducted groundbreaking work in this direction for the Bantu language Sambaa.

(11)   N-   za-   ji-   ona kui   na shimba.
        SUB.AGR.1SG- PERF- OBJ.AGR.V- see v.dog and IX.lion
        'I saw the dog and the lion.'

Such patterns are largely nonexistent from 'majority' European languages, which, as we now know, are overrepresented in linguistic theory. The oppression of groups such as the Xhosa and Zulu, during colonial expansion by the Dutch and English in South Africa and continuing through apartheid, yielded immeasurably negative effects for the people, their rights, their culture, and their languages. In the present moment, however, new identities, institutions, and initiatives are thriving. With the support of recently available research funding, we have launched a new collaborative project with a set of partners at three universities in South Africa – in Makhanda, Durban, and Bloemfontein, at which the majority of students are native speakers of Xhosa, Zulu, and Sesotho, respectively.

Among our initial goals in the development of experimental syntax within the region is an effort to study closest conjunct agreement in object position. What makes these studies very exciting is the fact that in these languages, not only can one study whether closest conjunct agreement for subjects patterns the same way that it does in South Slavic (where post-syntactic linear order enables gender agreement with one of the two conjuncts) but also whether object agreement works the same way! Nothing, after all, precludes the possibility of having a conjoined noun phrase in object position, and Southern Bantu allows objects to precede the verb as well, therefore enabling a fully crossed design – studying the rates of HCA and CCA for object agreement in preverbal and postverbal configurations. I would contend that this research is especially important as part of an institution-level partnership with the goal of expanding and diversifying the empirical base of linguistics, as well as attempting to create a multiplier effect in the region with a new generation of post-apartheid younger scholars. Ideally, these sorts of efforts can lead to microcomparative work to examine the extent to which Xhosa and Zulu differ from each other with respect to subject and object CCA and to compare both with Sesotho, already known to be linguistically a more distant baseline.

Further Reading

Compelling arguments for an asymmetric structure of &P, headed by the coordination itself, are presented by Zoerner (1995) and Johannessen (1998). For a detailed exploration of the markedness relations among the several noun classes of Xhosa, see Carstens (2019). One of the first comparisons between Bantu and Slavic conjunct agreement can be found in Corbett and Mtenje (1987). An exploration of closest conjunct agreement with disjunctions (as opposed to conjunctions) can be found in Foppolo and Staub (2020), and a discussion of why there is no closest conjunct case assignment in Weisser (2017).

5 Configurationality of Objects in Chichewa and Warlpiri

In this chapter, we see how our understanding of verbal argument structure (the relation of multiple objects to the verb) is in fact determined in large part by event structure: how non-core individuals may be related (benefactively or malefactively) to core verbal events. The empirical findings from Bantu languages have been so transformative for linguistic theory that they allow for unexpected consequences in languages traditionally thought to be 'nonconfigurational', such as Warlpiri.

5.1 Rethinking Direct Objects

A traditional way of thinking about the arguments of a verb, very much based on Latin and German grammars and their attendant notions of dative case-marking for the recipient (or benefactive) of ditransitives like 'I sent them a gift', is that there is an indirect object and a direct object. What makes one object more 'direct' than another, however? The intuition seems to be that, since the object in transitive verbs is marked with accusative case and is the affected 'theme' of the event, this direct objecthood simply 'stays the same' when one ramps up to ditransitives, where an additional case and thematic role is added. Nonetheless, this way of characterizing which object is 'primary' and which is 'secondary' is very much based on a kind of ontological priority for affected themes (or 'patients') – actions affect things – only subsequent to which can those actions involve transfer of possession or benefit to others. And as much as these notions might be valid, they aren't necessarily the way that every language encodes the relation between such objects in their syntax. Thus, Gary and Keenan (1977) pointed out that in some languages, the grammatical roles of indirect and direct object may be 'collapsed'. How can this be demonstrated?

Syntactic theory is all about comparing which operations can apply to which items under which conditions, and once one begins to look at a set of comparisons of the two objects in ditransitive constructions, there are at least five tests to consider (Mchombo, 2004). The first is word order: in an SVO language, which object is canonically right after the verb, and can the order of the two objects be flexibly reversed? The second is passivizability:

61

when the verb is passivized and the subject suppressed, can either object take over the subject position? The third is cliticization: if there is only one slot available for object-marking on the verb (recall the Bantu object-marking from Chapter 4), which of the two objects will be cross-referenced there? The fourth is reciprocalization, which 'takes away' the object, replacing it with a reciprocal marker indicating that the action is being performed by a plurality of agents on each other – which object is taken away in such circumstances? Finally, the fifth is question formation or relativization, which moves out of the verb phrase one of the objects for the sake of a question.

Posing diagnostics of this sort can be done for any kind of ditransitive construction. While benefactives (such as "I read them the book") are one type, there has been a rich tradition of examining a much wider range of such constructions in the Bantu languages, in which instrumental phrases (such as 'with a knife') can be introduced without any accompanying preposition. This is achieved via what is called an *applicative* construction,[1] which led to a renaissance in syntactic research in a number of Bantu languages in the 1980s, certainly the most prominent among them being Chichewa. Chichewa (also referred to as Nyanja) is the most widely spoken language in Malawi, a small, lush, landlocked country in East Africa, perhaps most well known in Europe because of the singer Madonna's adoption of Malawian children and efforts to help AIDS orphans there. Chichewa was one of the three Bantu languages sent into space on recordings of Carl Sagan's interstellar greetings on the Voyager record. Despite being treated with lower prestige than English throughout the colonial rule by the British – leading to problems of language education planning for years after formal independence (Kayambazinthu, 1998) – Chichewa is now a lingua franca throughout central and southern Malawi. There have been a number of prominent Chichewa-speaking linguists whose contributions have put the language in the spotlight, and for this reason the investigation of instrumental ditransitive constructions in the language deserves our attention. Let us start with a transitive sentence:

(1) Mavuto a-   na- umb -a mtsuko.
     Mavuto SUBJ.AGR.I PAST mold FV III.waterpot
     Mavuto molded the waterpot.

In the example above, the subject agreement with the class-I proper name 'Mavuto' (familiar from Chapter 4), the tense affix, the main verb, and the final vowel (abbreviated FV – usually -*a* in all examples besides negative or

---

[1] According to Jeong (2007), the term applicative may have originated in the Jesuit Carochi's (1645) grammar of Nahuatl, where "verbos aplicativos" referred to verbal forms indicating action intended towards another person.

subjunctive moods) pile up to form one agglutinative verbal form. However, in the following example, a new applicative suffix (sometimes called a 'verbal extension'), abbreviated APPL, appears after the verb stem. Suddenly, two morphologically unmarked postverbal objects are allowed:

(2)   Mavuto a-   na- umb -ir   -a mpeni   mtsuko.
      Mavuto SUBJ.AGR.I PAST mold APPL FV III.knife III.waterpot
      Mavuto molded the waterpot with a knife.

Let's consider (2) alongside another highly influential set of examples from Kimenyi (1980), a native speaker of Kinyarwanda (a Bantu language spoken in Rwanda):

(3)   Umugóre a-rá-som-er-a   umuhuûngu igitabo.
      woman   SUBJ.AGR-PRES-read-APPL-FV boy   book
      'The woman is reading a book for the boy.'

While a sentence like 'The woman is reading the boy the book' could pass in English as a double object construction (so called because both 'the boy' and 'the book' appear without any prepositional phrase but instead occur postverbally as ordinary noun phrases), something like 'Mavuto molded the knife the waterpot' could never pass muster or even make sense. Thus, something in Bantu languages such as Chichewa and Kinyarwanda allows these immediately postverbal objects – called the applied objects – to be either a beneficiary, as in 'the boy' in (3), or as an instrument, as in 'the knife' in (2). In English, the instrumental version would have to be expressed using a preposition like 'with', with this prepositional phrase (PP) occurring after the object 'the waterpot'. Indeed, even the beneficiary in (3) might be more comfortably expressed using a preposition like 'for' instead of with the double object version. 'The woman is reading the boy the book'. However, in these Bantu applicative constructions, there is no preposition, but instead all of the action in introducing these instruments or beneficiaries is accomplished by morphology on the verb itself.

Thus, in both (2) and (3), the verb itself has an additional affix, *-ir-*, the applied affix, which enables the presence of this additional applied object (AO) that comes before the basic object (or verb phrase object – let's call it VO). In both the benefactive example and the instrumental example, therefore, we see a kind of double object construction. However, as Bresnan and Moshi (1990) memorably put it, there are reasons to carefully study the AO in "the Bantu applicative construction, whose resemblance to the familiar dative object construction of English can be likened to that of the game of chess to checkers" (p. 148). Indeed, consider the use of the applicative verbal affix to introduce a *location* after the verb – as if it were presumptuous enough to occupy the direct object position as well!

(4) Alēnje   a-ku-pá-lúk-irá   pá-mchēnga mikêka.
    II.hunters SUBJ.AGR.II-PRES-weave-APPL-FV XVI-III.sand IV.mats
    'The hunters are weaving mats on the beach.' (Alsina & Mchombo, 1990)

Thus, Bresnan and Moshi (1990) observe that, far beyond the English dative object construction, the Bantu applicative can be used for "beneficiary, maleficiary, goal (recipient), instrument, location, or motive (reason or purpose), depending on the semantics of the base verb" (p. 149). What is a benefactive or a malefactive? These involve an argument that is not necessarily part of the core verbal event but which somehow benefits (or suffers) from it. For example, in "I couldn't be bothered to fill out the survey, so my son filled it out for me," the PP "for me" denotes someone who benefitted from the event of son-filling-out-form but wasn't a core agent or patient of the filling-out event (in fact, may not have even been present). Similarly, in "I was planning to attend the lecture, but my dog ran away on me this morning," the PP "on me" denotes someone adversely affected from the core dog-runaway event (with knock-on consequences lasting after the event itself). As we've just seen, in English these require the benefactive or malefactive prepositions "for me" or "on me." In Bantu applicative constructions, these again pattern like the immediately postverbal object of the verb – with no preposition or case-marking to be found. These noun phrases pattern like true arguments, in that they can participate in agreement and affect the verb's morphological form. Thus, in (3) from Kinyarwanda, repeated below in (5), the benefactive is right after the verb (Kimenyi, 1980):

(5) Umugóre a-rá-som-er-a   umuhuûngu igitabo.
    woman   SUBJ.AGR-PRES-read-APPL-FV boy   book
    'The woman is reading a book for the boy.'

This kind of benefactive argument is not really an argument of the verb 'to read' but an argument of the whole event of 'reading-a-book'. This also holds for the malefactive example above, where the dog running away is an event. A malefactive example from Chaga (a language spoken on the slopes of Mount Kilimanjaro), as researched by Bresnan and Moshi (1990) is shown below:

(6) N-ǎ-í-lyì-fí-à   m̀-kà kélyà
    foc-SUBJ.AGR.I-PRES-eat-APPL-FV I-wife VII-food
    'He is eating food on his wife' (e.g., to her detriment; can also be idiomatic for cheating on someone)

In other words, benefactive and malefactive arguments sometimes aren't really objects of the main verb at all but are rather put in a semantic relation with the verb phrase (VP). Let's say that this relation of benefiting from the VP event is mediated by the semantic head called APPL (for applicative) – the one we see the overt affix for on the Bantu verb stems above. This APPL sits higher in the tree (I know; try not to think of Isaac Newton here), and its job is to take the benefactive noun phrase like 'the boy' and relate it benefactively or malefactively to the action that takes place within VP:

(7)
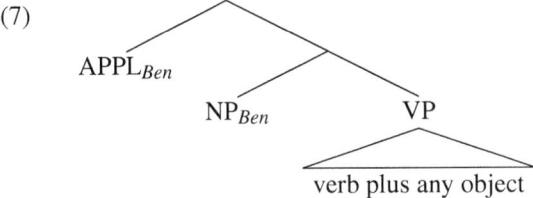
verb plus any object

If this is the right way to represent benefactives – as being external to a verb phrase and related to it by an external semantic link, namely the high APPL node in the syntactic tree – then it actually shouldn't matter at all what the internal contents of the VP are for whether or not the benefactive can be present. Thus, the VP need not even be *transitive* as long as this event can be benefactively related to someone.[2] Such cases of benefactives built upon intransitive verbs are rife throughout Bantu, as shown below for Chaga:

(8) a. N-ã-í-òṛòk-ì-à   m-ànâ
       FOC-1SG-PRES-stand-APPL-FV 1-child
       'He/She is standing for a child.'

In the intransitive VP 'to stand' in (8), there is no object at all in the VP, as foreshadowed in (7). In sum, Bresnan & Moshi's 'chess vs. checkers' analogy is quite apt; applicative affixes in Bantu allow for the introduction of benefactives or malefactives to verb phrases of all different types, as well as the possibility of including instruments (and even locations) in what looks like the position of just plain 'objects' to the verb – right after the verb itself, with no preposition or case-marker to set them off as 'indirect' objects of any sort.

But wait; given the tree structure in (7), how do these applicative objects like 'child', sand, or 'knife' come to be right after the verb? And are applicative arguments always 'right after the verb'? Delving into these two questions requires opening the lid a bit more on the structures involved.

---

[2] In fact, this logic also allows that the VP itself could be more internally complex than just a transitive, leading to a benefactive being related to a VP with an instrumental applicative. For such kinds of recursive application yielding multiple applicative affixes (of different types, such as benefactive and instrumental), see Kimenyi (1980).

5.2 Symmetries within Bantu Applicatives

Above, we saw applicative objects that were benefactives (and thus related to any kind of verbal event through a relation of 'benefiting' from it), but we also saw applicative objects that were instruments (and even locations). On all of these, the applicative affix *-ir* of Chichewa (which phonologically may vary slightly through Bantu, sometimes with realizations such as *-er-* or *-il-*) is found.

What Baker (1988) brought to the fore was the fact that within Chichewa, the status of the two objects with respect to the diagnostics above in instrumental applicatives exhibited *symmetry*. In other words, instrumental phrases like '(with) a knife' in Chichewa, with respect to running the tests for what counts as 'an object', patterned just like the 'direct object' itself. To give a sample, either order of the object and the instrumental is free (9):

(9) a. Anyani a- na- kwapul -ir -a agalu ndodo.
 baboons SUBJ.AGR- PAST whip APPL FV II.dogs IX.sticks
 'The baboons whipped the dogs with sticks.'
 b. Anyani a- na- kwapul -ir -a ndodo agalu.
 baboons SUBJ.AGR- PAST whip APPL FV IX.sticks II.dogs
 'The baboons whipped the dogs with sticks.'

This is also shown for cliticization (the presence of a cross-referencing object marker, within the single object agreement slot, that is obligatorily employed for an object that is not sitting right next to the verb), which can cross-reference either object in the instrumental construction (10):

(10) a. Mavuto a- na- chi- umb -ir -a mitsuko
 Mavuto SUBJ.AGR PAST OBJ.AGR.VII mold APPL FV IV.waterpots
 (chikwanje).
 VII.machete
 'Mavuto molded the waterpots with it (the machete).'
 b. Mavuto a- na- i- umb -ir -a chikwanje
 Mavuto SUBJ.AGR PAST OBJ.AGR.III mold APPL FV VII.machete
 (mitsuko).
 IV.waterpots
 'Mavuto molded them (the waterpots) with a machete.'

For relative clause formation (e.g., 'this is the NP that I think that Mavuto ...', where the NP is extracted from the verb phrase), with the instrumental, either object can be relativized (11):

(11) a. Uwu ndi mpeni umene ndi-   ku- ganiz -a kuti
        This is knife which SUBJ.AGR.1SG PRES think ASP that
        Mavuto a-   na- umb -ir -a mitsuko.
        Mavuto SUBJ.AGR.I PAST mold APPL ASP waterpots
        'This is the knife that I think Mavuto molded the waterpots with.'
    b. Iyi   ndi mistuko imene ndi-   ku- ganiz -a kuti
        These are waterpots which SUBJ.AGR.1SG PRES think ASP that
        Mavuto a-   na- umb -ir -a mpeni.
        Mavuto SUBJ.AGR.I PAST mold APPL ASP knife
        'These are the waterpots that I think Mavuto molded with a knife.'

All of these differences add up to the fact that in Chichewa, the instrumental object is treated symmetrically on a par with the basic object. When the applied object is an instrument or a location, it's able to be the higher or the lower object, as passivization shows (note the PASS morpheme following the APPL):

(12) a. Pa-mchēnga pa-ku-lúk-ír-idw-á   míkêka.
        XVI-III.sand SUBJ.AGR.XVI-PRES-weave-APPL-PASS-FV IV.mats
        'The beach is being woven mats on.' (Alsina & Mchombo, 1990)
    b. Mikêka i-ku-lúk-ír-idw-á   pá-mchēnga.
        IV.mats SUBJ.AGR.IV-PRES-weave-APPL-PASS-FV XVI-III.sand
        'The mats are being woven on the beach.'

These 'symmetric' applicative languages seem to pose a real problem for any attempt to say that the syntactic ordering of arguments from higher to lower within a syntactic tree must be introduced in the same kind of ontological thematic order that, say, always places them as follows: agents > benefactives > patients > instruments/locations. It seems that the ordering of patients with respect to instruments or locations, at least as far as a basic hierarchy of grammatical functions within the syntactic tree is concerned, may be variable and can be composed via different kinds of compositional "structurings of the verbal event," in the terms developed by Marantz (1993) and Pylkkänen (2008). These structurings of the verbal event are semantically composed via this high APPL head, available within the inventory of these Bantu languages (and also, it should be said, widely found beyond the African continent, in the western Pacific region within Austronesian languages and in North and Meso-America within Uto-Aztecan languages; Polinsky [2013])

In symmetric applicative constructions, this high APPL (HAPPL) node allows for the patient to 'leapfrog' up out of it and to a position that comes to be higher than the benefactive or instrumental. This potentially 'free slot' is represented by the word 'Spec-Slot' below. To this tree, let us also add the higher position that includes the Tense node.

(13)

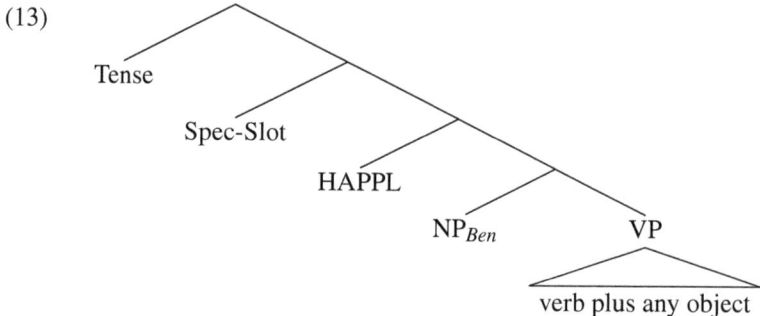

One of the guiding ideas in Marantz (1993) was that the main verb joins up with the higher APPL head via a kind of overt movement operation within the syntax and eventually moves from its lower position (together with the object) to join together onto the left of the APPL itself.

(14)

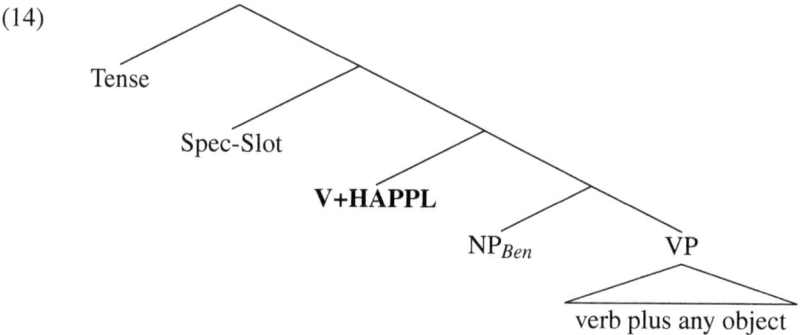

Finally, the V+HAPPL complex moves upwards to the tense position. This next step of what is called 'head movement' generates the complex agglutinative morphology characteristic of Bantu verbs.

(15)

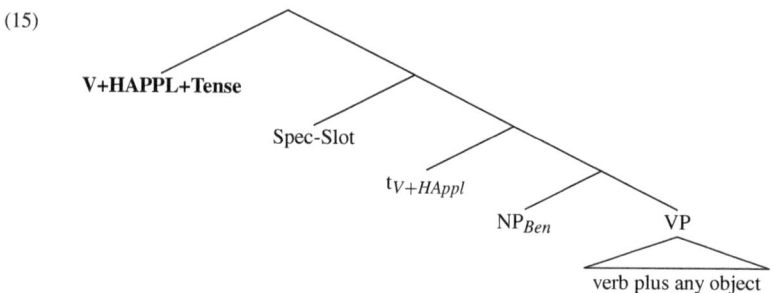

The consequence now is that this empty Spec-Slot, when it is used and moved into by the patient, will generate this symmetric ordering for applicatives. When the Spec-Slot is invaded by the patient, the object precedes the benefactive, and when it is not, then the object stays down low, after the benefactive. All of the above diagnostics that distinguished higher and lower objects will essentially follow from this optional decision for the patient to 'leapfrog' (in McGinnis's [2001] terms) over the applied argument.

When the object leaps up into this position, it becomes the higher object, whereas when it does not, the applied argument (be it instrumental, benefactive, malefactive, or locative) remains the higher object. As a result, either one becomes eligible for all of the further transformations above (e.g., onward promotion or movement in passivization and relativization).

What's important to distinguish here, of course, is why languages like Chichewa, Kinyarwanda, and Chaga have these high applicatives and why they have these symmetric applicatives. The answer to the first question bears on the nature of semantic operators that a language has in its inventory, and very much like our discussion of monstrous operators in Zazaki and Uyghur in Chapter 2, not all languages have the same inventory of semantic operators. High applicative languages have the ability to take an individual (like 'the chief', 'the knife', or 'the beach') and relate it to the event within a syntactic structure of this type. In English, explicitly stating such relations between events and individuals, of course, can be expressed with two clauses (even if it sounds a bit like the board game "Clue"):

(16)   a.   Mavuto sculpted a waterpot, and it took place with a knife.
         b.   Mavuto sculpted a waterpot, and it took place on the beach.
         c.   Mavuto sculpted a waterpot, and its taking place benefitted me.

By contrast, when an indirect object in an English ditransitive construction is a true object of the verbal event, the paraphrases in (16) cannot be extended:

(17)   *Mavuto sent a book, and its taking place was to me.

Instead, the 'goal' argument of English ditransitives truly is an object within the verb phrase. Putting things this way, beneficiaries are objects – and high objects – but they're event-external objects. This obviously makes core ontological notions like 'object' more nuanced. As Baker aptly puts it "The Chichewa applicatives suggest that there is no single notion of direct object that plays a central role in the grammar; rather NPs are simply grouped into natural classes in different ways depending on the specific concerns of the different modules of the grammar" (Baker, 1988, p. 382).

We can actually find other kinds of 'objects' that aren't patients but are still high objects: causees. In "I made the kids eat the spinach," the causee 'the kids' is, after all, the first postverbal noun phrase, but it's certainly not the patient. In "I made the kids swim," there's no patient at all. In Bantu, causatives also put this high object right after the verb:

(18) Umugabo a-r-uubak-iisha abakozi inzu.
man   SUBJ.AGR-PRES-build-CAUSE-FV workers house
'The man makes the workers build a house.'

The causee 'the workers' is an affected kind of object that is licensed by this causative affix on the verb. It's strikingly parallel to the Appl$_{Ben}$ tree we saw above:

(19)

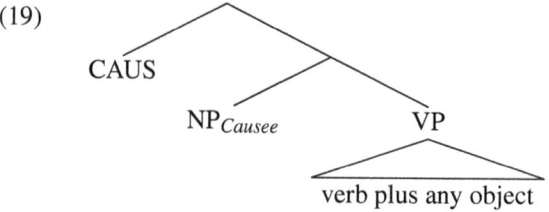

Given this parallelism in structures, it is no coincidence that a sentence like *Corleone had his partner killed* can have either a malefactive reading (the poor wretch, he was adversely affected by the killing event) or a causative reading (he made it happen – he sent out the hitmen himself), and as Marantz (1993) points out, APPL and CAUS may be realized by the same affix in some Bantu languages. Both involve high, event-related introduction of asymmetric objects. English simply does not have morphemes of this type that directly allow for introducing an event-external argument as part of the same extended verb, as the contrasts below from Venda versus English show (Pylkkänen, 2008):

(20) a. Mukasa o-se-is-a Katonga.
          Mukasa 3sg.past-laugh-cause-FV Katonga
          'Mukasa made Katonga laugh.'
      b. Mukasa o-amb-el-a Katonga
          Mukasa 3sg.PAST-speak-APPL-FV Katonga
          'Mukasa spoke for Katonga.'

(21) a. *Mary laughed Sue. (Intended meaning: 'Mary made Sue laugh.')
      b. *Mary spoke Sue. (Intended meaning: 'Mary spoke for Sue.')

What Chichewa, Chaga, Kinyarwanda, Venda, and dozens of other Bantu languages have shown is that there is a syntactic and semantic position for nodes like HAPPL above the VP. Languages that have it allow for the direct introduction of an object by means of a head that mediates the thematic relation between an individual and the event described by the VP. Additionally, the symmetric patterning of patient objects and applicative objects suggests that a mechanism such as 'leapfrogging', or any transformational equivalent that promotes the object into a higher position than the applied object, is available in an extra position furnished by the HAPPL head. This completely different tack for understanding cases of two postverbal objects in (20) has motivated a wholly new model. As Bresnan and Moshi (1990) again aptly put it within the historical context at the moment that Bantu applicatives came into their own right, changing the theory: "The syntactic structure of Bantu has long been assimilated to the grammatical model of standard European languages. In general, Bantu languages lack case and have a small, closed class of adjectives and few prepositions. Instead, the rich systems of noun class concords and verbal morphology are central to the syntax" (p. 180).

5.3 Transfer-of-Possession Is a Low Matter

What we've seen above is that Chaga or Chichewa sentences with a syntax like 'I carved the knife the waterpot' (with an instrumental understood), 'I stood the boy' (with a benefactive understood), or 'I wove the beach the blankets' (with a locative understood) have two morphologically unmarked objects following the verb. Superficially, these might look a lot like English double object constructions, such as 'I sent the tenant the package'. What, after all, enables the presence of the indirect object 'the tenant' right after the verb? Could it be just like the high applicative constructions seen above, simply with some restriction that says that only recipients can go in this position (and that English disallows HAppls introducing instrumentals or maleficiaries or locatives)?

We've already seen that the answer is no. First of all, even paraphrases don't seem to make such recipient arguments 'external to the event' in the same way:

(22)   a.   Mavuto sculpted a waterpot, and it took place with a knife.
        b.   Mavuto sculpted a waterpot, and it took place on the beach.
        c.   Mavuto sculpted a waterpot, and its taking place benefitted me.
        d.   *Mavuto sent a book, and its taking place was to me.

Second of all, the high applicatives seen above have all the syntactic properties that made them symmetric. This can't be done with English transfer-of-possession ditransitives:

(23)   *I sent the package the tenant.

Finally, English transfer-of-possession ditransitives are limited to a more restricted range of verbs (e.g., *sent, gave, mailed, threw,* or *baked*), and do not enjoy the freedom of being able to be used with any kind of verb (including intransitives like *stood*). Thus, there is no reason at all to think that English transfer-of-possession ditransitives should be modeled using the HAPPL that was discovered and exemplified in the Bantu languages above.

So how does one model such double-object verbs? Suppose that the transfer-of-possession relation is mediated by a low syntactic head that we'll call

Particle$_{HAVE}$. Such a head is apparently silent in English.[3] As (22) shows, its semantics is *not* to relate the recipient to an event but rather to make the transfer-of-possession part of the core verbal event. Thus, Prt$_{HAVE}$ relates two individuals (the recipient and the theme) to each other within a single event, inside the verb, with the structure below:

(24)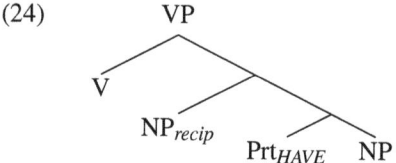

The structure in (24) (see, e.g., Pesetsky [1995]) immediately explains all the properties differentiated from high applicatives above. The recipient is not event-external; it is inside the VP and determined by the possibilities of the verb itself in enacting a transfer-of-possession relation (hence the restrictions on the verb). There is no relation like that of the benefactive or malefactive that is external to the event. Finally, there is no possibility of symmetry, because there is no Spec-Slot available in the structure in (24) to which the theme could shift above the recipient.[4]

Fine, so English transfer-of-possession constructions can be explained as above. Why mention them in the same breath as Bantu applicatives if their only similarity is having two unmarked postverbal NP objects? The answer is transfer-of-possesion structures of the type seen above are sometimes encoded in Bantu languages in a highly similar way. In fact, even in Chichewa, the transfer-of-possession equivalents of *I baked them the cake* are encoded with seemingly *the same applicative morpheme* as its instrumentals and locatives seen above. But looks can be deceiving. This *-ir-* morpheme and its two objects are not symmetric (Baker, 1988):

(25) a. Anyani a- ku- pang -ir -a atsikana mauta.
 II.baboons SUBJ.AGR PRES make APPL ASP II.girls VI.bows
 'The baboons are making bows for the girls.'

---

[3] Why call it a particle? Because English particle-shifting verbs, like *pick the kids up* allow an object to sit between the verb and a particle because transfer-of-possession constructions are learned together with particle verbs as a class (Snyder & Stromswold, 1997) and because both double-object syntax and particle-shift are only possible with morphologically Germanic, not Latinate, stems (Harley, 2009).

[4] As the spirit of any generatively minded inquiry would ask here, why *isn't* there the possibility of such a Spec-Slot for Prt$_{HAVE}$? There are a wealth of interesting proposals in the literature. I will mention one: Jeong (2007) suggests that even if a Spec-Slot existed, such movement would be 'too short'. Such restrictions against too-local movement exist elsewhere across a range of domains, including the ban on topicalization that would be too short (*I think that [John, t likes Mary]*).

b. *Anyani   a-   ku- pang -ir -a mauta atsikana.
   II.baboons SUBJ.AGR- PRES make APPL ASP VI.bows II.girls
   'The baboons are making bows for the girls.

Relative clause formation from the theme object is also disallowed with such recipient constructions in Chichewa (Baker, 1988):

(26) a. *Iyi ndiyo mfumu imene ndi-   ku- ganiz -a kuti
         This is   IX.chief whom SUBJ.AGR.1SG PRES think FV that
         Mavuto a-   na- umb -ir -a mtsuko.
         Mavuto SUBJ.AGR PAST mold APPL FV waterpot.
         This is the chief whom I think Mavuto molded the waterpot for.
      b. Uwu ndiwo mtsuko umene ndi-   ku- ganiz -a kuti
         This is   waterpot which SUBJ.AGR.1SG PRES think FV that
         Mavuto a-   na- umb -ir -a mfumu.
         Mavuto SUBJ.AGR PAST mold APPL FV IX.chief
         'This is the waterpot which I think Mavuto molded for the chief.'

There are thus good reasons to think that the tree in (24) for English has the equivalent in Chichewa where the morpheme Prt_{Have} is instead occupied by a version of the applicative morpheme called Appl_{Have}, as shown below for (27):

(27)
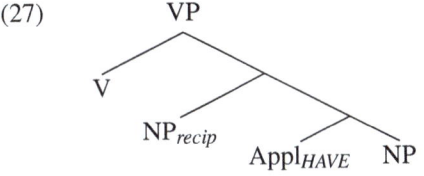

But wait a minute; this Appl_{HAVE} found inside the VP has a different syntax from the high applicative (which is above the VP). It also has a different semantics (event-internal vs. event-external). So why call both of these things applicative in the first place? Simply because they are morphologically realized with the same affix *-ir*? Essentially, the answer is yes. The high applicative and the Appl_{Have} have little in common, although they do both mediate and enable the presence of two postverbal objects. There is also, of course, a certain amount of semantic and pragmatic fluidity between recipients (of verbs like 'to send') and beneficiaries. After all, in *I baked them a cake*, the idea is that they benefitted from it (unless they were allergic!) as well as receiving it, and in *I read them the story*, they not only 'received' the content of the story auditorily, but also benefitted from it (unless it bored them to tears!). Nonetheless, while this fluidity may be the historical source of some of the overlap between benefactive applicatives and transfer-of-possession ditransitives, there are still very good reasons to think that beneficiaries are external and hence independent of the

VP itself. Recall that the Chaga benefactives can be employed with intransitive verbs like 'to stand'. In Chichewa, however, for which the diagnostics in (25) and (26) point to the structure in (27), seeming benefactive/recipients should be disallowed with intransitive verbs. Baker (1988) draws attention to exactly these differences between the instrumental (modeled with an HAPPL above) and the benefactive/recipient in Chichewa:

(28) Msangalatsi a-   ku- yend -er -a ix.ndodo.
     i.entertainer SUBJ.AGR- PRES walk APPL FV stick
     'The entertainer is walking with a stick.'

(29) *Mkango u-   ku- yend -er- -a anyani.
     iii.lion SUBJ.AGR- PRES walk APPL FV ii.baboons
     'The lion is walking for the baboons.'

What Chichewa crucially shows is that the same language can have a high applicative, with symmetric syntax for its objects and an event-external semantic relation for the applied object, and an Appl$_{Have}$, employed for recipient objects (with occasional overlap for benefactive semantics, depending on the verb). In fact, there is now a great deal of burgeoning work on microvariation within the Bantu languages as some have high, symmetric applicatives for every kind of applied object (e.g., Chaga), while others have the low, asymmetric Appl$_{Have}$ for benefactives (e.g., Chichewa), and yet others have low, asymmetric applicatives even for instrumentals (e.g., Chimwiini, see Henderson [2018]). In Kinyarwanda, benefactives are symmetric, but locatives are not (Kimenyi, 1980; McGinnis, 2001). In some cases, an overt preposition can be found to introduce locatives and instrumentals. In others, the lack of such a preposition sometimes invokes the need for code-switching, and thus isiXhosa has integrated English 'for' into its benefactive applicatives (Simango, 2019). Modeling this microvariation is of great excitement to current syntactic theory and has ushered in new work on parametric correlations between one construction and another, as recently explored in van der Wal (2022).

5.4 Warlpiri: A 'Nonconfigurational' Language with Asymmetric Objects

The symmetric patterning of high applicatives discussed for Kinyarwanda, Chichewa, and Chaga were fundamental in positing a structure with high applicatives introducing such event-external arguments alongside a syntax that allowed for symmetric shifting of the patient to become the higher of the two objects. Subsequently, modeling the Prt$_{Have}$ structure of lower, asymmetric structures like that of Chichewa and English led to Pylkkänen's (2008) semantic differentiation of the two structures and a burgeoning exploration of symmetric and asymmetric applicatives in languages far beyond Bantu, including rich re-examinations of the structures in more familiar languages, such as Spanish (Cuervo, 2003), Japanese (Miyagawa & Tsujioka, 2004), and Modern Greek (Anagnostopoulou, 2003).

Of perhaps most interest for refining our notions of seemingly typologically 'far-flung' languages is when the results of models based on symmetric and asymmetric Appls from Bantu bear out as valid far beyond – such as diagnosing the presence of structure in Warlpiri. Warlpiri is a Pama-Nyungan language spoken by an indigenous group around Alice Springs, Australia. Their territory was invaded by European settlers, and they now mostly reside on government-launched settlements. The language has an imposingly complex vocabulary for kinship terms, based on dihedral groups splitting into eight relational mappings (Laughren, 1982). Numerous aspects of its syntax have been described, such as relative clauses and pronominal clitic clusters. It is perhaps among the most well-studied Australian languages within linguistic theory. It is estimated that when Europeans invaded Australia, there were 250–350 distinct languages; today, perhaps only fifteen of these are still being actively learned by children – although as of 2019, Warlpiri is one of a handful that shows few signs of decline (Simpson & Wigglesworth, 2019).

With the early 1980s notion of generative grammar in terms of large-scale macroparameters governing massive differences in language types (e.g., the correlations between VS inversion and having null subject pronouns within Western European languages; see Rizzi [1982]), one of the seemingly largest looming differences was that of 'nonconfigurational' languages, with a parameter of configurationality set to 'on' or 'off' within a language (Hale, 1983). Modeling Warlpiri specifically, Hale proposed that NP arguments to a verb could appear wherever they wanted to (e.g., with no notion that a VP must contain pairing of verb and object NP) and that verbs and their arguments had no imposed ordering. The only phrase structure rules written at the time within the X-bar formalism were the following (where X* indicates 'anywhere from zero or more'):

(30) a. $\overline{X} \to \overline{X}* \overline{X}$
      b. $\overline{V} \to \text{AUX } \overline{X}* \text{ V } \overline{X}*$

The first rule is to accout for the fact that noun phrases and infinitival phrases are always head-final. The second requires an auxiliary to be in clause-initial position in finite clauses and everything else to be freely generated. Hale (1983) noticed Warlpiri's extremely nonconfigurational (as opposed to, say, Western European languages) properties of free word order, the ability to pro-drop (i.e., not pronounce at all) all arguments and adjuncts, and having discontinuous noun phrases. He suggests "these characteristics follow in some natural way from the combination of 'flat' structure (i.e., projection of lexical categories just to the one-bar level) and categorial non-specificity in the initial, prelexical, definition of phrase marker" (p. 10), which is accomplished by the rules above.

Let us observe some of these properties. As long as the auxiliary is in second position, (31a), as well as completely scrambled variants such as (31b–c), are interchangeable equivalents (whereas 'speared has kangaroo the man' is clearly not so in English).

(31) a. Ngarrka-ngku ka wawirri panti-rni.
man-ERG AUX kangaroo spear-NONPST
'The man is spearing the kangaroo.'
b. Wawirri ka panti-rni ngarrka-ngku.
kangaroo AUX spear-NONPST man-ERG
'The man is spearing the kangaroo.'
c. Panti-rni ka ngarrka-ngku wawirri.
spear-NONPST AUX man-ERG kangaroo
'The man is spearing the kangaroo.'

NPs that can be torn asunder into discontinuous parts of the sentence are shown below, where the demonstrative 'that' and its associated 'kangaroo' appear at opposite ends of the phrase.

(32) Wawirri kapi-rna panti-rni yalumpu.
kangaroo AUX spear-NONPST that
'I will spear that kangaroo.'

Over time, research on languages such as South Slavic has shown numerous discontinuous noun phrases of this sort, leading to the analysis of what is called 'Left Branch Extraction'. But at the time of Hale (1983), these had not yet been widely studied, and of course they may differ significantly in the details from what is permitted in Warlpiri.

Finally, the ability to pro-drop any pronoun in the sentence in Warlpiri is shown below, where only a verb and auxiliary are pronounced, but the subject and object are implicitly understood.

(33) Panti-rni ka.
spear-NONPST AUX
'He/she is spearing him.'

While the phenomenon of subject pro-drop is common in Italian, and that of object pro-drop is common in, say, Brazilian Portuguese, it is virtually unheard of to be able to suppress both subject and object pronouns (including any and all pronominal clitic remnants of them) at the same time in Western European languages.

Hale's research led to a wealth of alternative, more refined attempts to describe the precise mapping between verbs and their NP arguments in Warlpiri. Could subject, object, and indirect object really float around in whatever order they wanted? Was there evidence that this was the result of directly generating things however one wanted, as opposed to resulting from transformational movements out of a core, structured VP? Many answers came forth. One, originally developed by Jelinek (1984), was that no large-scale abandonment of the local verb–argument relation was necessary. Instead, everything that looked like an NP argument in Warlpiri was a dislocated adjunct. A very loose analogy would be with the structuring of adverbial NPs around a core verb phrase (underlined) with all pronominal arguments, as in English (34a), or with appositive phrases freely interpolated after pronouns, as in (34b):

(34) a. As for the mermaid, and speaking of the captain, <u>he finally sent her it</u>, the letter, you know?
      b. He, the doctor, tells me, the patient, what to do. (Jelinek, 1984, p. 50).

Jelinek's proposal related Warlpiri to the kind of structures that can be found in languages with heavy reliance on pronominal clitics that are tightly clustered around the verb. In Italian, for example, the phenomenon of left-dislocation (and verbal resumption by clitics) and of right dislocation have been widely studied (Samek-Lodovici, 2015). The Pronominal Argument Hypothesis suggested that in Warlpiri, all arguments were always pronominals.[5] Under this view, there should never be any detectable hierarchical ordering differences between any NP arguments because they all are adjuncts freely stacked atop the VP in any order.

A different instantiation of the nonconfigurational approach was developed by Austin and Bresnan (1996):

(35)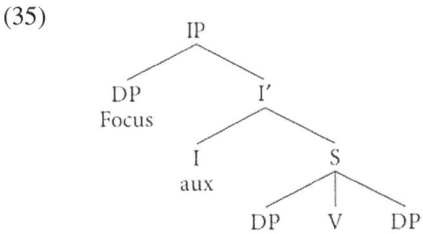

For them, there is a completely flat (e.g., binary, ternary, or quaternary branching) S node, where everything inside is freely generated in whatever order. Only the second-position auxiliary has a fixed hierarchial position, as well as the element that is chosen to occupy the first position (so that something is to the left of the auxiliary), but this can be a verb, an NP, or anything, as long as it is discursively in focus.

---

[5] Baker (1996) took this idea even further, arguing that the Pronominal Argument Hypothesis could be extended to a range of languages with full obligatory agreement morphology for both subjects and objects, except that their pronominal clitics were always *null*. These languages, for which the polysynthesis parameter was set to 'on', included Mohawk, Tiwa, Nahuatl, Chukchee, and many others, though Warlpiri was not analyzed as such.

The claim that all arguments of the VP are flat and symmetrically joined up with a constituent in any order should now start to bring into one's memory the notion of *symmetric objects*. If a verbal recipient (e.g., an indirect object) and a direct object could be generated in either order, shouldn't we now expect all those properties of high applicatives in Chaga?

This flat-structure approach turns out to face difficulties, as documented by Legate (2001), precisely on the basis of double object versus what are called 'ethical' dative constructions (essentially, benefactives and malefactives) that show evidence for a hierarchically organized verb phrase in Warlpiri. Legate (2001) demonstrates that Warlpiri has a class of ditransitive verbs with asymmetric applicatives. In ditransitives, the dative-marked argument, rather than the absolutive direct object, triggers object agreement. Thus, no third-person agreement or agreement in paucal number (referring to 'several', but not all or many, plural objects) is found on the verb. Only the asymmetrically higher object – the dative recipient – controls this agreement slot.

(36) Ngajulu-rlu kapi-rna-ngku   karli-patu   yi-nyi
      I-ERG   FUT.C-1SG.SUBJ-2SG.OBJ boomerang-PAUC give-NONPST
      nyuntu-ku.
      you-DAT
      'I will give you the several boomerangs.'

This kind of ditransitive verb construction, with asymmetric agreement marking of the dative object, is only found with the classic set of transfer-of-possession verbs: of giving, sending, communicated messages, ballistic motion ('throw'), and so forth. Semantically, we are back to where we saw low transfer-of-possession in Chichewa and English. Recall that Appl$_{HAVE}$ requires an animate beneficiary. Thus, one can 'send a package to the border', or one can 'send a tenant (or a boarder) a package', but one cannot say:

(37) *I sent the border a package

This animacy restriction is also found with Warlpiri's class of Appl$_{HAVE}$ verbs with dative case assigned to the recipient. When inanimate, an allative case-marking variant (i.e., a different structure, akin to English *to*-NP) must be used instead.

(38)   a. Purturlu kala-rla   yilya-ja.
           backbone PAST.C-3.DAT send-PAST
           'He sent her the backbone.'
       b. Marnkurrpa-rna yilya-ja   Yalijipiringi-kirra.
           three-1sg.S   send-PAST   Alice.Springs-ALLAT
           'I sent three to Alice Springs.'

Finally, there's an interesting phenomenon of 'Switch Reference' marking on the complementizer of adverbial clauses headed by 'while' that indicates whether the subject they introduce is coreferential with one of the arguments of the main clause, and if so, which one. Now, the embedded infinitival complementizer -*kurra* indicates that this coreferentiality is with the matrix object. When used with the Appl*HAVE*, this indicates coference with the asymmetrically higher object – the dative recipient.

(39)   Karnta-ngku ka-ju   kurdu miliki-yirra-rni
        woman-ERG PRES.IMPF-1SG.OBJ child show-put-NONPST
        nguna-nja-kurra-(ku).
        lie-INF-SR.OBJ-(DAT)
           'The woman is showing the child to me while I am lying down.'

What have we learned? All the symmetric properties encountered in Chaga are not found with Warlpiri's Appl*HAVE*. Instead, it has a clearly hierarchical ordering between the recipient and the direct object:

(40)
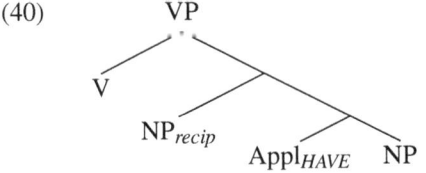

This is not the end of the story, however. Symmetric constructions like that of Chaga's beneficiary introduced by HAppl*BEN* are *also* found in Warlpiri, as Legate (2001) shows. These high applicative constructions involve what is sometimes called an 'ethical dative' in the literature on European languages, essentially referring to an event-external beneficiary.

When these are used, now both the ethical dative *and* the object of the verb will trigger object agreement. This suggests that the object is the highest object within its verb phrase. Thus, in (41), *warri-rni* 'seek' selects a dative object, and the auxiliary agrees with both this VO object and the dative AO:

(41)   Ngarrka-ngku ka-ju-rla   ngaju-ku karli-ki
        man-ERG   PRES.IMPF-1SG.OBJ-3.DAT me-DAT boomerang-DAT
        warri-rni.
        seek-NONPST
           'The man is looking for a boomerang for me.'

Recall that the ethical dative is introduced outside the VP. Symmetric patterning comes from when the theme migrates up to a higher position made available with high applicatives.

Similarly – and symmetrically – either object can control into adjuncts, as shown for the malefactive below, where the object controls the switch-reference marker in (42a) but the maleficiary does in (42b):

(42) a. Maliki-rna ramparl-luwa-rnu Jakamarra-ku parnka-nja-kurra.
dog-1SG accident-hit-PAST Jakamarra-DAT run-INF-SR.OBJ
'I accidently hit (his$_j$) dog$_i$ on Jakamarra$_j$ while it$_i$ was running.'
b. Jakamarra-ku-rna-rla maliki ramparl-luwa-rnu
Jakamarra-DAT-1SG-3.DAT dog accident-hit-PAST
jarda-nguna-nja-kurra
sleep-lie-INFIN-SR.OBJ
'I accidentally hit Jakamarra$_j$'s dog on him$_j$ while he$_j$ was sleeping.'

The symmetric constructions above, with a beneficiary or maleficiary, also involve possession, but they don't involve possession as part of a core verbal event of transferring possession. Instead, they involve an affected possessor – someone who, event-externally, is affected, benefactively or malefactively, by whatever happened to their possession within the VP. Being introduced outside the VP by a HAPPL head, they also allow object leapfrogging into the high Spec-Splot, and thereby symmetric properties.

Ironically, therefore, the true symmetry in Walpiri is not found within the core VP. The core VP is hierarchically structured, with a higher and lower object. Any symmetry found between the two objects is in another construction, built *outside* of the VP:

(43)
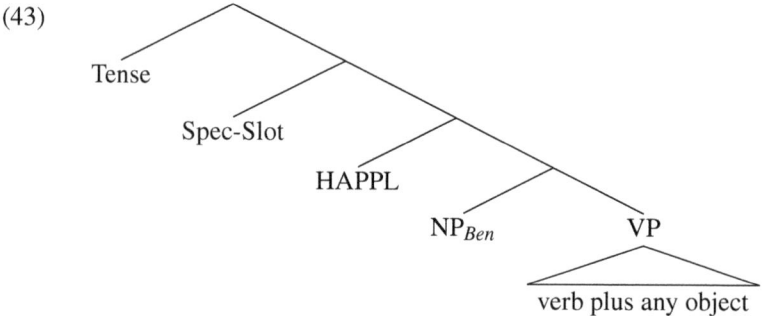

Recall that symmetric NP patterning is found when the theme object migrates up to the Spec-Slot that HAppl$_{Ben}$ furnishes for optional availability. No such slot is found with the Low Appl$_{HAVE}$. Walpiri has configurations entirely akin to the ones found in Bantu. Each of them has their own structural properties.

Symmetric applicatives involve a high introduction of a beneficiary. They relate this argument, semantically, to a core verbal event. They have much fewer restrictions on verbal semantics or on the transitivity of the verbs than transfer-of-possession verbs.

The transfer-of-possession cases involve a relation between the recipient and the object. There is a closely mediated, hierarchically defined semantic relationship of possession between them, and they are contained entirely within the VP.

All of these distinctions are understandable in terms of syntactic structure (as opposed to, say, two lexical classes of verbs – beneficiaries can be added to any kind of verb!). Crucially, it was only once these two kinds of applicatives were compared and analyzed in Bantu that one could make sense of their distribution in a way that allowed Legate (2001) to apply this entire suite of diagnostics and compare them within Warlpiri. The result was that a flat, nonconfigurational, fully symmetric VP as the only structure for Warlpiri verb phrases is untenable.

5.5 Be Wary of Flatland

Where have we arrived? I would say the general lesson, to recall one of my favorite nineteenth-century mathematical novels (thinly veiling its criticisms of Victorian society), *Flatland* by Abbott (1884), is to be wary of the notion that what appears to be one-dimensional or two-dimensional actually is. Usually when flat structure is posited in linguistic theory for a given language, L, it simply means that not enough diagnostics have been run yet on the language. (Or that the field has still not developed a fine-grained enough set of diagnostics yet).

We've learned that one must be wary of any kind of reification of grammatical functions like object as kind of primitive of argument structure, conferring a status that somehow works independently of where these NPs are found in the structure. Properties of a given NP in a sentence, like whether it has the right to participate in agreement, control, relativization, word order, passivizability, and many others, cannot be solely deduced based on the semantic relation between the verb and its object. The structure within which objects are placed is crucial to determining their grammatical patterning for an extremely wide range of phenomena, as reviewed above. The configurationality of two objects, whether in a structure mediated by an Appl$_{Have}$ node or instead in a structure determined by a HAppl node, yields specific hierarchically determined properties of asymmetry vs. potential symmetry. The fervor of activity on Bantu morphosyntax (and its variation within the family) led to transformative tools for linguistic theory that have enabled breakthroughs in the understanding of double-object structures in by now dozens of languages, applied far beyond the Bantu language family.

There is even more evidence for configurationality in Warlpiri syntax – much of it only enabled by the application of diagnostics that were simply not available in fine enough detail at the time that earlier researchers had posited flat structures for the language. A fully flat structure of everything (except, potentially, one focus NP, and a second-position auxiliary) would lead one to expect no restrictions on the placement of adverbs within the clause.

However, Warlpiri has a set of adverbs that must appear in initial position: *kari* and *kula-nganta*. These mean something like 'noticeably to me' (evidential), or 'misleadingly to me' (counterfactual) and must appear initially, preceding topicalized or focused constituents, complementizers, and second-position clitics; any other ordering is ungrammatical.

(44) a. Kari ka-lu wangka-mi.
EVID PRES.IMPF-3PL speak-NONPST
'I can see/hear that they are speaking.'
b. Kula-nganta kaji-npa nyuntu pantu-rnu.
CNTF NONFACT.C-2SG you spear-PAST
'I thought (wrongly) that you must have speared it.'

Only the speech acts, evaluatives, evidentials, and epistemics in Warlpiri must be in this high fixed position. Other adverbs, akin to 'possibly', 'now', 'perhaps', 'often', and 'completely', have lower structures in the clause – exactly where Cinque (1999), in his proposal about the syntactic ordering of adverbs, based on semantic classes, places temporal, modal, completive, and frequentative adverbs – hierarchically lower than the speech acts, evaluatives, evidentials, and epistemics. Warlpiri divides its adverbs into these higher and lower classes, in general accord with cross-linguistic tendencies, but it is only when one systematically compares them with respect to other elements, as Legate (2001) has done, that one can diagnose that the structure isn't in fact all flat. Thus, the lower adverbs, like *-lku* 'now', are placed after the second-position auxiliary:

(45) Kari ka-rna maju-**lku** nyina.
fact PRES-1sg bad-**now** be.NONPST
'I know that I'm now very ill.'

Finally, within the same 'cartographic' tradition, Rizzi (1997) makes the proposal that the high, left periphery of the clause has multiple, distinct projections for topic and focus, and specifically that there is a higher position for topic than for focus (observable broadly cross-linguistically, and exemplified below for English):

(46) a. As for pizza, who will eat it?
b. *Who, as for pizza, will eat it?

The position of a topic must come higher than one of focus in Walpiri too. When both are present, the second-position clitic appears immediately after the topic:

(47)   Pikirri-ji   npa nyarrparla-rla warungka-ma-nu-rnu?
       spearthrower-TOP 2sg where-LOC   forget-cause-PAST-hither
       'Where did you forget the spearthrower on your way here?'

The typological space of languages doesn't seem to include flat, unconstrained, nonconfigurational trees of the type originally posited by Hale (1983) and refined through subsequent work on Warlpiri. Flat structures are simply inadequate to account for the facts. When we look at cases of more than one object, more than one adverb, or more than one topic and focus, we find asymmetries. Hierarchical differences between subject and object have been known for as long as grammatical reasoning has taken place. The crystallization, on the other hand, of the theory of structure below the position of the subject, and a wide variety of multi-tiered relations between different kinds of objects, has only come to maturity within the last few decades and would not have happened without the contributions and comparisons enabled by the Bantu languages with which we started.

Further Reading

Beyond the ditransitive literature itself, there are many interesting directions to read further, related to the morphosyntactic expression of multiple objects. On the relations between instrumentals and objects outside of applicatives, in what are called 'serial verb' constructions, see Baker (1991). To read about the relations mediated by particles somewhat like applicatives with a different morphosyntax, called linkers, in the Khoisan languages Ju|'hoansi and ǂHoan, see Baker and Collins (2006). Finally, for uses of applicatives within Bantu for purposes other than introducing additional objects – instead as intensification of verbal action akin to particle constructions like 'to dress up' – see Marten and Mous (2017).

6 Partial Nasality in Maxakalí and Kaingang

This chapter explores the contributions of the minoritized indigenous languages of Brazil, Maxakalí and Kaingang, to representations of nasality gestures akin to musical scores, as well as the right way to frame the universality of "mama" and "papa" in light of a phonetic model called Enhancement Theory.

6.1 What My DoktorGroßVater Proposed, and What He Didn't Have a Chance to See

My doctoral advisor's doctoral advisor, Roman Jakobson, wrote a short paper called 'Why "mama" and "papa"?', which is one of my favorites to teach undergraduate phonology with. The observation in Jakobson (1962) starts with a survey of kinship terminology across 1,057 words for father and mother across languages compiled by Murdock (1959), finding that the vocative words for male and female parental units is something like *papa* and *mama* in nearly all of them (even when *mama* means 'dad', as in Georgian).

As I explain to my students in my own exegesis of the paper, it's not that infants are even necessarily talking about their parents when they say "mama" and "papa" – it's just that these are their first *syllables*, and parents have a tendency to think, "Oh, they must be calling *me*." Why are these the first syllables? In Jakobson's conception, /p/ is the most consonantlike of all consonants (it has the most complete closure of the vocal tract), and /a/ is the most vocalic of all vowels (as it has the most open aperture of the vocal tract). It is therefore not only that /pa/ is 'easiest to produce', but in fact, in Jakobson's more acoustically based characterization, it displays the most optimal polarization between two binary opposites in perceptual space.

This was part of a much larger project, related to Jakobson's investigation of what is called markedness – or, more appropriately, unmarkedness – of the most unmarked consonants, unmarked vowels, and unmarked syllables. Markedness refers to the nonsymmetrical treatment of what would otherwise perhaps be a symmetrical choice in a system – think of turning right at a North American intersection, as opposed to turning left. The idea was that /pa/ is one of the first syllables produced by a child, as well as one of the syllables most likely to be retained during aphasias, lesions, and language loss (to which Jakobson had a great deal of data from postwar trauma studies, drawing in part on work by Alexander Luria). It is also one of the most common syllable types cross-linguistically. This recurrent choice of /pa/ as opposed to, say, /uz/ shows that not all choices are equal. Uniting these three seemingly disconnected threads of empirical inquiry formed the synthesis of his monograph *Kindersprache, Aphasie, und allgemeine Lautgesetze* – literally, 'child language acquisition, aphasia, and universal sound laws'. The third of these domains pivoted upon what were called implicational universals about language inventories, arrived at through large-scale typological comparison (an enterprise initiated with his good friend Nikolai Trubetzkoy, who engaged in comparison of vowel systems across the Eurasian continent).

To put it in a playful way, one could say phonologists are keen to develop intuitions about universal patterns within the phonological inventories of a given language that could be useful for placing bets. Thus, if you tell me that a language has the sound /z/, I will safely bet that it also has /s/ (as English and Portuguese do). But if you tell me it has /s/, I will not be willing to bet it has /z/ (for it could be like Spanish, which has the former but not the latter). And if you tell me it lacks /s/, I surely won't bet it has /z/ (for it could be like Arrernte and other languages of Australia, which have neither). One thing is for certain on this view: It is impossible (or, at the very least, highly statistically unlikely) for a language to have /z/ without having /s/. Abstracting from these specific examples, the point is that the presence of the *marked* member of an oppositional pair within a given language will necessarily imply the presence of the *unmarked* pair (in this case /s/) but not vice versa. Jakobson's overall goal within this enterprise was to develop an interconnected theory of marked and unmarked consonants, vowels, and syllable types. Among syllable types, CV (consonant–vowel) structures such as /pa/ are unmarked compared to VC structures – for this reason, I often joke that Jakobson's paper *could* have been called 'Why Not Amam and Apap?', as his aim was not only to define the unmarked types but, in doing so, to implicitly characterize their marked opposites as well.

Returning to *mama* and *papa*, these are not only composed of (a) the most unmarked of all consonants (as both feature a bilabial closure, the most articulatory and indeed visually complete obstruction of airflow through the vocal tract), (b) the most unmarked of all vowels (for there is a reason that dentists ask us to open up and say [a]), and (c) the most unmarked of all syllable types (as languages such as Hawaiian, or *'Ō.le.lo Ha.wai.'i*, as its speakers call it – where each ' is a glottal consonant – have only CV syllables) but they also contain (d) reduplication of the same syllable type twice, as this repetition is one of the most economical ways to achieve a disyllabic target template with only one consonant and one vowel. Babies all over the world are simply experimenting with optimal syllables when they say *mama*, and their mothers take this to be a referential form of address. (Formal terms like *mother* and *father* are not inherently vocative.) Thus, *mama*, when babies utter it, doesn't at first 'mean' mother but ends up doing so as it pairs the most basic phonological sequence with the first intended referent.[1] So what about *papa*, or *tata* (as /t/ is also one of the maximally unmarked consonants)? According to the logic, these next-most-easy-to-articulate sequences end up getting paired with the next-most-present referent, the other caretaking parent: father.

Sticking now to consonants, the voiceless stop consonants /p,t,k/ and the nasal stop consonants /m,n,ŋ/ form the six most unmarked ones, most easy to draw kinship terms from (including maternal grandmother terms like /nana/). According to Jakobson's work and subsequent investigations into phonological unmarkedness, both voiceless stops and nasals are virtually ubiquitous across languages and feature in early acquisition, and it is for this reason that there seems to be no sharp preference for /p,t,k/ vs. /m,n,ŋ/ as the two least marked consonantal sets.

However, there is clearly a second tier of markedness, where one can then extend further to the voiced stop consonants /b,d,g/ (which are indeed found in kinship as one goes 'a step beyond' the core nuclear family, say in uncle terms, like Russian /d'ad'a/). Not all languages possess voiced stop consonants, and even when they do, these are often more limited in where they can occur. Jakobson definitively set the foundation for work in phonological theory still being done to this day, including a stepwise determination of how contrasts are gradually unfolded in a given language (with particular resonance in work such as Dresher [2009]). Nonetheless, I would contend that as Chomsky appeared on the scene, he ushered in a new set of questions in linguistic theory: what we *don't* find in languages. Contemporary linguistic theory is arguably equally preoccupied with delimiting the set of impossible languages – patterns never spoken. Thus, it turns out that, given the three-way contrast between voiceless stops, voiced stops, and nasals (hereafter characterized by /p,b,m/), there are languages with /p/, but no contrast between /b∼m/ (when I say no contrast, I mean in the way that, say, Spanish or Russian lack a contrast between the vowels in English *ship* and *sheep*). In other words, certain languages don't choose from all three of /p,b,m/ within their inventory of consonantal building blocks.[2] But there are not languages that choose /b/ but lack a contrast between /p∼m/. In other words, /b/ (more generally voiced stops) really is 'dispreferred' among these three. Thus, a language may have /p,b,m/, or /p,m/ without /b/, or /p,b/ without /m/. But it won't have /b,m/ without /p/.

---

[1] In a likely parallel manner, the syllabic mantra *aum* pairs these same segments.
[2] Recall that these are stand-ins for the entire class of voiceless, voiced, and nasal stops. Thus, while Arabic famously lacks the sound /p/, it does not lack all voiceless stops.

We can thus find languages that, when choosing their set of building blocks, drop /b/ or drop /m/. But no language will drop /p/ (the voiceless consonants) while retaining /b,m/. However, it turns out that the right way to express this isn't necessarily in terms of /b,m/ being equally marked consonants, but instead in terms of the inventory containing /b,m/ (with no use of /p/) as a marked *system*. Jakobson's ability to draw on diverse sources of empirical data and to find unexpected connections in unifying them was truly remarkable (and extended well beyond phonology, including his analysis of "Nevermore" in Poe's 'The Raven' as containing 'never' (Keyser, 2011), an example of the rhetorical mechanism of 'chiasmus' as it contains a near inverse of 'raven'[3]), but at the time of his research, the field did not have sufficient depth in the descriptions of /p,b/ or /p,m/ languages, to which we turn below after a bit more discussion.

6.2 The Trouble with /b/

Jakobson's paper was called 'Why "mama" and "papa" '? and did not feature "baba" in the title. What's wrong with /b/ compared to these other two? Voiced stops are simply more challenging to produce for aerodynamic reasons because voicing (vibration of the vocal cords) requires airflow from higher to lower pressure across the glottis – producing a stop (creating an 'obstruent') requires closure in the vocal tract, which eventually equalizes the pressure and makes this voicing-producing airflow difficult to sustain. (In nasal stops such as /m/, airflow through the nose allows this pressure differential to continue.) In fact, when languages seem to have a contrast between words like *cap* and *cab*, as English does, it turns out that a lot of the actual acoustic contrast is not carried by the consonants themselves but by the preceding vowels. Thus, if one measures the duration of vowels in *cap* and *cab* (or any pair of words differing only in the voicing of the final consonant, such as *ape* and *Abe*), the vowel before the voiced consonant will always be the longer one. This vowel lengthening is a cue that English speakers 'redundantly' encode for the benefit of the listener alone. Voiced stops will always be shorter than voiceless stops, for the reasons mentioned above; they are harder to sustain given the aerodynamic trade-off between voicing and obstruency. When speakers enact vowel lengthening before voiced consonants, they are creating a 'contextual' perceptual effect: If you make a vowel a little bit longer than usual, the consonant following it sounds a little bit shorter than usual, reinforcing the percept that it is voiced.

Not all languages, however, go to these lengths to maintain the contrast between /p,t,k/ and /b,d,g/ in syllable-final (aka 'coda') position. Thus,

---

[3] An example with particular resonance for me, as my own papa's self-abbreviation, Ray Nev, led to his first company's name, Raven Research.

languages as diverse as German, Polish, Catalan, and Turkish disallow /b,d,g/ from word-final position altogether, a phenomenon called final devoicing. Interestingly, English-speaking children also go through a stage where they enact final devoicing, pronouncing words such as *bad* with a final [t]. In a short but very influential paper, Stampe (1969) proposed that final devoicing comes from a constraint *D# (where * is a constraint banning a configuration and the banned configuration is D, any voiced stop, before the end of a word, notated by #) that is universal in nature across all languages but can be 'turned off' during the course of language acquisition. Thus, children acquiring English eventually learn to turn off the constraint *D#, while those acquiring German never need to turn it off (or learn it in the first place).

We mentioned that voiced stops like /b/ are difficult to sustain because the pressure differential between 'upstairs' (above the glottis) and 'downstairs' quickly equalizes once there is an obstruent consonant made upstairs. This is because a closed oral cavity, with no airflow escaping from it but air flowing into it, will quickly accumulate pressure. There are a few imaginable ways to keep this airflow going a little longer, however. One is cheek-puffing, as expansion of the walls of the cheeks will increase the volume upstairs and thus allow the pressure to build up for a little longer; indeed, this has been observed as a strategy employed in some languages to sustain the voicing-producing airflow needed for voiced stops. Another strategy, one that is widely employed by many languages of lowland (i.e., east of the Andes) South America, is 'prenasalization', so that instead of /b,d,g/, one may observe in certain contexts [^{m}b,^{n}d,$^{\eta}$g].

For example, Maxakalí, a language of the Macro-Jê family, spoken in Minas Gerais, Brazil, turns these 'dispreferred' consonants /b,d,g/ in loanwords from Brazilian Portuguese into prenasalized variants [^{m}b,^{n}d,$^{\eta}$g]. One of the ways that this can be graphically displayed is through a method of using earbuds – the round in-ear headphones that come with cellphones – as a recording device placed under the nostrils.

Together with Mario Coelho da Silva, an expert on the Maxakalí language, we brought the earbuds technique to a Maxakalí village. Although it seems relatively unusual to ask speakers of an indigenous language who live with traditional village organization to place earbuds under their nostrils for the purposes of recording prenasalized voiced stops, it turns out to be one of the most practical, noninvasive, and easy ways of verifying the presence of nasality on such consonants beyond simply impressionistically trying to tell with the naked ear alone. The method, developed by Stewart and Kohlberger (2017), in fact uses two microphone sources: one is the two earbuds positioned below the nostrils, while the other is a plain microphone for the oral track. By recording the two tracks at the same time and then normalizing them using a straightforward software script, one can create graphs, superposed in time,

Partial Nasality in Maxakalí and Kaingang   89

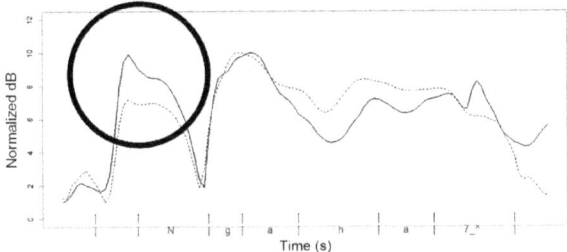

Figure 6.1 Nasalance track of prenasalization in Maxakalí voiced stop loanwords: Solid line is nasal intensity; dotted line is oral intensity

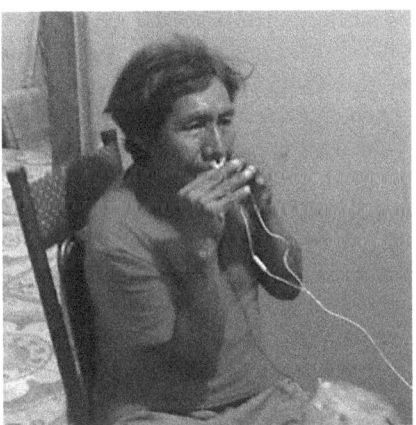

Figure 6.2 Earbud methodology for nasalance

representing the amount of nasal and oral intensity. As an example, Figure 6.1 shows a recording of the word [ᵑga.haw] (a loanword from the Portuguese word for 'bottle', *garrafa* [ga'fia.fə]).

As you can see in the graphic, nasal intensity is only greater than oral intensity for this initial segment, the prenasalized portion preceding the voiced stop [g]. This loanword is of interest to our overall study of prenasalization as a kind of 'hypervoicing' of voiced stops, because we know that it didn't just "come directly descendent all the way from ancient Proto-Macro-Jê" with prenasalization – in its original Brazilian Portuguese variant, *garrafa* [ga'fia.fə], there is no nasalization at all. Loanword adaptations of this type are of prime interest to phonologists because they show that certain tendencies are *productive*: Maxakalí speakers have actively *imposed* nasalization on the loanword that did not contain it because they prefer to have prenasalization before all voiced stops that occur word-initially (Figure 6.2).

6.3 Enhancement Theory and Hypervoicing

As opposed to languages like English, French, or Portuguese, why does Maxakalí reliably impose audible prenasalization on all word-initial voiced stops? Because it can. Maxakalí can get away with prenasalization of /b,d,g/ to make them easier to produce and perceive because its inventory lacks phonemic nasal consonants (see also World Atlas of Language Structures Online, 2013, chapter 18.). In other words, this language does not have the syllables in *mama*! (We will come back to the nature of this gap in more detail below.)

When a language lacks a contrastive phonemic property G altogether in its inventory, this feature G is, interestingly enough, 'still available' in the language for other purposes. This forms part of the discovery of Enhancement Theory (Keyser & Stevens, 2006). Enhancement refers to this phonetic process of recruiting a noncontrastive feature G in a language in order to enhance a contrast between a binarily opposed pair of sounds distinguished by, say, +F and −F. One of the classic examples is lip-rounding with English /ʃ/. The /s-ʃ/ contrast in English, as we know from the existence of numerous tongue-twisters playing upon it (e.g., *she sells seashells by the seashore*), is difficult to maintain in perception as well as production, but it turns out that it is often enhanced by lip-rounding (visualize yourself saying the word *shirt* right now, for example). This is the additional 'trick' of redundantly using G, lip-rounding on consonants, which is not otherwise contrastive in English, to enhance a featural contrast that, strictly speaking, is based on tongue position along the roof of the mouth alone. Enhancement is kind of like the fact that the messages at a traffic light aren't coded by red-yellow-green alone but also by the fixed vertical position of each of the three distinct lights.

Another language that wanted to enhance the /s-ʃ/ contrast, however, might not have lip-rounding 'available' anymore. This would be because lip-rounding on consonants is already being used in the inventory, as it is, for example, in Mandarin Chinese (in which words such as [kʷai] 'fast' have a rounded initial consonant). In order to enhance the /s-ʃ/ contrast in Mandarin, therefore, the language resorts to a different enhancing feature, namely retroflexion (not only the point of contact of the tongue on the roof of the mouth but also the tongue tip's position, curled backwards).[4]

Keyser and Stevens's (2006) Enhancement Theory provides a way of understanding when one phonetic feature is recruited to help 'redundantly' enhance a contrast. In Maxakalí, the contrast between voiced and voiceless pairs /g~k, b~p, d~t/ has the opportunity to recruit nasality, specifically prenasalization, because this language lacks phonemic nasal consonants. By venting part of the

---

[4] Thus, to a discerning ear, Mandarin [ʂ] sounds different from English [ʃʷ] because the former employs tongue retroflexion as an enhancing gesture, while the latter employs lip-rounding as an enhancing gesture.

airflow across the glottis through the nose, in addition to what's flowing into the oral tract, voicing can be sustained for longer without running into that pesky problem of the pressure eventually equalizing due to the closed volume in the mouth. Nasal venting of this sort is a tendency that one can find across many languages to minor degrees (or even major degrees during singing and other moments of emphatic vocalization; just listen to the realization of the initial [g] in the refrains of Leadbelly's 'ŋGoodnight, Irene'), but in Maxakalí it can be reliably used across all initial voiced stops because it's a feature that isn't being used otherwise.

Thus, Maxakalí is a language with only /p-b/ (what about the name of the language, you might say? As in many cases, this is an exonym, given by outsiders, and not what the speakers of the language call it). Does that mean there are no instances of the syllables [mama]? Yes, indeed, as already said above. However, there are instances of the syllables [mãmã], with nasal vowels. Maxakalí does allow nasal consonants like [m,n,ŋ] but not freely – only when they precede nasal vowels. In Maxakalí, the vowels control the consonants. When a vowel is nasal, it will turn all the consonants that it can into nasal within the same syllable. Thus, nasality of [m,n,ŋ] is allophonic, that is, predictable. These consonants are only found as predictable, mutated variants of underlying /b,d,g/ – and this in where square brackets (for predictable allophonic realizations) vs. slashes (for true underlying, unpredictable contrasts) play a crucial role in how to notate these differences in linguistic status.

In summary, when vowels are nasal, as in [mãmã], underlying /b/ turns into its predictable allophonic variant [m], but the language lacks /m/ as an underlying phonemic contrast. Lacking /m/, therefore, Maxakalí can recruit nasals for other purposes, as in the case of enhancement of the voicing contrast /p-b/ to achieve hypervoicing. Fair enough – chalk up another case for enhancement among the dozens of examples. But what is really interesting is that nasal contours – sequences of [mb] – can be used for other enhancing purposes in other languages.

In particular, Leo Wetzels and I argued for a crucial difference between *prenasalized* [^{m}b] and *postoralized* [m^b] (Wetzels & Nevins, 2018), where the apparently typographic distinction in what is superscripted actually reveals ontologically which is the basic segment and which is the enhancing part. Thus, prenasalized stops are essentially voiced stops with enhancement-related prenasalization. But what would a language use *postoralized* nasals for? Well, for when nasals themselves need to have oralization added to them for some reason.

6.4 Nasal Shielding

Now, the theory of enhancement as developed above already says that a language will only use enhancing [b] if it doesn't have /b/ in its inventory elsewhere. Thus, in Kaingang, another Macro-Jê language of Brazil, the underlying inventory contrasts nasals with voiceless stops: /p-m/ without /b/. The voiced stop series can be recruited for other purposes. But nasals are easy to perceive and don't face the troubles discussed above. Why would enhancement come in handy for nasals?

The answer lies not in nasal consonants themselves, which Kaingang has, but in nasal *vowels*. The vowels need to be protected, and in particular, this is a kind of altruistic enhancement. We've already seen altruistic enhancement above, in the case of English vowel lengthening before voiced stops in order to increase the percept of their short duration. Altruistic enhancement usually involves an adjacent sound J making a K next to it sound even more K-like, like the lengthened vowel making the short voiced obstruent sound shorter. But in the Kaingang case, it might be thought of as a prophylactic enhancement: it prevents K becoming less K-like by *shielding*. Specifically, in Kaingang, the contrast between oral and nasal vowels is so important that one wouldn't want an oral vowel to become 'accidentally' nasalized. A nasal consonant can easily accidentally nasalize a vowel. By sacrificing its edge as an oral stop, as in [m^{b}a], the nasal /m/ ensures it won't accidentally turn the /a/ into an [ã]. This shielding is necessary on either side of a nasal consonant and can thus lead to preoralized, postoralized, or even circumoralized nasals. Thus, Kaingang doesn't have *mama*; it has [m^{b}a^{b}m^{b}a]!

In order to prevent the natural tendency of 'contaminatory' accidental nasalization of a vowel by an adjacent nasal consonant, the nasal consonants 'sacrifice' part of their nasality, and they can do so in Kaingang precisely because the language lacks underlying voiced stops like /b,d/. Voiced stops are thus available to be recruited for this other purpose – altruistic, enhancing shielding of adjacent oral vowels. The complete set of allophones for nasal /m/ and the environment in which they are found are presented below, along with a sample word as recorded by Dr. Marcia Nascimento Kaingang – the first native speaker of this language to obtain a doctoral degree in linguistics.

(1) Allophones of underlying nasals in Kaingang

env.	allophone	example	gloss
# _ ṽ	[m]	[mãn]	'hold'
ṽ _ #	[m]	[ŋãm]	'break'
# _ v	[m^b]	[m^{b}a]	'carrying'
v _ #	[^{b}m]	[hi^{b}m]	'frog'
ṽ _ ṽ	[m]	[mõmæ̃ŋ]	'fear'
v _ v	[^{b}m^b]	[ke^{b}m^{b}a]	'try out'
ṽ _ v	[m^b]	[ɸũm^{b}u]	'tobacco'
v _ ṽ	[^{b}m]	[ha^{b}mæ̃]	'listen'

Notice that there is no allophone of [b] alone – this is simply never found. The voiced stop [b] is only found as part of a preoralized, postoralized, or circumoralized nasal contour with /m/ as its core.

There is no pure *mama* in Kaingang or Maxakalí. Jakobson did not have access to data at the time to know that a syllable like [ma] or [na] would be explicitly banned in Maxakalí (where [m,n] are only found before nasal vowels) or in Kaingang (where an [m,n] must sacrifice its edge towards orality before oral vowels). What's interesting is that even when Maxakalí lacks /m/, it still 'uses it' to help /b/, and even when Kaingang lacks /b/, it still 'uses it' to help /m/. The theory of enhancement had not yet been developed in Jakobson's time, nor had the existence of languages that lack underlying /m/ been adequately described.

How are the allophonic contrasts above represented, in terms of the articulatory timing that is necessary for a single consonant to bear preoralized, postoralized, and/or circumoralized portions? This directly catapults us into the theory of timing representations in phonology.

6.5   On the Timing of Contoured Consonants

One of the first topics in learning phonetic transcription usually involves affricates such as [t͡ʃ], where the ligature tie at the top reflects a direct borrowing from musical notation. As the transcription of the contrasting pair *white shoes* [wajt ʃuz] vs. *why choose* [waj t͡ʃuz] makes clear, these two sequences are completely identical in terms of the segments they contain but differ only in their timing. In the former, each of [t,ʃ] occupies its own dedicated timing slot, whereas in the latter, the two have to share the same timing slot, and thus each get only around half the amount of time that they would as fully fledged consonants. For this reason, the latter, called an affricate in the literature and represented in early literature as /č/, was formerly treated as a single consonant and, in early phonological work, such as Chomsky and Halle (1968), was represented by a special feature, [+delayed release]. However, subsequent work (see, for example, Sagey [1986]) demonstrated that consonants like [t͡ʃ] pattern as if they had a /t/ and an /ʃ/ inside them within a sequenced change in the feature [±continuant], simply with these two crammed into a single unit of timing.

While this development of phonological theory is fairly well known, it was actually the case that before affricates were problematized and reanalyzed in this by-now standard manner, contour nasals were treated this way first. Anderson (1976), with specific reference to languages such as Kaingang, points out that "when the full range of consonant types in which nasality is involved is considered, then, it seems unlikely that any independently motivated feature, involved in making distinctions among the purely oral segments, can be used to distinguish fully nasal, prenasalized, and postnasalized consonants" (p. 332), as "they differ from one another only in relative timing" (p. 333). Instead, Anderson proposes that a parameter such as [± nasal] (with its negative value recognized as an explicit instruction to close the velopharyngeal port and shut off nasality) may vary in its value within the scope of a single segment. Anderson draws inspiration from the modeling of contour tones in languages such as Mandarin Chinese, in which what is traditionally called the 'third' of four tones (the falling-then-rising contour present in each individual tone-bearing unit [TBU] of the greeting *nǐ hǎo*) in work such as Woo (1969) is treated not as a unitary, primitive 'third tone' within an inventory of options but rather a contour tone, with the three-note sequence [mid]-[low]-[high]-sequenced and transitioning over the duration of a single syllable.

Diphthongs within vowel systems (as in the affirmative syllable *aye* [aj]) are treated as two vocoids within a single syllable, and rounded consonants such as [kʷ] mentioned above are also treated as complex articulations within the scope of a single consonant rather than a cluster of two consonants.[5] Anderson suggests that nasality, like tones, can vary within its value (say, from negative to positive to negative) with in a single segment, in representations that Sagey's (1986) work crystallized as follows:

(2)   Affricate (e.g., t͡ʃ):

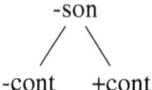

-son
/ \
-cont   +cont

(3)   Rising contour tone:

TBU
/ \
L   H

(4)   Postoralized nasals (e.g., mᵇ):

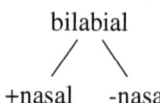

bilabial
/ \
+nasal   -nasal

Interestingly enough, Anderson mused that "internal structure in terms of the feature [continuant] is not the correct way to describe affricates, though further investigation is required before a definitive conclusion can be reached" (p. 343),

---

[5] For this reason, the Latin *aqua* /akʷa/ became *apa* in Romanian, reducing a single complex consonant to a simplex version of a single consonant.

Partial Nasality in Maxakalí and Kaingang   95

although, as time would tell, autosegmental representation of the type shown above in (2) proved the most widespread for affricates, probably in large part because these are found as nearly 'Euroversals' throughout languages familiar to university-employed linguists, while postoralized nasals are not.

It is probably not well inscribed within the annals of phonological history that Kaingang had such a crucial role in triggering a rethinking of the representation of phonological timing, such that many-to-one relations between feature values and their hosting timing units of the type in (4) eventually became the bread and butter of linguistic theory. But scientific work is often like that – a germ of an idea lies in one paper on nasality in Kaingang that mentions the problems it poses for the representation of timing, whereas in parallel, a non-autosegmental solution in terms of [+delayed release] still lingered on for affricates for years, until the relevant evidence from different corners attained a critical mass. By and large, I think it is fair to say that the indirect role that Anderson's contribution based on Kaingang had on the representation of timing faded a bit into collective amnesia once affricates were treated this way.

As we have reviewed above, however, Kaingang turns out to have had fundamental consequences not only in understanding how circumoralized nasals such as [ᵇmᵇ] can arise but also *why* they do. Enhancement Theory provides a way of understanding that this kind of altruistic denasalization on both sides of what remains, at its core, a [+nasal] consonant can only happen in languages that don't have /b/ already enshrined as a phoneme.[6]

The 'altruistic,' vowel-perception-based motivation of postoralization in Kaingang vs. the 'greedy,' aerodynamic-based motivation of prenasalization in Maxakalí makes the difference between [ᵐb] and [mᵇ] far from notational.[7] Instead, as Steriade (1993) proposed, one must distinguish between the articulatory moments of minimal (indicated with a zero as A_0) and maximal oral aperture (indicated by A_{max}).

(5)

nasal stop	prenasal stop	postnasal stop
[nas]	[nas]	[nas]
/ \	|	|
A_0 A_{max}	A_0 A_{max}	A_0 A_{max}
[m]	[ᵐb]	[bᵐ]

---

[6] Loanwords, too, provide confirmation for this, as the word *padre* 'priest', is rendered in Kaingang as [panᵈcr] because there is no way to have a [d] without it being an offshoot of nasality.

[7] Interestingly, work such as Riehl (2008) suggests that these two cannot be reliably distinguished by the relative duration of the oral vs. nasal portions alone, a conclusion that in Wetzels and Nevins (2018) we pushed further to argue that the difference can only be sought in the underlying status of each within the phonological system as a whole.

However, as we now know, (5) should label the rightmost case as a preoralized nasal. A circumoralized nasal would be similar, with A_0 on both sides. What is important here is the incorporation of the notion of aperture into phonological representations. Most phonological theories did not explicitly distinguish closure from release phases in the description of stop consonants. In fact, Steriade points out that affricates can be described by a sequencing of A_0 and A_{fric}, where the latter is a degree of aperture sufficient to produce the turbulent airstream characteristic of fricatives. Unreleased stops – like the final [p̚, t̚, k̚] of Cantonese – are represented by *only* having an A_0 phase.

What the inventory of Maxakalí and Kaingang bring to the fore is the fact that languages don't seem to be 'content' with just two-way contrasts and a very clean divide between them. There are languages with /p,t,b,d/ only, such as Maxakalí with [papa] and [ᵐbaᵐba] and languages with /p,t,m,n/ only, such as Kaingang with [mᵇaᵇmᵇa] and [papa]. But if they lack /b/, their /m/ may still take up some phonetic space from a [b], and if they lack /m/, an [m] may still encroach upon their /b/. This is akin to what happens with vowels: Languages without a difference between *sheep* and *ship* will have an /i/ that floats between these and is opportunistically used where it best suits the speaker.

This allows us to revisit the notion of contrast in a radical way. Rather than Jakobson's most unmarked consonants, we can instead move towards asking what are the most unmarked consonant *systems*? The result, based on a sampling of South American languages not well studied in Jakobson's time, is the finding that /b,m/ is never chosen as a two-way system. These two can be chosen, but only if /p/ is chosen first.

(6) (a) [±voiced] ≫ [±nasal]   (b) [±nasal] ≫ [±voiced]

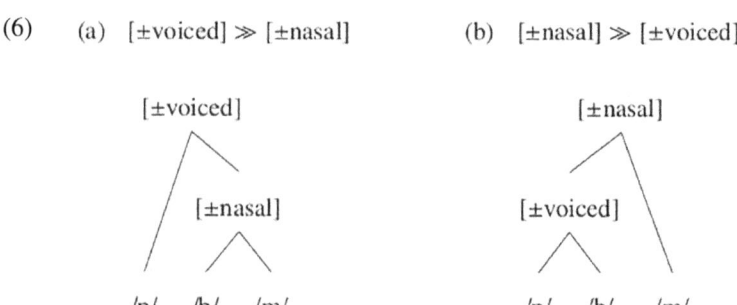

With a closer study of /p,m/ vs. /p,b/ systems, we move towards understanding consonants in a parallel way to what has already been achieved with vowels in *dispersion theory* (see Liljencrants and Lindblom [1972]): the finding that if a language has only three of the five most basic vowels, these three will be /i,u,a/.

Once contrastive choices are made within a system, what are the best ways to enhance contrasts? The answer is that contour nasals can be chosen to enhance [b] in a /p-b/ system or to protect oral vowels in a /p-m/ system. Enhancement by noncontrastive features is a recurrent mechanism recruited across phonological systems, but the Maxakalí–Kaingang comparison is most likely the first case of the same type of consonant – a nasal–oral contour within the scope of a single segment – being employed for two vastly different types of enhancement in two different systems.

The study of these two Macro-Jê languages within the context of these issues is rather recent: As I mentioned above, the pursuit of a PhD in linguistics by Marcia Nascimento Kaingang (alongside a number of recent Kaingang speakers pursuing masters and doctoral degrees in anthropology and linguistics in Brazil) is a relatively recent phenomenon, in part encouraged by the presence of affirmative action funding programs intended to broaden inclusion. Anderson's own awareness of Kaingang was through reports by Bible translation experts, who, whether or not they focused on instrumental phonetic work, generally did not pursue comparisons of phonological representation between indigenous languages in Brazil. Comparisons of this sort bring about questions that can be raised for new languages, always bearing the transformative power to change the theory. For example, preliminary work on Oro Waram by Apontes (2018), a massively underdocumented language of the Txapakura family of languages in Brazil, suggests that post-oralization of nasals occurs optionally, even though the language does not have nasal vowels, but obligatorily when another consonant follows the nasal. In Wetzels and Nevins (2018) we suggested this may be implicating the presence of a *third* kind of enhancement, neither shielding nor venting: one to enhance the place of articulation of the consonant (labial vs. coronal vs. dorsal), made all the more imperceptible and fragile when placed before a consonant (instead of a vowel). But this work in turn raises predictions about the relative perceptibility of /mr/ vs. /nr/ as compared to /br/ vs. /dr/ before one can even think of placing down the theoretical brick on which it is written that postoralization improves the place of articulation, among the thousands of building stones to yet be shuffled and reconfigured within the edifice of phonological theory.

Further Reading

Dresher (2009) presents a comprehensive discussion of phonological contrast and its representation, including the unfolding of contrasts in inventories of different shapes. For detailed studies of the aerodynamic and perceptual mechanisms underlying venting, see Westbury (1983) and, on shielding,

Herbert (1986). Of great interest as well to the question of labials as the most consonantlike of consonants is the challenge posed by analyzing labiovelar stops such as [k͡p]; see Ohala and Lorentz (1977) and Connell (1994) for an overview of their phonetic characteristics and timing in languages such as Ibibio.

7 Symmetric Hands in Sign Language Phonologies

In this chapter, we examine the phonological representation of the two hands in sign language phonology, and in particular the limited independence of the nondominant hand. Striking evidence from the variety of Black ASL and its comparison with white ASL reveal patterns of allophony that suggest a specific implementation of deletion analysis is at work in one-handed versions of otherwise two-handed signs. Coupled with findings on the limitations of two-handed versions of signs made near the visually salient location of the face that implicate an important role for nonmanual marking, these results suggest that the real locus of simultaneity in signed languages that differentiates their phonologies from spoken languages is not necessarily amongst the two hands but rather between the hands and the prosodic and intonational layers of nonmanual marking.

7.1 Sociohistorical Variation as a Window onto Sign Language Structure

This chapter takes a look at sociolinguistic variation – as resulting from sociohistorical factors that differentiate people into groups – and how it interfaces with phonological differences. The specific phonological difference under study is the use of two hands versus the use of only one as an aspect of sublexical structure (i.e., as a phonological feature) in individual signs and their overall patterning throughout the lexicon and morphophonology. Sign languages, it goes without saying, are fully fledged human languages in terms of having richly structured syntax, semantics, pragmatics, morphology, phonology, and phonetics (see Sandler and Lillo-Martin [2006] for a comprehensive overview), and like all languages with highly complex amounts of structure, there is always room for individual variation, particularly in the domains of connected discourse. It is also well known that sign languages differ greatly from each other, and thus that, as Klima and Bellugi (1979) compellingly show, the meaning of signs in ASL cannot be guessed by signers who use Chinese Sign Language or vice versa, thus putting to rest any suspicion that there is a more universally transparent base that makes all sign languages essentially alike.

Nonetheless, given the way that signing communities have often historically formed – through educational, religious, or social groups that unite Deaf people within a given region as part of a community in which deafness is a unifying force in creating linguistic networks, one might not necessarily expect the traditional sociolinguistic variables (e.g., maintaining the pre-World War II process of rhotic deletion in American English among working classes in New York in Labov's [1966] classic study) to have such obviously stratified effects on the phonology within Deaf communities.[1]

As it turns out, there is a glaring case at hand in which sociohistorical factors have massively guided distinct phonological trends in dialects isolated from each other, and this is the case of Deaf individuals in America who, given the appalling course of legalized segregation based on skin color for separate cemeteries, libraries, restrooms, parks, and waiting rooms at bus stations, also had, over the course of nearly a century, Black schools for the Deaf and white schools for the Deaf, with separate educational and social environments for sign language. Given the Supreme Court's Plessy vs. Ferguson decision in 1896 that racial segregation was a constitutional right with separate (but not equally funded) schools, these two communities remained isolated from each other within eighteen states of the Southern USA.

Not only were the Black schools for the Deaf and the white schools for the Deaf segregrated from each other as generations of signers went through education and social group formation, but the policies among these schools turned out to be different. White schools for the Deaf followed a highly flawed and influential educational idea of oralism, after the infamous International Conference for the Deaf in Milan in 1880 declared "that the oral method should be preferred to that of signs in the education and instruction of deaf-mutes" as Alexander Graham Bell's antisigning policy won out over that of Thomas Gallaudet and others. An immediate result of the Milan Conference resolutions was the large-scale firing of Deaf teachers and their replacement with nondeaf teachers, who trained students to vocalize and lip-read instead of signing. In the United States, this large-scale setback for the unfettered continuity of ASL as a natural language was largely only implemented in white schools for the Deaf. In contrast, Black schools for the Deaf continued with Deaf teachers and with the use of sign as opposed to oralism. Desegregration of schools for

---

[1] I follow the distinction in works such as Padden and Humphries (1988), in which Deaf with a capital D is for individuals (who may in fact be hearing) that identify as Deaf in terms of cultural identity and in use of a shared sign language, distinct from the physiological condition of deafness. In what follows, I also adopt the label (Southern) Black ASL, following McCaskill et al. (2011) and the recent protagonization of the term in the Black Lives Matter movement, while fully aware that there are contexts of historical focus where the term African-American is preferable.

the Deaf occurred in the 1960s, a period that roughly coincided with the end of oralism policies and a return to treating ASL as a medium of instruction, most notably at Gallaudet University in Washington, D.C. Even with these changes, however, sociohistorically based differences between Black and white ASL communities were not going to change overnight – and in fact, persisting race-based disparities within ASL continue through the present day (Player, 2021), given the systemic racism that has disproportionally impacted Black Deaf people for so long.

As a result of having nondeaf teachers in white schools, not only the medium of instruction but countless other factors were bound to be different, including the notion of Deaf Space (Johnson, 2014; Kusters, 2015), as laid out within the schools. For example, as signed languages are visual languages, students sitting in a circular arrangement will be infinitely easier for sign language perception than an arrangement where students sit in rows, which is more likely to be enforced by hearing teachers oblivious to the effects of spatial arrangement. Some consequences of these two markedly different educational policies for white and Black Deaf students are more obvious than others – for example, a sociolinguistic comparison of Black ASL and white ASL conducted as recently as Lucas et al. (2001) revealed that Black signers employ far less mouthing (the silent pronunciation of corresponding words in English) than white signers, a clear long-term difference based on the historical emphasis on oralism within white schools for the Deaf. But other linguistic differences within the two communities seem to be more indirectly influenced by aspects of sign language structure resulting from the fact that Southern Black ASL essentially suffered less interference from oralism as a language than white ASL, and in maintaining more continuity as a linguistic community did not undergo some of the more drastic shifts that affected the phonology of the latter. As McCaskill et al. (2011) state, "A paradoxical effect of racism and misunderstanding of a scientific theory caused many Black deaf children to receive an education that was more comprehensible than the education their white deaf counterparts received" (p. 107).

To summarize the discussion more broadly, what one can observe in comparison of Southern Black ASL and white ASL is perhaps one of the most stark cases of two Deaf communities within the same larger sign language being isolated from one another and undergoing distinct types of social and educational influences on language interaction and structure. It is usually the case that deafness unites people of distinct backgrounds into the same overall linguistic community, and outside of perhaps the case of Belfast in Northern Ireland (where in the same city, religious and political differences govern the use of British Sign Language vs. Irish Sign Language), the literature is generally thin on cases that are as polarized along ethnicity as the differences between these ASL communities. The combination of factors in segregated schools created the conditions for the development of a unique sign language variety in the USA, distinct from that used by white Deaf students. The disgraceful effects of Jim Crow laws in the USA created, as a result of racism and educational policies, two communities ('lects', as they are called in sociolinguistics) of the same sign language that can be analyzed in terms of contrasting phonological variables, with the possibility to observe whether there is an overall directionality to phonological processes that sign languages undergo with external interference and accelerated change. As it turns out, the most salient such phonological variable is the difference in two-handed versions of ASL signs, and the findings provide one of the key puzzle pieces to help understand the representation of two-handedness in sign language more generally.

Anticipating the theoretical repercussions to follow, the representation of the weaker hand in sign language (i.e., the left hand for right-handed people, or vice versa) must be represented as an aspect of phonological structure that can undergo deletion, assimilation, and markedness reduction. This is a striking result, as arguably one of the most immediately noticeable differences between sign language structure and spoken language structure is the fact that one has two independently articulable hands that can, in principle, be fully autonomous from one another but not two independently articulable mouths. The fact of the matter is, however, that the phonological representation of the weaker hand in sign language (henceforth, the nondominant hand [NDH] or H_2 to represent its secondary status) is simply not a fully independent tree of phonological features. Sign languages don't use – and thus we must conclude don't have – the ability to represent the left hand and right hand as two articulators that are carrying out their own motor plan in full-blown simultaneity. It is not like playing the piano, where the two hands can go their entirely separate ways in terms of finger configurations and movement. Indeed, as Battison (1974) aptly summarizes, "We have one tongue, but two independent hands. This independence is constrained, however, by the need to simplify manual–visual signals in a rapid transmission context" (p. 3).

The phonological representation of H_2 has been one of the most theoretically complex aspects of sign language phonology. It involves the phonological encoding of both articulatory and perceptual constraints specific to this channel – thus undergoing *phonologization*, in Hyman's (1976) sense of the term: turning gradient phonetic trends into generalizations over the lexicon. Like all empirical matters in phonology writ large, studying the generalizations about the phonology of the NDH has required the inspection and analysis of evidence from sources as broad as acquisition, psycholinguistics, allophonic processes in connected speech, and the direction of sociolinguistic change. In order to unpack these arguments and better understand the current state of the art in sign language phonology, we first turn to an overview of the sublexical elements that compose sign language structure.

7.2 From Cheremes to the Asymmetry of the Two Hands

American Sign Language was brought to Hartford, Connecticut by Thomas Gallaudet in 1817 and was based on French Sign Language after Gallaudet's unsuccessful visit to England first. Even before that, however, there were extant sign languages in use in places like Martha's Vineyard, and through language contact and change (see Woodward and DeSantis [1977]), ASL quickly adapted and went its own way – perhaps much like Brazilian Portuguese began to dramatically diverge from that of Lisbon once it took its own diachronic path on a new continent with new language contact, with ensuing changes in prosody, morphology, segmental phonology, syntax, and even pragmatics. ASL was, however, rapidly suppressed and interfered with by oralism thereafter (particularly in schools for the Deaf reserved for whites, as mentioned above) and never received any systematic study until the work of Stokoe, a professor at Gallaudet University, who published a paper in 1960 that radically changed the study of ASL and went on to develop a structuralist dictionary of the language organized in terms of 'cheremic principles'. What is chereology? It was Stokoe's term for the phonology of signed languages. Stokoe's historically important contribution was to show that ASL had a "syntactical, morphemic, and sub-morphemic structure different from that of English" (1960, p. 10). He focused on minimal pairs, and on demonstrating that "operating for each user of the language, in the midst of an almost infinite variety of movement, is the principle of significant contrast" (p. 24). In so doing, he provided evidence for what Martinet (1957) and Hockett (1960) called 'duality of patterning', one of the fundamental properties of human language: having a combinatorial system of phonology to build words out of sublexical elements, alongside a combinatorial system of syntax to build phrases out of sub-phrasal elements. Minimal pairs demonstrated that handshape, location, and movement are among the recurrent components drawn from finite sets (of, say, forty-five handshapes, twenty-five locations, etc.) that, when combined, could generate a vastly more efficient model of the lexicon than thousands of globally differentiated whole signs.[2]

More refined theoretical developments would come shortly thereafter, with a focus on phonological *processes*. Phonology, considered as a combinatorial system for creating meaningful elements out of meaningless elements, could be applied to sign language, with insights into descriptive and explanatory generalizations about recurring patterns used to form the lexicon out of smaller sublexical elements. Battison (1978) explicitly decides to apply the notion of *phonology* to sign language for three reasons: "to avoid confusion between

---

[2] Note that these particular sublexical primes can be combined simultaneously, but many aspects of sign language phonology turn out to require *sequential* specification; see, for example, the discussion of two-handed alternating signs below, in which the dominant hand moves first.

Stokoe's structural analysis and the present study in a generative phonological framework, to avoid using a new term where a familiar one seems adequate and appropriate, and to highlight existing similarities between speech and signing" (p. 14). His decision proved immensely fruitful, and the theoretical dialogue between spoken and signed phonology has been mutually informative for both subfields, as well as enriching for a more complete understanding of what a phonological component is, after all. Prior to this era, as Battison (1974) points out, it is puzzling that interest in sign languages had focused primarily on syntax. He notes that the misconception that sign languages are "ideographic, lack duality of patterning, or are even universal" (p. 1) had led to a focus only on the order of signs themselves in sentences, particularly when educators' main preoccupation was the use of Sign English, which imposed English word order and morphology on ASL. Battison instead argued strongly in favor of a detailed study of sign language phonology – in part, in fact, to counter the failed coinages of neologisms. Battison (1978) shows how the contrived neologisms coined by proponents of 'manual English' undergo restructuring by children, noting, "These signs are apparently odd because of their discernible phonological instability, and some of them actually violate the morpheme structure constraints we have posited. These signs undergo radical restructuring by signers to make them fit ASL patterns of articulation" (p. 46).

Under this view, the phonology of a sign language – like the function of phonology in general – is to systematically delimit the set of manually executed gestures used to represent meanings in a given sign language from the larger subset of all possible manually executed gestures producible by the human body. As Battison (1974) says, this will necessarily involve "constraints on underlying forms (morpheme structure conditions) and constraints on surface variation, expressed by phonological rules" (p. 2).

Even before Stokoe, formal analyses of sign language in terms of duality of patterning were already underway in the work of anthropological linguists. The Plains Indian Sign Language of North America was an intertribal lingua franca used for communication as a secondary sign language by nondeaf people, presumably because learning one new language among n such tribes in constant interaction would not require learning $n-1$ other languages for communication, but only the one. As a secondary sign language, of course, it may have some properties distinct from those when intended as a primary language, though we must recall that situations of 'bimodal bilingualism' are common, particularly with hearing children born to Deaf parents, who acquire the sign language from birth, although it may not continue as their primary language at later stages in life. The Plains Sign Language was famously studied in the nineteenth century by Mallery (1886) during post-Civil War excursions into Dakota territory, and his work inspired language scientists worldwide, including Wilhelm Wundt in

Leipzig. Some seventy years later, the language was almost extinct, but based on the dissertation by West (1960), there was fieldwork with William Shakespeare Arapaho, and this work informed discussions by Kroeber (1958), who conducted phonological analyses involing the numbers of one-handed versus two-handed signs and their free variation, and Voegelin (1958), who explicitly argued for duality of patterning in the language on empirical and conceptual grounds in his article 'Sign Language Analysis, on One Level or Two?'.

The 1970s witnessed a renaissance in sign language studies across all areas. Woodward, who we will encounter below, was working in Stokoe's research lab and wrote the first linguistics dissertation about ASL in 1973. As mentioned above, Battison's (1974) work explicitly applies the term phonology to ASL and develops generative models of phonological processes in the language, such as deletion. Countless other works focused on phenomena such as acquisition, diachronic change, loanword phonology, compounding, slips of the hand, psycholinguistic studies of iconicity, and beyond. The most far-reaching synthesis and state of the art was Klima and Bellugi (1979), in some ways equivalent to what Chomsky and Halle (1968) was for the crystallization of the generative phonology program. The authors add a more complex set of sublexical features to Stokoe's (1960) main three parameters of handshape, location, and movement, thereby launching the eventual field of studying the hierarchical feature geometry of signs in a manner akin to Sagey's (1986) model for spoken language phonology (Figure 7.1); see Brentari (1998) for what remains one of the most articulated such models to the present day. Among the parameters that Klima and Bellugi (1979) added was *hand arrangement* to indicate a range of the following properties: one-handed versus two-handed, two-handed symmetric or two-handed alternating, or simply having the NDH as a base hand. They included compelling evidence from 'slips of the hand' for phonological processes affecting H_2 and leading to greater symmetry among the two hands, to which we return below.

The representation of the H_2 as a base hand received one of its most important formalizations in the work of Battison (1974), who proposed the Symmetry and Dominance Conditions as phonotactic constraints on well-formed signs in ASL. Attributing to Frishberg (1975) the discovery that "historical changes in sign language do not necessarily maintain iconicity, but rather operate according to the physical dynamics of the apparatus which produces the signs" (p. 3), Battison observed a drastic effect of symmetry in the way the two hands were used phonologically, as part of a larger pattern of motoric constraints on signing. For example, signs originally involving contact with the elbow might undergo phonological reduction (akin to lenition) and touch only the other non-moving hand. On the perceptual side, in processes of language change, signs might move the point of contact from the center of the face (an otherwise phonetically 'crowded' region of space) to a more peripheral

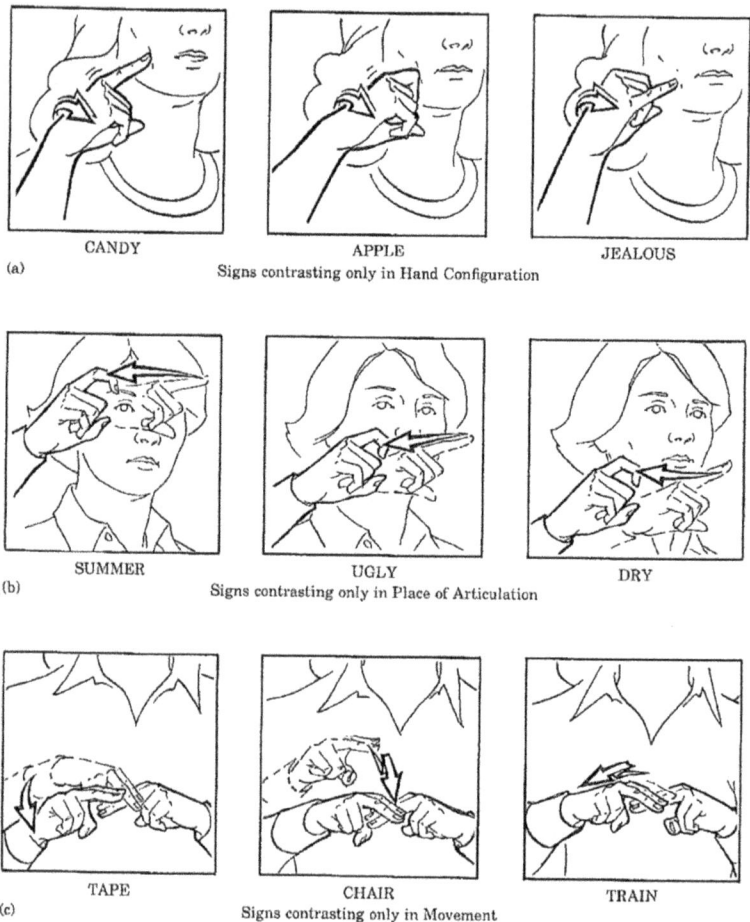

Figure 7.1 Minimal pairs based on handshape, place of articulation, and movement (Klima & Bellugi, 1979, figure 2.2, p. 42)

region. An example of peripheralization on the face can be seen in the following example of ALIVIO 'relief' in Brazilian Sign Language (Figure 7.2) (Xavier, 2014).

Both of these processes have clear analogues in spoken phonology, making them at the same time both very easy to study within the light of existing spoken language phonology and radically confirming of a more general cognitive master plan underlying the unconscious design of both.

One recurrent process Battison described, however, has no obvious analogue in spoken phonology, and it was the following: symmetry is unmarked, while

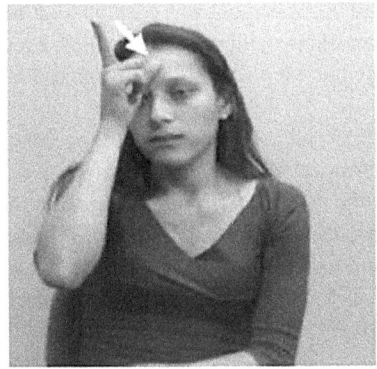 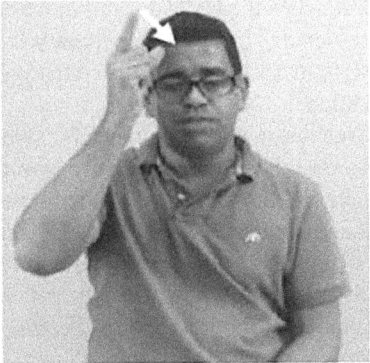

Figure 7.2 Peripheralization of ALIVIO by the signer on the right (Xavier, 2014)

asymmetry between the two hands is marked.[3] This kind of markedness, like all phonological markedness studied from Jakobson (1941) to McCarthy and Prince (1993), would lead to alternations in which faithful surfacing of potential contrasts would be eliminated and reduced. The Symmetry Condition, therefore, required H_2 to be identical to the dominant hand (both in its handshape and in its movement type and trajectory) if both of them were in use. In other words, it became impossible to specify the NDH for its own location or its own movement.[4] Battison viewed this in a way that contemporary models of the phonetics–phonology interface would find right at home: "In terms of a production model of signing, symmetry would appear to reduce the programming load" (1974, p. 20). This view is supported by work on the underlying 'phonetics' of interlimb coordination, such as Kelso et al. (1979), who contend that "the brain produces simultaneity of action not by controlling each limb independently, but by organizing functional groupings of muscles that are constrained to act as a single unit" (p. 1029). Similarly, infants acquiring sign languages natively strongly prefer symmetrical two-handed signs and are often less accurate in producing handshapes of one-handed signs when they can produce exactly the same handshapes in two-handed signs (Siedlecki & Bonvillian, 1993b).

---

[3] In addition, ipsilateral contact (touching the same side of the body or head as the acting hand, as when a right hand conducts military salute on the right side of the forehead) is unmarked compared to contralateral contact (e.g., putting one's right hand over one's heart).

[4] Crasborn (1995) brings in the four major limb joints as phonetic parameters providing a fine-grained definition of symmetry, and Napoli and Wu (2003) focus on movement symmetry, contending that the hands must be in identical or inverse positions along their respective paths.

Now, when the NDH doesn't move at all but is present as a base hand, it must be restricted to one of seven unmarked handshapes, the nature of which we will return to in Section 7.3. This constitutes what we will call the Unmarked Base Condition.[5]

Given this overall preference for symmetry, what can we make of the deletion of H_2 overall? That isn't really symmetric, is it? Well, the point is, it's not *asymmetric*. In purely one-handed signs, the two hands *aren't* doing something different from each other. Difference is contradiction, and as the old work on formal set theory goes, as long as the intersection of A and B doesn't have anything in it different from the union of A and B, there is no contradiction between them. In other words, *deletion of H_2 also yields nonasymmetry of the two hands*.

But $A \cup B = A \cap B$ is not enough because in this case, A has a necessarily more privileged status than B in cases of nonequal contents. This is what makes it the *dominant* hand. One striking result of this view is the prediction that the NDH can never act on its own. How could it? (Unless it *becomes* the dominant hand, say, for example, when the right hand is somehow occupied). But the NDH is an abstract phonological category, and in perception of left-handed signers by right-handed signers (or vice-versa), perception is automatic (often without even noticing that a particular signer is left-handed, as I have found while conversing with my own research teams). There are also no attested minimal pairs involving solely one-handed signs in which, say, one lexical item is realized with the left hand but the other realized with the right hand. As Blevins (1993) points out, "In reality, discourse and pragmatic factors will often result in a situation where signers whose right hand is dominant will use the left hand for single-handed signs, and vice versa. Further, most of the constraints discussed below hold of underlying representations, that is, they are morpheme structure constraints" (p. 52). What is crucial, therefore is that H_2 alone cannot be the sole articulator specified in the underlying representation of a sign language morpheme. It cannot be emphasized enough that this is an entirely linguistic constraint. Nothing prevented Alexander Skriabin, for example, composing an entire piano nocturne to be played entirely and only with the left hand. However, in sign language, there is no way to do this; as Battison (1974) states, "Deletion of the dominant moving hand in an asymmetric sign, i.e. where the two hands are not identical, is ungrammatical" (p. 9).

This asymmetrically dominant role of the dominant hand (DH) over the NDH, and exactly how to model it, led to an explosion of research. For example, how do we model the fact that H_2 can be optional, while the DH must always be present? As Battison noted, "Although the phonetic basis of signing has different dynamics, the constraints on form are rather familiar at

---

[5] Battison called it the Dominance Condition, but as it is specifically about the NDH, we rename it more transparently here.

the lexical level" (1974, p. 11). Just like Halle's example of *bnick, there are possible and impossible words in sign language phonology, and there are formal generalizations that govern entire swaths of impossible words instead of listing them one by one or expecting historical change to freely introduce any kind of new pattern.

As it turns out, the model of Onsets–Nuclei vs. Codas in syllable structure – at least abstractly, while not literally mapping onto the DH vs. NDH – turns out to be very instructive. In a great many languages exemplifying Jakobson's unmarked syllable templates, Onsets must be present, whereas Codas are banned. In others, such as Japanese or Italian, Codas can only be present when they are from an extremely limited set or are entirely identical copies of neighboring Onsets. This led Brentari and Goldsmith (1993) to posit that H_2 was formally identical to a Coda Constituent, in the sense of depending upon a restrictive set of Licensing Conditions – in some languages, not licensed at all, while in others, only licensed by very unmarked elements or by being identical to their neighbors. Other researchers demurred; Blevins (1993), for example, treats H_2 as a feature geometric node that is necessarily a daughter of the DH in the tree, thereby inheriting all of its handshape and movement specifications when present. On this view, H_2 can be seen as phonologically 'underspecified', obtaining its features by default on the way to phonetic implementation.

Yet other researchers suggested that a feature such as [two-handed] alone would be sufficient to capture symmetric uses of H_2. Under this kind of proposal, of course, uses of the NDH as a nonmoving base hand would have to treat it as a location and not as an instance of [+bimanual], as we will call it here. Blevins (1993) thus points out that "The two functions of H2, that of articulator and location, are analogous to the two functions of the glottis in some views of spoken phonology: it can function as the major articulator, as in a glottal stop, or it can function as the airstream mechanism, as it does in ejective and implosive sounds" (p. 59, fn. 16). Sandler (1989) developed these representational differences in a highly articulated feature geometry for sign, including a node for H_2–Place: the NDH as a base.

Before discussing in further depth these various proposals for the representation of H_2 – clearly a novel kind of challenge for phonological theory – we must look at some of the details of its role as a location, namely when it is the base hand, statically held in place as a passive articulator for the DH to tap, rub, or generally execute movement on. These constitute the Unmarked Base Condition and are considered in the next section.

7.3   A Paucity of Unmarked Shapes of the Base Hand

The use of H_2 as a static (nonmoving) base hand that the dominant hand makes contact with is quite widespread in the lexicon of all signed languages, as even a cursory look at the alphabet of fingerspelled letters in British Sign Language

Figure 7.3 The two-handed BSL alphabet

(BSL) reveals. In Figure 7.3, the NDH is either a copy of the dominant hand or uses one of a few restricted set of unmarked handshapes.

According to Battison (1974), only seven handshapes are possible in ASL when the NDH is a base hand that is not a copy of the DH. As he says, "In these cases, a relative complexity in one part of the sign (two hands vs. one hand moving; different handshapes vs. identical ones) is counteracted by a reduction in complexity somewhere else (symmetry; one hand remains still)" (p. 12). The seven unmarked handshapes, referred to by the letters B, A, S, C, O, 1, 5 are shown in Figure 7.4.

These seven handshapes (mnemonically 'BASCO 15') are maximally dispersed articulatorily and perceptually, in that they involve either no selected fingers (in the case of A, S), one selected finger (in the case of G), or all selected fingers (in the case of O, C, B, 5) — note that the thumb falls outside the set of selected *fingers* in the relevant denitions. Furthermore, as Blevins (1993, fn.17) says, "I have yet to find true minimal pairs in ASL for A vs. S, B vs. 5, or C vs O in monomorphemic signs, suggesting that the inventory of possible handshapes for H2 as a location might be reduced to four: {S, B, O, 1}" (p. 59, fn. 17) – mnemonically just 'SOB 1'.

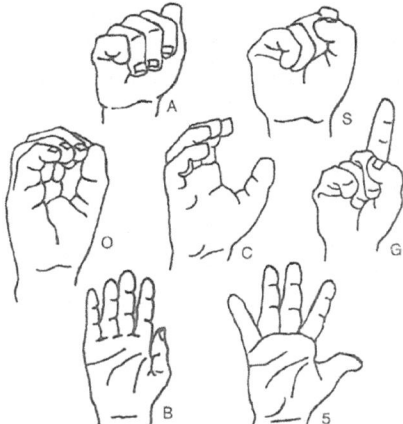

Figure 7.4 Battison's proposed seven unmarked NDH base handshapes

These would correspond to no selected fingers, all selected fingers with thumb contact, all selected fingers, and one selected finger. On this view, as Blevins points out, {A, 5, C} would be 'open, spread, or extended' allophones for the first three handshapes. The view that selected fingers can be understood in dispersion-theoretic terms, akin to Liljencrants and Lindblom's (1972) perceptual disperson of the vowels i, u, a in auditory space, is developed in Stoianov and Nevins (2017), based on van der Hulst's (1996) specification of fingers as 'all', 'none', or 'one' (with the index finger chosen by default for the latter). As Johnston and Schembri (2007) put it, "They form a set of basic visual–geometric shapes: the S is a maximally compact hand configuration; the B handshape is a simple flat surface; the 5 has the fingers spread and extended to the maximum extent; the 1 has a single finger projecting from a fist; the C is an arc and the O handshape is a full circle (Brennan, 1992). They are the most basic possible handshapes, and appear to be the easiest to produce and perceive (Lane, Boyes-Braem and Bellugi, 1976) ... Research shows that young children learning signed languages use the unmarked handshapes in place of the more marked configurations in the early stages of signed language acquisition (Marentette & Mayberry, 2000). It is common in children learning Auslan, for example, to replace the H handshapes in the sign FATHER with the less marked 1 hand configurations" (p. 106).

Subsequent research has shown that these unmarked handshapes have a high frequency of occurrence in type and token frequency (Klima & Bellugi, 1979,

p. 64). Napoli & Wu (2003), in a more thorough corpus study of ASL, find that ninety-five percent of the signs in which H_2 is a stationary base fall into one of these seven unmarked handshapes.[6] They are also found among the first handshapes mastered by deaf children acquiring signs (Boyes-Braem, 1973; Siedlecki & Bonvillian, 1993a). Battison's criteria for unmarkedness thus take into account the classic Jakobsonian evidence from typology, acquisition, and even aphasia, where relevant (see below). Importantly, like additional studies of markedness, such as Greenberg (1963), markedness in one domain also limits the range of orthogonal contrasts that can be expressed. Thus, Battison (1974) observes that the NDH's point of contact is relevant and that "these unmarked handshapes may contact other body parts in a greater variety of ways than marked ones, which may be restricted to one or two contact points. For example, the relatively unmarked B (flat hand) may contact other body parts, including the other hand, at a number of points–the fingertips, the heel, the palm, both top and bottom edges of the hand, the back of the hand and the back of the fingers. The relatively more marked R (the familiar cross-your-fingers handshape) has only two points of contact: the fingertips, and less often, the heel of the palm" (p. 7).

In fact, the BSL alphabet above also includes a third type of sign, one in which H_2 is not taken from one of the seven unmarked handshapes but is a copy of the DH, although it is not moving. This is also found in signs such as ASL 'SIT', which involves two selected fingers (the index and middle), with the dominant hand making curved contact on the NDH (akin to legs sitting on a chair).

Does this exhaust, then, the entire range of possibilities for the NDH: simply a copy of the DH – whether moving or not – or taken from one of the seven unmarked handshapes? In other words, does no 'true independent simultaneity' exist? There are, in fact, a very interesting range of exceptions in which the two hands do go their separate ways – and they are related to prosody, morphology, or verbal play.

Battison (1974, p. 9) notes that, for example, one can make the sign for 'TIME SIX' ("six o'clock"), then maintain the handshape for 'SIX' with one hand while the other hand signs information about, say, what happened at six o'clock. This prosodic continuation of a fixed discourse topic intersects with the notion of a 'buoy' in sign language. Liddell (2003) elaborates the use of H_2 'buoys' that are held constant as conceptual landmarks while the other hand

---

[6] Confirmation of Battison's phonotactic constraints outside of ASL have been widely found; for example, Eccarius and Brentari (2007) found evidence that the Symmetry and NDH Unmarked Base Conditions were upheld in Hong Kong Sign Language.

Figure 7.5 NDH classifier for airplane in NGT (Crasborn, 2011)

continues to sign, whether by iterating through a list of elements in a sequence or by holding a topic constant. Krifka (2007) views the interplay between the two hands in such cases as a topic–comment structure, and Lillo-Martin and Klima (1990) explore the use of H_2 in maintaining discourse referents. Geraci (2014, pp. 123–134) provides suggestive evidence from Italian Sign Language that each hand can map the distinct thematic roles in transitive verbal clauses, with the ipsilateral hand used for agents and the contralateral for patients, independently of word order.

Another, above-the-word-level use of the NDH as an independent morpheme is when a classifier signed by the NDH can be maintained while the dominant hand signs new information. Thus, the use of two hands with different configurations (in particular, with the NDH base in the Y-shape of an airplane for 'human stands on an airplane') would not be considered a monomorphemic sign, and thus not a phonotactic violation of the NDH base condition (any more so than compounds present phonotactic sequences not found in single morphemes in spoken languages), as shown in the example in Figure 7.5 from NGT, the sign language of the Netherlands (Crasborn, 2011).

Eccarius and Brentari (2007) develop a revised version of Battison's Dominance Condition to further restrict such cases, and van der Kooij (2002) also posits that a large majority of H_2 base shapes constitute a separate morpheme, such as the mug in the sign for 'TEA'. Additional uses of the NDH base that violate symmetry with the DH include cases where the NDH is maintained for the extent of an entire prosodic phrase while the DH continues to sign (see Crasborn [2011] for examples from NGT). As such, the NDH is used as a marker of prosodic phrase boundaries.

Perhaps some of the most striking independent uses of the two hands are in verbal play and poetry. For example, Crasborn (2011) cites the example of a poem by NGT signer Wim Emmerik, in which the left hand signs 'GUN, SHOOT-GUN, HUMAN-FALL' while the right hand simultaneously signs 'HOPE, DO, LIFE'; the poem was intended to express the two sides of the coin about cochlear implants. Tracking such simultaneity proves perceptually difficult outside of these artistic domains (perhaps akin to the subtle use of acrostics and inversions in spoken-language poetry), and Napoli and Sutton-Spence (2010) specifically argue that the limitation on the number of simultaneous propositions is not motoric but due to attention tracking, and they construct similar hypotheses about the limits on perceptual processing of simultaneous propositional information based on studies of gesture.

Spoken languages do not have two identical articulators that could, in principle, pattern in the same way that the two hands do in signed languages. However, as we have seen, the two hands in general do not act like independent articulators in two-handed signs. Even though there might be great advantages to being able to separate at-issue content from comments on a speaker-oriented, expressive, or 'meta' level, the perceptual system does not harness this potential of the two hands on a regular basis. Now, nonmanual marking on the face (e.g., eyebrow-raising or mouth movements) are treated separately from the phonology of the hands by all sign language researchers and are often treated akin to intonation (Sandler, 2012), as used for purposes of clause-typing, scope-marking, or gestural expression, but the articulatory programming of the face is treated sufficiently separately from that of the hands that this kind of nonmanual marking is, perhaps, the most simultaneity one finds in signed languages – much more so than what might be expected from the two hands alone.

In fact, a recurrent tendency is that the NDH base is often eliminated in slips of the hand, acquisition, and diachronic change, and that in such cases, H_2 assimilates to the handshape of the DH. This is a further move towards symmetry, as it eliminates an additional locational specification for the NDH and simply replaces it with the feature [+bimanual]. Klima and Bellugi (1979, p. 77) note that, based on records from 1918, the sign 'DEPEND' was formerly nonsymmetrical with the DH index finger on the edge of the open NDH, but in contemporary ASL both hands assume extended index fingers (Figure 7.6).

Based on these and other similar examples, they generalize that "In each of these cases, a base hand has assumed the hand configuration of the dominant or active hand" and that "the tendency towards symmetry appears in the errors made by children and second-language learners" (p. 77).

What about in cases of language impairment? In a study by Hickok et al. (1996) of a patient with aphasia named RS, her divergent signs all appeared

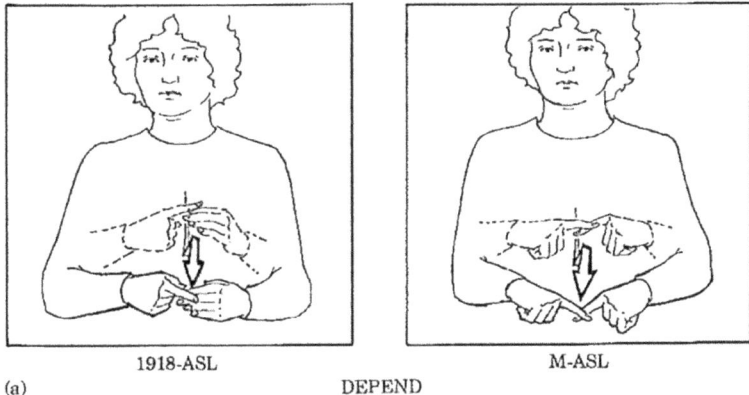

(a)   1918-ASL   M-ASL
                        DEPEND

Figure 7.6 Diachronic change towards base hand symmetry in ASL 'DEPEND' (Klima & Bellugi, 1979, figure 3.7, p. 78)

with two-handed signs. For example, on signs that require the two hands to assume different handshapes, RS would incorrectly mirror the movement of one hand with the other. Notably, RS's coordination difficulties did not show up on nonlinguistic limb movement tasks, and she had no difficulty in everyday bimanual tasks, such as knitting. In acquisition, H_2 base hands are underrepresented in early signs as compared to their frequency in ASL; Cheek et al. (2001) found less than ten percent of these 'unbalanced signs' in a corpus of early child signing.

Concluding so far: H_2 does not have total freedom. Even when it acts as an NDH base and assumes one of the handful of unmarked handshapes (perhaps only four, if Blevins's [1993] observations bear out), even having H_2 as an unmarked base is, in a sense, marked, as evidence from acquisition, aphasia, and diachronic change tend to favor replacement of the NDH base with the feature [+bimanual], imposing a copy of all specifications of the H_1.

Now, like all phonological features familiar from spoken-language phonology's distinctive feature theory, a phonological feature like [+bimanual] must yield minimal pairs – akin to the work done by [+voice] in the initial consonant of *bin* and *pin*. Similarly, we expect cases of neutralization, where in specified phonological contexts, the conditioned deletion of this feature yields identity and even homophony, as in Russian final devoicing between *luk* 'onion' and *lug* 'bow' in the nominative but not the genitive. What are the minimal pairs, what are the contexts for deletion of [+bimanual], and what is the potential evidence that deletion is of [+bimanual] versus, say, [+unimanual]? We turn to these matters now.

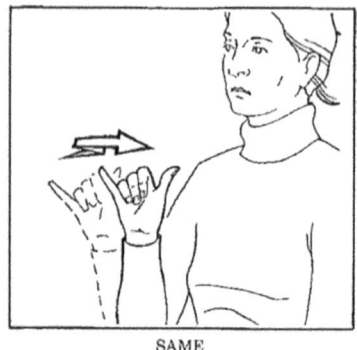 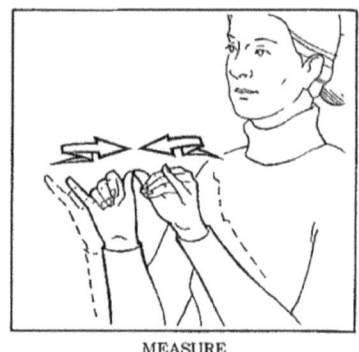

Figure 7.7 Minimal pair for [+bimanual]: ASL 'SAME' vs. 'MEASURE' (Klima & Bellugi, 1979, figure 2.11, p. 50)

7.4 The Feature [+bimanual] in Minimal Pairs and Allophony

For [+bimanual] to be a feature, there must be minimal pairs, as are found in ASL for words such as 'SAME' and 'MEASURE' (Figure 7.7).

However, as Klima and Bellugi (1979) observe, "Such minimal pairs are rare in ASL; the use of one as opposed to two hands rarely distinguishes between semantically unrelated lexical items, but it plays a major role in morphological processes" (p. 50). Indeed, this would suggest that the addition of [+bimanual] can afford morphological derivation – much in the same way that addition of features such as [+voice] or [+nasal] do in Welsh consonant mutation or Terena inflection. In ASL, one of the most well-known uses of [+bimanual] as a derivational morphology feature is to form reciprocals. An example from the reciprocalized form of the verb LOOK-AT is shown below in Figure 7.8.[7]

Authors such as Kuhn and Aristodemo (2017) have developed extensive theories of the semantics of adding [+bimanual] to verbs in order to yield pluractional semantics (such as distributivity and iteration; see Chapter 8 for more discussion of pluractionality), and in particular differentiate between fully mirrored use of [+bimanual] and the additional specification of a feature called [alternating]. This feature, which we can consider an additional specification only of signs already [+bimanual], can be seen in signs such as the ASL verb 'TO MILK' (Figure 7.9) (Padden & Perlmutter, 1987, p. 340).

---

[7] Like all cases of derivational morphology, the result may, over time, become frozen and lexicalized without the original base form being present. Interestingly, Lepic et al. (2016) finds that a great deal of lexically [+bimanual] verbs cross-linguistically have reciprocal semantics.

Symmetric Hands in Sign Language Phonologies

LOOK-AT   LOOK-AT[R:'each other']

Figure 7.8 Reciprocalized semantics in 'LOOK-AT' by derivational [+bimanual] (Klima & Bellugi, 1979, figure 12.4, p. 280)

(7)   MILK (verb)

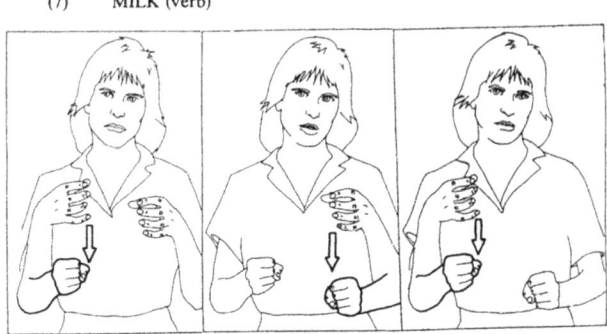

Figure 7.9 Alternating [+bimanual] signs start with DH: ASL 'TO MILK' (Padden & Perlmutter, 1987)

In this sign, the two hands do not move simultaneously but rather alternate in which one is moving when. One must start with the strong hand, for which the handshape changes from being open to a closed fist as it moves down. Then, while the strong hand is paused in its downward position, the same change and movement are executed by the weak hand. Finally the strong hand comes up again and then executes the third movement. In other words, for signs like this (which require a movement path specifying a upward starting point moving down), the hands alternate in terms of movement (and in this case, also in terms of handshape changes).

Now, how do we know that direction of neutralization is to delete [+bimanual] from lexically specified signs, as opposed to the opposite

INTERESTING

LIKE

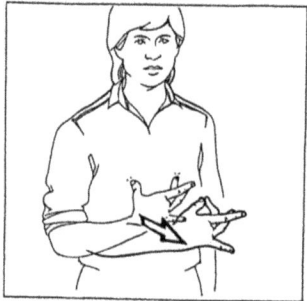

Figure 7.10 Weak Drop in ASL 'INTERESTING' yields neutralization with 'LIKE'

(say, adding [+unimanual])? The most thorough set of arguments come from Padden and Perlmutter (1987). They show that not all one-handed signs become two-handed under free variation, while the opposite, namely two-handed signs becoming one-handed, is highly productive – particularly under conditions of encumbrance (having one hand occupied while driving, eating, or carrying a bag) or under conditions of rapid signing. In fact, deletion of [+bimanual] on the sign for 'INTERESTING' yields a form that becomes homophonous with 'LIKE' (Figure 7.10).

Crucially, while 'INTERESTING' has a one-handed variant (neutralized by phonologically deleting [+bimanual]), the sign for 'LIKE' *has no two-handed variant*. (They additionally cite pairs such as 'PARTY' and 'PURPLE', 'NOTHING' and 'FURNITURE', and 'PLAY' and 'YELLOW'). This is a knockout argument against there being a feature like [+unimanual]. If the relevant phonological deletion process can only delete [+bimanual] (in what is called 'Weak Drop'), there should be no way to add two-handedness to a unimanual sign as a purely phonological process – although it may of course be added for *morphological* derivation, in a way akin to Welsh consonant mutation, as mentioned above.

Indeed, the compelling diachronic and sociolinguistic studies conducted by Woodward and DeSantis (1977) with Southern Black ASL – a more conservative variant of ASL – using the 'apparent time' method of sociolinguistics (Labov, 1963) that compares older, more classical variants of the language with more recent diachronic changes – find that the direction of change involves deletion of [+bimanual], leading to more one-handed variants of signs among white signers and among younger Black signers as the direction of change. Like coda neutralization of [+voice], however, there is almost always a conditioning context for processes of neutralization and feature deletion. Before we can engage in the comparison between [+bimanual] preservation and deletion between Black ASL and white ASL, therefore, we must consider the phonological contexts in which this feature interacts.

The phonologization of perceptual factors turns out to play a crucial role in understanding the contexts in which [+bimanual] is deleted, which come from one of the most influential (and potentially surprising) findings in the study of sign language perception: Signers are typically not looking at the hands of their interlocutors as the default fixed focal point in their visual field but rather their face. This focal point of visual perception in a visual–manual language turns out to render the face as a location in signing that has the highest degree of visual salience – perhaps most akin to an initial syllable or stressed syllable in spoken language in terms of having the greatest amount of acoustic and psycholinguistic salience.

It was Siple's (1978) work (originally circulated since 1973) that found that signs articulated near the face tend to disprefer two-handedness, whereas signs articulated lower than the face tend to prefer two-handedness. These phonetically motivated trends have caused diachronic changes, whereby some signs have had [+bimanual] added to their underlying representation, while others have removed it. The first landmark study of these trends for ASL was conducted by Frishberg (1975), who shows that the direction of historical change is for one-handed signs articulated below the neck to become symmetric. Why? Presumably to reinforce their otherwise weak perceptual status. Siple proposed that in the areas of lowest visual acuity (e.g., away from the central focal point of the face), there will be more unmarked handshapes because their perceptual recoverability is reduced – akin to the phenomenon of vowel reduction (i.e., *reduction* of the number of *contrasts*), whereby only the most dispersed corner vowels *i, u, a* survive. In the same regions, Siple proposed there would be a greater proportion of two-handed signs in order to increase the perceptual redundancy in these less salient locations.

Like many aspects of phonology, phonologization represents the symbolic, formal instantiation in grammatical terms of real-time phonetic trends, both articulatory and perceptual. We can certainly learn a lot about why phonology has the constraints and representations that it does by studying the motoric side, but arguably just as much by studying the perceptual side. Napoli and Sutton-Spence's (2010) work shows that two different handshapes are too much to process (see also Blevins' [1993] remarks to this effect). At the same time, the complete elimination of the NDH would sacrifice the perceptual redundancy that Siple (1978) argues for and that historical change supports.

In a comparison of ASL signs from a 1918 dictionary with those of contemporary 1970s ASL, Frishberg (1975, p. 703) arrived at the following generalizations:

(1) Perceptual strengthening in [−facial] location:
   a. For signs made below the neck,
      (i) one-handed signs become two-handed;
      (ii) the location becomes more centralized about the line of bilateral symmetry and moves up toward the hollow of the the throat

(2) Decrowding in [+facial] location:
   a. For signs made in contact with the face,
      (i) two-handed signs become one-handed; and
      (ii) the specific location on the face changes historically from the center to the perimeter.

Let's examine these in turn. (1) is driven by concerns of boosting recoverability through redundancy (recall, in part, the notion of enhancement from Chapter 6). As Frishberg (1975) observes, "Symmetry eases perception in that the viewer can predict many characteristics of the sign just from seeing the shape and movement of one hand" (p. 701), thereby "increasing redundancy by presenting the same information to both halves of the visual field. Such formational redundancy is crucial in a linguistic system. In some sense, these sorts of implications or probabilities built into ASL are comparable to morphotactics in oral languages. The more we know about a segment in English, the more we can predict about the following or preceding segment" (p. 706). By doubling the hands in the lexical representation of a [−facial] morpheme and by centralizing movements towards the visual focal point, therefore, perceptual strengthening occurs for signs that would otherwise be less salient, given Siple's (1978) default visual focal point on the face. In other words, we can view (1) as akin to phenomena in spoken languages, such as vowel harmony, in which a crucially contrastive feature is passed onwards within a prosodic domain to guarantee its redundant encoding and recovery (see, e.g., Suomi [1983]).

But if symmetry and redundancy are so helpful for signs (and indeed, motorically easier to program, as suggested in Battison's [1974] remarks and psychomotoric studies such as Kelso et al. [1979]), then why does it show a diachronic tendency to become lost on the face, as encoded in (2)?

Recall that one of the true loci of simultaneous phonology in signed languages is not the independent action of the two hands but rather the simultaneous deployment of nonmanual marking by the eyebrows and mouth, as used for a wide range of prosodic, grammatical, and gestural encoding. As Frishberg (1975) observes, "Displacement to the perimeter of the face, as well as the reduction of hands from two to one in this area, opens the face for paralinguistic information (analogous to intonational cues)" (p. 707). In other words, when there is too much going on in an already highly salient phonological environment, reduction of some kinds of phonological information can be sacrificed more easily than others. This can be likened to what happens in cases like Ticuna tone-stress interactions (Skilton, 2021), whereby the stressed syllable is actually the place in which tones that need to be reduced or deleted for dissimilatory reasons are sacrificed – precisely because there is already other suprasegmental information to focus on. The face, being a locus of default visual salience, does not need the extra redundancy afforded by the feature [+bimanual] and would prefer to have decrowding to peripheral regions of the face and lesser movement.

The two tendencies in (1)–(2) follow the same logic: Cut redundancy in salient and crowded positions, and employ redundancy in less salient positions where perceptual cuing may be needed. Adding a second hand can also be thought of as a way of enhancing perceptual cuing of prosodic boundaries, and indeed Mantovan (2020) finds addition of [+bimanual] on a phrasal phonological level as a correlate of phrase-final lengthening, a prosodic strengthening process used to demarcate constituents (similar to the view of Iverson and Salmons [2007] that many cases of fortition in spoken language phonology can be understood in these terms). Indeed, in a study of formal vs. casual registers, Zimmer (1989) found that [+bimanual] version of signs are used more in formal registers (such as signing to a crowd in a public speaking event) and less in casual ones, which is consistent with the trends in spoken language phonology by which 'careful enunciation' (e.g., increased fortition) leads to hyperarticulatory trends for the sake of perceptual reinforcement. Conversely, when deletion of [+bimanual] as an encroaching phonological rule (arguably representing phonologization of contingent patterns of encumbrance, which is even more widespread these days with the use of holding a cellphone while signing in video chats) and other forms of spatial interference begins to take place, arguably deletion as a phonological process would first be allowed in those areas already most salient to vision.

Frishberg's study was based on diachronic comparisons between an older ASL dictionary and then-contemporary versions of signs, and like much diachronic work, its insights are complementary when convergent results are found in the laboratory and in synchronic variation going in the same direction. At just around the same point in time, Battison (1974) began to study allophonic variation (in other studies, e.g., Battison et al. [1973], looking at conditions on allophonic inclusion of the thumb in handshapes unspecified for thumb position), and asked signing participants whether they could enact Weak Drop when conversing casually. He found that signs near the face allowed deletion of [+bimanual] as well as peripheralization. He also found constraints on deletion in the presence of [alternating] movement, in which the arms cross each other and move to the contralateral side of the body, a conclusion later upheld by Padden and Perlmutter (1987). Presumably these are due in part to not only perceptual constraints but also motoric tendencies related to alternating movements; see the discussion of Tkachman et al. (2021) below.

Arguably the most striking results confirming deletion of [+bimanual] as a historically developing process was found not only through comparison with synchronic variation and with dictionary comparisons, but with studies of living signers, particularly if sociolinguistic patterns afforded a view onto differences between lects, with external factors likely to have large effects on their rates of change. The studies by Woodward and DeSantis (1977), to which we now turn, provided this crucial piece of confirming evidence to complete the jigsaw puzzle.

7.5   Empirical Contributions of Black ASL Phonology to the Model

As Woodward and DeSantis (1977) immediately noted, some of the signs that Frishberg (1975) pointed out as having become one-handed in Stokoe et al.'s (1965) ASL dictionary were not, as a general rule, one-handed in all varieties of ASL. "We noticed while doing research in the Southern United States, however, that these latter signs are still in the process of undergoing change" (p. 332). What kinds of language-external factors, however, would be responsible for the trend that Black Southern ASL would be slower to undergo the diachronic process of [+bimanual] deletion?

In establishing the criteria to evaluate vertical racism versus horizontal racism, Telles (2004) points out the high degree of the latter in the United States over the last two centuries, demonstrating that as a result of legal and cultural enforcement of segregation, white and Black communities have often historically lived in separate neighborhoods, avoided intermarriage, enjoyed different cuisines, listened to different music, and spoken with distinct vernaculars. It may thus come as no surprise that signing in these two communities has been historically different. Croneberg (1965) and Woodward and Woodward (1976) were among the first to trace dialect differences in white ASL and Black Southern ASL to historically segregated schools for the Deaf. Hill (2021) documents a period of over ninety-nine years as seventeen states and Washington, DC had segregated schools for Black Deaf children over a period stretching from 1869 through 1978. Some states had laws requiring that Black Deaf students be taught only by Black teachers; Tennessee, for example, passed such a law in 1901. As McCaskill et al. (2011) state, "Not surprisingly, Black Deaf people were affected both by the same racial discrimination of the era that affected Black hearing people and by the same social isolation and marginalization due to race that contributed to the development and maintenance of African American English" (p. 15).

The rise of oralism – the belief that spoken language is inherently superior to sign language, of which Alexander Graham Bell was one of the most pernicious proponents (Booth, 2021) – motivated schools across the USA to replace Deaf teachers with hearing instructors who would speak to students rather than sign with them. Strikingly, however, this emphasis on oral education was not extended to Black Deaf students on the same basis as it was to white Deaf students. As of 1940, eleven of sixteen schools for Black Deaf students still used an entirely sign-based approach (Baynton, 1996). And this policy-based apartheid among the Deaf was not limited to schools; Tabak (2006) notes that "Deaf African-Americans were also excluded, systematically and mercilessly, from those educational, economic, and social institutions that were established by white hearing and white Deaf Americans. The National Association of the Deaf, the National Fraternal Society of the Deaf, and Gallaudet College all excluded African-Americans until the latter half of the twentieth century" (p. 97).

The historical roots for there being distinct varieties of Standard ASL and Black ASL are clear, but only very recently has the study of Black ASL taken on a new renaissance of study and popular celebration. As Woodward and Woodward (1976) pointed out, the situation fifty years ago was one in which, as arguably a doubly-minoritized language, Black ASL was not broadly used with pride in interlocution with researchers "because all the researchers who have observed Black Southern signing are white, hearing, non-native signers, we have not as yet been perceptive enough to notice it. The situation is also compounded by the fact that Black signers attempt to approach White signing in conversation with White signers and also attempt to approach English when in contact with hearing people" (p. 212). Despite these challenges, it turns out that Woodward and DeSantis were able to make what I would contend is one of the most significant contributions to the study of diachronic phonology of signed

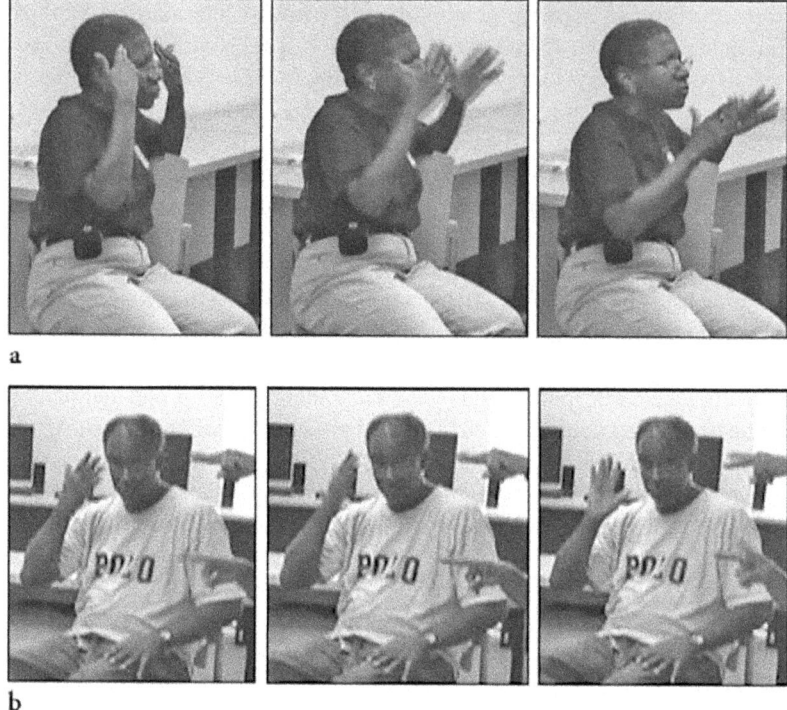

Figure 7.11 Two-Handed vs. one-handed versions of 'DON'T KNOW' in BASL (McCaskill et al., 2011)

languages through the study of Black ASL. Aside from documenting lexical variation (virtually inevitable in the comparison of any two sign language varieties within the same country) and phonological variation that was related to the feature of location (e.g., centralization towards face and/or torso), Woodward and DeSantis compared the rates of two-handed (henceforth 2H) versions of signs (e.g., symmetric execution of the same handshape, movement, and location by the NDH) to their one-handed (1H) versions. An example of 2H vs. 1H variation is shown in Figure 7.11, based on McCaskill et al. (2011, p. 76)

In studies of ASL varieties in Georgia and Louisiana (and comparing them with Northern varieties of ASL, as well as the older, historically-related French Sign Language), Woodward and DeSantis (1977) found the factors conditioning allophonic deletion of [+bimanual] were age and ethnicity. Specifically, at the time of their publication, white signers above the age of forty-seven were found in the lect groups in which more 2H, older, variants were used, while overall, younger white signers were found in the lect groups in which the newer 1H variants occur. Importantly, however, Black signers under forty-seven patterned in the same lect groups as the older white signers. Finally, where cognate comparison was possible with French Sign Language, it was found that French SL used 2H allophones more. This pattern of results allowed Woodward and DeSantis to conclude: first, that by means of the apparent time methodology in sociolinguistics, the 2H versions were older (as they were used by older signers); second, that the 2H versions were historically the original forms (as they were used more in the cognate French Sign Language forms); and finally, that signers of Black ASL maintained greater preservation of the historically older forms.

It's been more than forty years since then, with the internet and innumerous societal changes occuring, but sociolinguistic maintenance of in-group features appears to have, unconsciously or not, retained two-handedness as a characteristic feature of Black ASL varieties. As Woodward and Woodward (1976) report, attitudes about Black ASL have varied since the 1970s among its own signers, ranging from 'wanting to learn correct signs' to maintaining the sociolinguistic identity of the lect, as "assimilation with a pressure to leave behind language and culture is not integration" (p. 217). The present and future development of Black ASL is a lively topic in contemporary debates, with popular videos by young people, such as Charmay's viral (2020) two-minute video about Black ASL, who point outs immediately "With BASL we sign with both hands, and ASL is more like one hand" (0:55)[8] For particularly insightful discussions and resources on continued issues of linguistic identity within the Black ASL community, see Player (2021) and Hill (2021).

Central to the current discussion about the richness and depth of contributions to sign language phonology from Black ASL is the fact that Woodward and DeSantis's (1977) results are more nuanced than simply reporting 1H vs. 2H variants, in that they look at the interaction with other phonological features such as [+facial] as a conditioning environment for the deletion. These findings were replicated in McCaskill et al.'s (2011) extensive Black ASL project, where they report that older signers who attended segregated schools are less likely to choose the 1H variant than younger signers who attended school after integration, and showed interaction of the conditioning of this feature in terms of contact location. (McCaskill et al. also point to replication of these trends in Lucas et al. [2007]). Consider for example, lowering of 2H signs away from the face, a phonological resolution of a cooccurrence constraint on *[+facial,+bimanual] that, instead of deleting the latter, deletes the former – as a phonological process that McCaskill et al. report is "disfavored

---

[8] Strong Black Lead, www.youtube.com/watch?v=3HDm3kx3rhY.

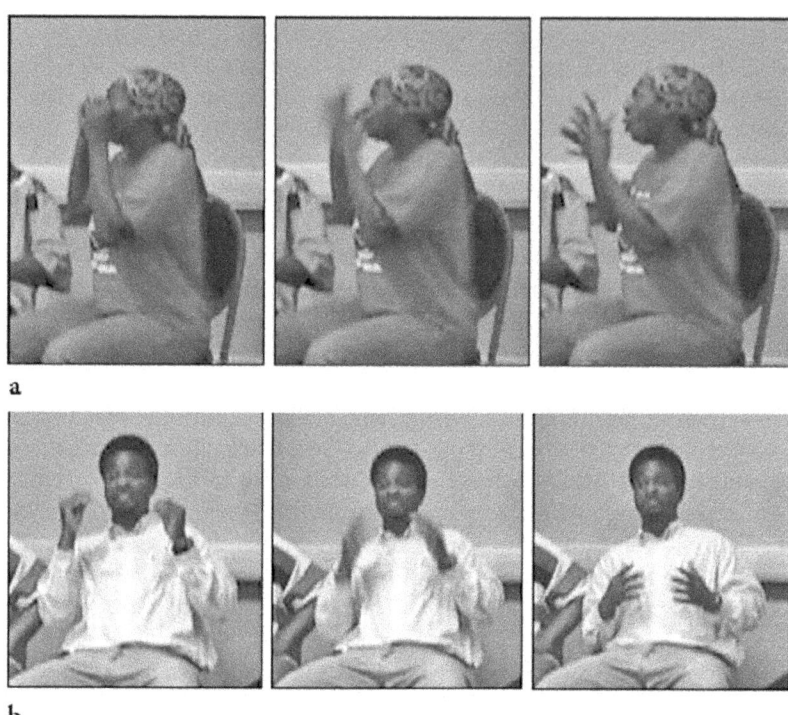

Figure 7.12 Deletion of [+facial] in BASL 'TEACHER' (McCaskill et al., 2011)

by working-class Black signers" (p. 89), who maintain the raised and bimanual forms, as shown in Figure 7.12.[9]

Deletion of [+bimanual] is a natural direction for phonological change for a number of reasons. First, the insertion of [+bimanual] is reserved for morphological derivation of intensity, plurality, pluractionality, or aspect, and having an 'inverse' operation (to, say, form singulars out of inherently plural nouns or plural verbal events) seems unnecessary from the point of view of morphological markedness. Secondly, there are numerous phonetic pressures for deletion of [+bimanual]. Signs whose underlying forms involve two hands may be made without the articulations of one hand under several conditions. One may be because H_2 is holding the final articulation configuration of another

---

[9] Interestingly, Schembri et al. (2009) report a parallel deletion of [+facial] as a lowering change-in-progress among younger urban more than older signers of Australian and New Zealand Sign Language – noting that signers of Maori descent are less likely to use these noncitation forms than Deaf New Zealanders of European descent.

sign, as with discourse buoys. Another may be that the signer may choose to converse with only one hand to make the conversation inconspicuous, where there is danger of eavesdropping (or 'eyedropping') (Battison, 1974). A third is that one hand may be involved in a nonlinguistic task and may be partly or completely unavailable for sign articulations. This last trend may be particularly exacerbated in spatial or educational environments not specifically designed for the Deaf, as in schools with oralist, nondeaf teachers, and classroom or spatial layouts that often require one hand to be occupied.[10] On the other hand, Black Southern ASL, without the artificial imposition of mouthing, oralist pedagogy, and nondeaf teachers, presented an interaction with the apparent-time method of age-graded changes in ASL, whereby younger signers that identify with Black ASL retain the contrastive lexical feature of [+bimanual], resisting its phonetic erosion. Here, we have a powerful case in which the careful study of a doubly-minoritized language presents us with extremely valuable empirical findings to refine and inform our models of hand symmetry in ASL phonology.

If we can generalize from these results, then given that [+bimanual] deletion is the unidirectional phonological change found in sign languages, what can we conclude with respect to the overall view of symmetry as unmarked? Imagine a language with vowel harmony, such as Uyghur or Yoruba, in which a pattern of sociolinguistic interference causes massive apocope of final high vowels in disyllabic roots. (This example is not entirely artificial, as both languages have processes in which there is reduction to high vowels or deletion of high vowels). A lexicon of harmonic roots such as *modu* and *temi* now faces massive change in progress with final high vowel deletion, leading to relexicalization as *mod* and *tem*. Is the language any *less* harmonic now? It doesn't seem right to say yes here. I would contend that, given the definition of symmetric hands based on having a phonologically dominant hand, the issue is entirely parallel when it comes to Weak Drop. If the relevant definition of symmetry for sign language phonology is that $N \cup D$ cannot differ from $N \cap D$, then undergoing Weak Drop does not induce less symmetry. Like vowel harmony, the crucial issue is noncontradiction with a more prominent or dominant position. This is the insight that Brentari and Goldsmith (1993) aimed to capture with their notion of a prosodically dependent position. Now, just like in vowel harmony languages, there can be disharmonic words, typically derived from compounds or borrowing, and in signed languages, the words that violate Battison's Symmetry Condition tend to be complex compounds (see Napoli & Wu [2003]), contrived neologisms, or borrowings. In Brentari and

---

[10] As Battison (1974) points out, skilled signers may utilize the object they are holding (e.g., a Bible or a steering wheel) as if it were part of the hand itself; "according to the ingenuity of the signer in the use of space, he may mime the presence of the hand, just as one can mime the presence of a wall" (p. 10).

Padden's (2001) model, these are akin to the strata of different phonological layers found in languages like Japanese or English, in which different historically distinct aspects of the lexicon have led to different constraints holding over morphologically distinct subparts of the morphemic inventory.

Deletion of [+bimanual] as a post-lexical process should have no effect on the morphological interpretation of a sign. Indeed, in their study of addition of [+bimanual] for semantic or even stylistic purposes Johnston and Schembri (1999) note that "If appropriate to the semantics of the individual sign, doubling can also be an index of 'intensification' of the sign's meaning, but the vast majority of one-handed citation lexemes also require the addition of internal sign modification involving nonmanual features (such as 'grimacing' or widening the eyes) and/or manual stress to unambiguously achieve the intensification of meaning. That is to say, doubling alone is usually insufficient for intensification" (p. 161). For example, some signers report that the doubling of 'BAD' implies 'very bad'. Crucially, however, the singled forms of normally double-handed lexemes do not represent a meaning attenuation, that is, the form of lexically 2H 'DEAD' with [+bimanual] deletion does not end up meaning 'very sick' or 'almost dead'. What this means is that *the addition of [+bimanual] to an underlyingly 1H form can be a derivational morphological process, whereas the deletion of [+bimanual] from an underlyingly 2H form is phonologically conditioned and post-lexical.*

What we know about post-lexical processes from Kiparsky's (1982) work on the life cycle of grammaticalization and phonological change is that post-lexical processes are the easiest to enter the grammars and begin a process of eventual lexical change. As Padden and Perlmutter (1987) argue from evidence based on interaction with morphological processes, Weak Drop is a post-lexical process in this model. This connection of post-lexical [+bimanual] deletion as a process of recent phonologization, at least in ASL, finds strongest support in the window afforded onto the language by comparison of synchronic and diachronic variation in the language, which through an unexpected twist of fate, is most sharply delineated in the US through a comparison of Black ASL and white ASL, given the abhorrent history of segregration and educational policies that have ended up apparently inducing phonological change in one variety much more quickly than in the other.

7.6 Modeling the Restricted Status of H_2: Features vs. Prosody

The deletion of H_2 as found in Weak Drop, as we have seen, is not freely variable and is highly conditioned by location features such as [+facial]. There

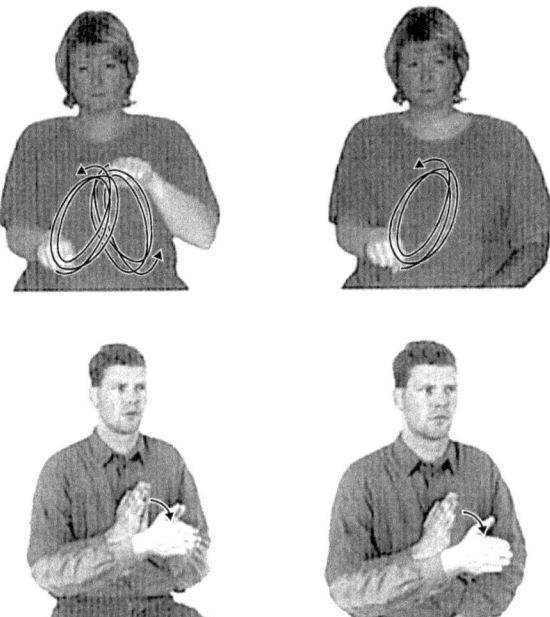

Figure 7.13 Two-handed signs with [contact] or [alternating] resist Weak Drop in ASL (Brentari, 1998)

are additional restrictions on this deletion process as well. Brentari (1998) formalizes the fact that 2H signs with *contact* between the two hands (such as 'WITH') cannot undergo Weak Drop. In addition, research such as Padden and Perlmutter (1987) argue that [alternating] signs do not undergo Weak Drop as freely (Figure 7.13).

In a model based on the Optimality–Theoretic notions of faithfulness (i.e., the imperative to preserve certain features from the input representation), Brentari (1998) argues that specific high-ranked (though violable) constraints demand the preservation of the features [alternating] and [contact] that are part of [+bimanual] signs in which the two hands move. In this sense, the notion of preservation of features as a faithfulness constraint, in conflict with deletion of other features due to markedness constraints against them, suggests a featural treatment of all of these specifications. Indeed, throughout the discussion above, I have treated the relevant phonological specification as a contrastive feature, namely [+bimanual], as the one that undergoes deletion in Weak Drop.

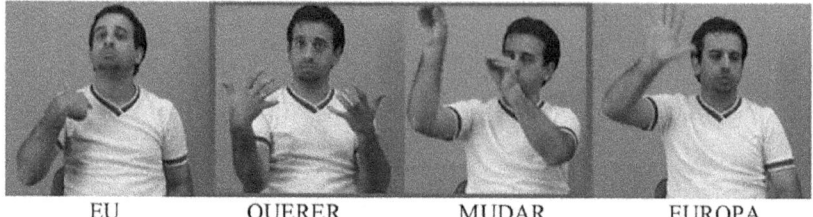

| EU | QUERER | MUDAR | EUROPA |

Figure 7.14 Assimilation of [+bimanual] in connected discourse (Xavier, 2014)

My decision to do so is based on additional phenomena, such as assimilatory feature spreading, which is generally easier to model through features rather than higher-level prosodic constituents. One of the most compelling phenomena that suggests the two-handedness of a sign is an abstract property that is represented independently of the specific visual configuration or holistic trajectory of the sign itself comes from processes like the one exemplified in Figure 7.14 in Brazilian Sign Language. In this connected discourse, the sign 'QUERER' ('want'), usually 1H, is suddenly turned [+bimanual]. This is obviously a post-lexical, not morphological, phenomenon, as it is found in rapid discourse specifically when the following sign is lexically [+bimanual], as shown in Figure 7.14.

These kinds of anticipatory assimilations in fast speech phenomena are characteristic of post-lexical assimilation and are easily modeled as feature-copying of the abstract property of [+bimanual] from the sign 'MUDAR' ('move home') to the preceding sign. They are also found in 'slips of the hand' (transpositional speech errors, akin to spoonerisms in speech), that is, performance errors that occur under conditions of tiredness or performance demands (but which, of course, pave the way for recurrent context-sensitive mutations that may lead to diachronic change), as found in Figure 7.15 (from Klima and Bellugi [1979], p. 135), where 'MUST', which is 1H, anticipates the feature [+bimanual] of upcoming 'TRY'.

A number of syntactic phenomena (perhaps akin to raddoppiamento sintattico in Italian) appear to condition assimilation of [+bimanual], especially the syntactic category and prosodic closeness of the two items involved. Thus, according to Johnston and Schembri (1999) "A doubled form of WHAT may be more likely after (or before) a double-handed sign than a two-handed sign, and much less likely after (or before) a one-handed sign than either a double- or two-handed sign" (p. 159) in Australian Sign Language, and in Shanghainese

Symmetric Hands in Sign Language Phonologies 131

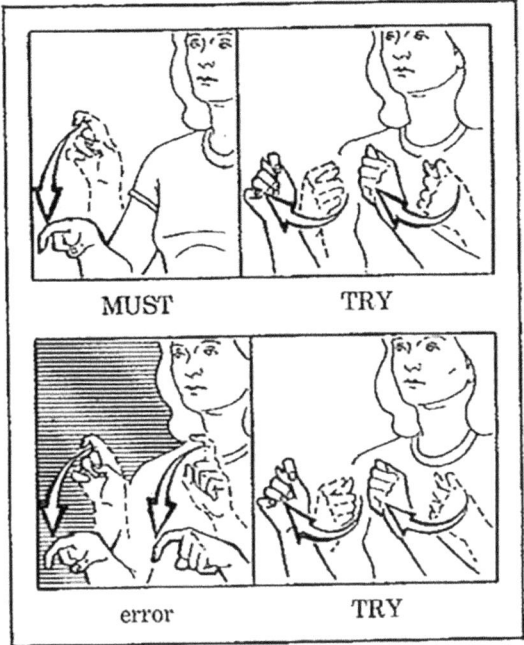

Figure 7.15 Slip of the hand: Anticipation of [+bimanual] (Klima & Bellugi, 1979, figure 5.7, p. 135)

Figure 7.16 Assimilation of [+bimanual] in compounding (Gu, 2018)

Sign Language compounds (Figure 7.16), such assimilation may be lexicalized as progressive (Gu, 2018, p. 162).

Nonetheless, like many complex empirical phenomena as found in spoken language phonologies there are a rich set of approaches to assimilation phenomena, underspecification, and dependency quite generally, in terms of autosegmental approaches, in which the delicate balance of overgeneralization, undergeneralization, and being just right in terms of empirical coverage lead

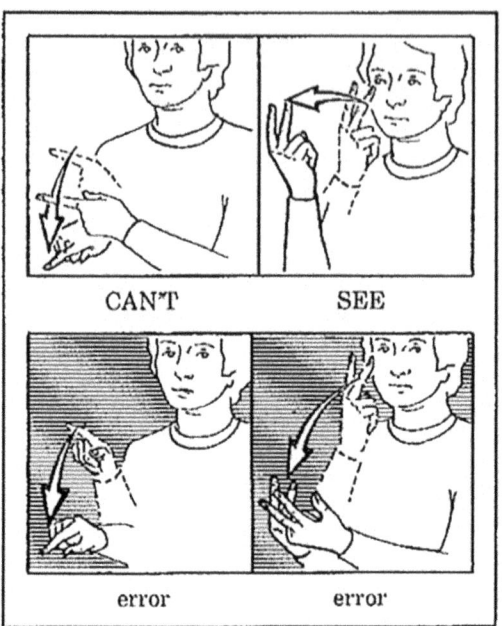

Figure 7.17 Slip of the hand involving metathesis of nonmoving identical H_2 specification (Klima & Bellugi, 1979, figure 5.4, p. 132)

to very detailed comparisons of distinct, abstract approaches to structure. Thus, Brentari (1998) proposes that H_2 patterns like a weak additional branch of prosodic structure, akin to a syllable appendix in spoken languages. This generalized notion of 'weakness' underlies the fact that the NDH is restricted in terms of either bearing identical content to the DH, no content, or unmarked (and nonmoving) content. For example, another kind of slip of the hand, shown in Figure 7.17, involves metathesis (e.g., switch of the feature between two adjacent signs) not of the feature [+bimanual] that would generate symmetric moving hands but rather the presence of an NDH base hand (Klima & Bellugi, 1979, p. 132).

On the one hand (alright, please pardon the unintentional pun!), it would seem tempting to unify the metathetic slip of the hand in Figure 7.17 with that of assimilation, as found in Figure 7.15, and if the uses of NDH as an unmoving base do not involve [+bimanual], this cannot be done. On the other hand, given that Brentari's (1998) work above shows that the features [alternating] and [contact] must be subordinate to [+bimanual], perhaps a feature such as [staticNDH] could be added, and indeed the cases of diachronic change, such as in Figure 7.6, would then be analyzed this way.

More broadly, whether one captures the nonautonomous, restricted, and often assimilatory status of H_2 in terms of a dependent-level prosodic constituency, such as a coda, or in terms of featural specifications with subspecification for properties such as [alternating] continue to be a topic of fruitful research. In a phonetic study of cyclic motion, Tkachman et al. (2021) claim, for example, that "signs produced with alternating movements (as in locomotion) show more resistance to change than signs produced with symmetrical movements" (p. 2), and draw support from work by Sanders and Napoli (2016) that phonological processes may be grounded in physiological factors such as 'torso balance'.

Indeed, one reason to perhaps treat all of the features related to the NDH in a single, hierarchically organized feature-geometric node such as H_2 are the restrictions that Brentari (1998) has noted on ASL compounds, in which the two members of the compound cannot contain different handshape specifications for the NDH. Thus, a potential compound such as 'CHECK-VOTE' (which would be syntactically and semantically well formed to refer to a vote recount and parallel to existing compounds such as 'CHECK-READ' 'to proofread') is phonologically ill-formed, as the handshapes on the NDH would be different in the two members of the compound. Brentari (1998) proposes that the H_2 node should thus be handled as a word-level phenomenon, with scope over the entire compound. It might, however, be possible to model this restriction as parallel to the phenomenon in Japanese surname compounds, in which voicing specifications in the left-hand member affect the initial consonant of the right-hand member (Tanaka, 2017).

In summary there are a number of overall tendencies for phonotactic and dynamic patterns of H_2 specification that are now inevitably part of any complete theory of phonology, as they arise in connected discourse, diachronic change, language acquisition, and slips of the hand:

(3)   a.   Signs with a static NDH that has a different handshape may become fully symmetrical with the handshape of the DH;
        b.   Two-handed symmetrical signs may become one-handed (Deletion of the [+bimanual] feature); and
        c.   Deletion is favored by the feature [+facial] and disfavored by the features [alternating] and [contact].

There is no doubt that the question of the phonological representation of symmetric hands in signed languages (which we must recall, have only been treated within the purview of linguistic analysis using the same theoretical tools as spoken languages for a bit over a half-century) has become one of the most important challenges and sources of insights for our notions of dependent units of phonological organization.

7.7 Conclusion

The hands are biologically asymmetric, reflecting a lateralization preference throughout the vertebrate kingdom even found in the jaws of whales (MacNeilage et al., 2009). This leads the phonological system to a definition of symmetry that is very specific: namely, a 1H sign is not a violation of symmetry, but a 2H sign where the weak hand is moving and doing something different from the strong hand *is* a violation of symmetry. We have concluded that a feature like [+bimanual] is necessary for encoding minimal pairs such as 'LIKE' vs. 'INTERESTING', but that this feature can be allophonically deleted under a range of phonological, morphological, and sociolinguistic conditions. As a result, asking whether a sign is 1H or 2H isn't the right cut to make, any more than, say, asking whether a word is monosyllabic or disyllabic is relevant in a vowel-harmony language. Instead, like final high vowel devoicing or apocope (which depends on stress placement or surrounding consonants), the allophonic deletion of [+bimanual] relies on a host of interacting features, such as location on the face and pattern of movement.

As Brentari (1998, p. 248) argues, a purely hemispheric asymmetry alone (or purely articulatory phonetic considerations) cannot explain the structure of 2H signs because for nonlinguistic tasks, individuals can develop equal dexterity in both hands. Similarly, a definition based on phonetic recoverability alone is insufficient as the amount of symmetric redundancy found between the two hands is equal whether or not they are articulated in the [+facial] region or not; nonetheless, this feature is crucial in conditioning the rates of deletion of the feature [+bimanual], Brentari (1998) concludes that "An arbitrary, grammatical definition of complexity and redundancy is required, not simply a definition that refers to physiological or phonetic complexity" (p. 250).

Recall the definition in set-theoretic terms from Section 7.2, which is 'arbitary' in the sense that it is specific to the logic of human phonological systems (be they spoken or signed). According to this grammatically based logic, the informational content of H_2 must be a subset of that of H_1 (where an empty set still counts as a subset), and the exceptions to this are limited to the four maximally unmarked and dispersed handshapes 'SOB 1'.

It is often said that syntax undergoes linearization because we have only one vocal tract, but we would thus expect a great deal more parallelism and simultaneity among the hands in sign languages (which we know is motorically possible).[11] However, it is evident from the discussion above that restrictions on perception may be at play. As Frishberg (1975) states, "We have seen that historical tendencies in ASL have been to limit the characteristics of possible signs. At the same time, we note that these processes are creating systematicity, giving the perceiver ways to predict signs in 'noisy' (e.g., badly lit) environments" (p. 717). Any phonological system, be it visual or auditory, employs phonotactics in order to cut down the overall range of possible signs in order, increasing the predictability of combinations in a noisy channel and in lexical access more generally.

As Brentari and Goldsmith (1993, p. 20) point out, the same analytical paths that have led phonologists of spoken languages to such concepts as the feature, the segment, the syllable, the foot, and the phonological word will likely turn out to reveal that these notions may have counterparts across modalities in terms of how phonological information is organized into units of different complexity. Thus, as spoken language phonology has shown, codas (as well as the second member of onset clusters, in Baertsch and Davis [2003]) have a more restricted range of contrasts: the syllable is not symmetric on both sides of the nucleus. Brentari and Goldsmith (1993) suggest that the findings about distributional asymmetries in the two hands in signed language allow us in turn to rethink the theoretical bases of units such as the syllable in spoken language as potentially more abstract units that organize amounts of phonological complexity.

It appears that the truly simultaneous level of signed language phonology is not between the two hands articulating independent, autonomous handshapes but rather in the amount of information conveyed by nonmanual marking as a system of visual prosody, akin to the additional level of grammatical information carried by intonation in spoken language. Nicodemus and Smith (2005) find combinations of up to seven distinct nonmanual markers used to signal prosodic phrase boundaries. Indeed, perhaps the overarching view is that there is not duality but triality of patterning in human language, as syntax, phonology, and intonation act in parallel as combinatorial tiers. The two hands, however, involve representational challenges in terms of the need for asymmetric physiology balanced with symmetric, redundant perceptual and lexical organization, thereby enriching the overall logic of tradeoffs that form the hallmark of all phonological systems.

---

[11] However, extremely rich phonological systems are just beginning to be theoretically explored in the phonology of Protactile, a form of Tactile ASL in which DeafBlind signers interact with interlocutors by means of both signers' pairs of hands, and in Edwards and Brentari (2020), this involves all four articulators, arranged in a hierarchy in which the DH of the signer is more active than the DH of the receiving signer, followed by the NDH of the conveying signer, and finally the NDH of the receiving signer.

Further Reading

Sign language phonology has reached such a state of crystallization and maturity in empirical richness and theoretical depth that there is no longer any doubt that 'phonology' can be applied to 'signed languages' or, indeed, vice versa. Areas that interface with sign language phonology and have the potential to inform theories of symmetric handedness can be found in adjacent studies on L2 acquisition of phonology, and the acquisition of cospeech (nonsign) gestures. See Ortega and Morgan (2015) on findings for symmetry and two-handedness in L2, and Pettenati et al. (2010) on symmetry in infant gesture. For a particularly prehistoric glimpse onto the earliest visual communication system – cave paintings – and their interface with the phonology of the NDH, see Etxepare and Irurtzun (2021).

8 Number-Encoding on Verbs in Hiaki and Chechen

Allomorphy (i.e., the different realization of the same morpheme based on local context) is well known for affixes and functional nodes but not for roots. In fact, it has been explicitly claimed not to exist for roots. Hiaki provides empirical evidence that root suppletion exists and therefore, in turn, that even roots are phonologyless within the allomorphy approach in the framework of Distributed Morphology. By considering potential counteranalyses to number-conditioned root suppletion in Hiaki, we examine the distinct phenomena of pluractionality in Chechen, in which events show a parallelism with the count-mass distinction in the nominal domain. Crucial evidence for modeling the count-mass distinction in the nominal domain in terms of properties of the numeral system itself, and not in terms of nominal mapping, is then exemplified by the Athapaskan language Dëne Sųłiné.

8.1 Roots and Suppletion: How Marginal?

If there is one domain of linguistic structure that is more uniform in Indo-European languages than possibly any other, it is at the level of the word – morphology – and in fact, the highly 'inflectional' character of Western European languages (in which tense and subject agreement are often fused into single verbal suffixes), within Humboldt's (1836) influential typology of morphological word-types, has led to certain expectations about the most likely forms of what are called 'paradigms'. What is a paradigm? You might recall the arrangement of verbs into neatly ordered rows, such as first-person singular, second-person singular, and so on, from whatever second language you formally studied. But the notion of paradigm permeates grammatical thinking, even for categories such as the comparative and superlative form of adjectives. Thus, triplets like *good, better, best; fun, more fun, most fun; silly, sillier, silliest;* and *bad, worse, worst* all form paradigms of adjectival morphology, the topic of an entire cross-linguistic study by Bobaljik (2012). We can see from these English examples that some of them are *analytic*, such as 'more fun' (for whatever reason, **funner* is shunned), others are synthetic (meaning that they include comparative and superlative suffixes, such as *sillier, silliest*), and yet others are both synthetic and *suppletive*.

What does it mean to be suppletive? In this case, it doesn't refer to the analytic vs. synthetic difference between freestanding *most* and suffixal *-est* but rather to a modification of the form of the root itself. Thus, the comparative form is *better*, not *gooder*, suggesting that alongside the suffixal *-er* is a comparative-specific form of this adjectival root, something like *bett-*. Similarly, the root form of *bad* changes to a wholly different surface shape in its comparative and superlative guises, something like *wors-*. This kind of suppletion is found in English for these two adjectives alone and is found in the singular vs. plural pair of nouns like *one person* ~ *lots of people*, **lots of persons*. Similarly, in English verbs, despite the well-known patterns of irregularity found in *sing~sung, catch~caught, bring~brought*, these cases all maintain some degree of identity between the root forms in present and past (and often fall into fairly regular subclasses, such as *ring~rung* and so forth). The only true case of suppletion in English lexical verbs (i.e., outside of the system of auxiliary verbs such as *be*) is found with the verb pair *go* ~ *went*, in which there is no phonological overlap at all between the two forms and no other verb with which this falls into a remotely similar subclass.

The limited nature of suppletion has led authors such as Mel'čuk (2003) to call it "a rather marginal phenomenon in all languages" (p. 180). This intuition, without a doubt based on what is called 'sampling bias' in our work as linguists, has not only led to characterizations of suppletion as 'rare or not' at the observational level by scholars but has even elevated this rarity to the point of being one of the architectural cornerstones of the theory. Thus, in Distributed Morphology (a theory of how words are built and how the lexicon is decoupled across separate and dissociable syntactic, phonological, and semantic levels), as it was originally developed by its founders in publications such as Marantz (1997) and Embick and Halle (2005), explicitly states that roots – the stuff of which suppletion is made – cannot actually undergo the kind of morphological competition that one finds for suffixes such as *-ity* and *-ness* (e.g., in the relevant adage, it wasn't *curiousness* that killed the cat but rather *curiosity*). To understand how allomorphy for affixes works (and how it eventually must all be generalized to all items given the existence of root suppletion in languages like Hiaki), let's go into a little more detail on the notion of *competition*.

8.2 The Subset Principle: Back to Warlpiri

Remember those second-position auxiliaries in Warlpiri, which were, in Hale's (1983) conception, the only items to have a decidedly fixed and predictable position within the clause? We never went into much detail as to their actual morphological makeup, which is itself pretty interesting (and formed the topic of the detailed and still essentially maintained as correct analysis of Hale [1973]), because these auxiliaries themselves show enclitics that can agree across three number categories – singular, dual, and plural, for both subject and object. Now, let's look at the enclitic forms for first and second person:

(1)   1st   2nd
    sg   ṇa   npa
    dl   ḷitjata   npa-pala
    pl   ṇa-lu   nku-lu

Looking at the plural row, we can deduce that *-lu* is the plural number ending. For the 1dual form, it looks irregular in not bearing a suffix, so let's assume that the dual number ending is *-pala*. The question is, why is the form of the second-person morpheme *nku* only in the plural row? According to Halle (1997), this is a case of 'competition among the most specific'. The intuition, formalized there in terms of number of features mentioned in the description of allomorphs, is that the one that matches the highest number of features wins. Thus, consider the list below of what are called 'vocabulary entries' in this theory:

(2)   Partial list of vocabulary entries for Warlpiri subject enclitics:
       a.   /-nku/ ↔ 2, in the context of Pl
       b.   /-npa/ ↔ 2

The idea is as follows: for the second-person singular and dual forms, (2a) cannot be used because it is *too specific*. Thus, (2b) is used. However, for the second-person plural form, while both (2a) and (2b) are compatible, (2b) is *not specific enough*. This just-right amount of competition sets things up so that there is a *default* item, such as (2b), and a more highly specified item, such as (2a). Default items can be 'underspecified' – not mentioning the context of number at all. But they will be 'beat out' in the competition when more specific items that do mention the context of number are appropriate to use, by what Halle (1997) calls 'The Subset Principle'.

An application of the Subset Principle for items such as enclitics involving person–number features has led to literally dozens of analyses of individual languages within Distributed Morphology, across features as wide-ranging and complex as the interaction of conjugation classes with tense that are familiar within any study of inflection. It is very easy to set up such an analysis, as long as one can set up features like '2' and 'Pl' above (and the proper characterization of such features has led to extremely detailed research programs in themselves). But how can such logic be applied to the roots found in *good ~ bett*? That is to say, if *nku* and *npa* are exponing a morphological feature like [+addressee], what kind of feature are *good* and *bett* (the root allomorph that shows up in *bett-er*) exponing?

8.3 Speech Errors to the Rescue

The study of inflectional morphology in contemporary linguistic theory has always lumbered behind advances in theoretical phonology, almost like an eager younger sibling. Thus, the great breakthroughs in feature theory in phonology, leading to representational understanding of feature geometries, contrast, assimilation and dissimilation (see Chapters 6 and 7) have only recently (since Noyer [1992]) led to a flurry of debates about what the exact set of features is for person, number, gender, case, tense, and other inflectional categories, a partial inventory of which are shown below:

(3)   a.   Person: [±author], [± participant], [± addressee], ...
        b.   Number: [± singular] [± augmented] [± additive], ...
        c.   Gender: [± femine], [± common], ...
        d.   Case: [± governed], [± oblique], [± higher-role], ...

With features like these as a tool for decomposing pronouns such as English *they* or Spanish *ellas* into their constitutive features, all of the inflectional competition can be dealt with using the Subset Principle. Pronouns like these are, in fact, composed of one or more discrete morphemes, at least one of which realizes [−singular], and these compete with other morphemes for insertion according to the principles of specificity discussed above. Thus, the third-person plural feminine in English is not *she-s* (although first and second language learners may occasionally construct such cases if they have not yet fully acquired the more specific form that blocks all others from being usable). In the set of forms below, while items (4)a and b both realize two of the three features composing third-person feminine plural, (4)a is chosen − presumably because, given a choice between gender and number, the latter is more important to break the tie.

(4)   a.   [−participant, −singular] ↔ /ðej/
        b.   [−participant, +fem] ↔ /ʃi/
        c.   [−singular] ↔ /-z/

Now let's try this for *good* and *bett*. What binary features would go on the left?

(5)   a.   [+beneficence] ↔ /gʊd/
        b.   [+beneficence] in the context of [+comparative] ↔ /bɛt/

Nobody has explicitly proposed anything like (5). But authors such as Marantz (1997) and Embick and Halle (2005) have implicitly proposed something akin to this as they attempt to maintain the idea that only the kinds of nouns, adjectives, and verbs that can undergo this kind of competition (and hence suppletion) are necessarily ones based on semantic features that are somehow very basic, universal, and almost 'functional' in character. Thus, Marantz's (1997) tack was to say that apparent root suppletion only occurs with items that are suitably 'light' in character, arguably encoding adjectival, verbal, and nominal universal features. In the case of specific examples, *person* ~ *people* realizes a 'light noun' functional category n (perhaps bearing a universal feature [+human]); *go~went* realizes a 'light verb' functional category v (perhaps bearing a hypothetical universal feature [+path]; and *bad~worse* realizes a 'light adjective' category a (perhaps bearing universal features [+negative, +evaluative]). If this could be maintained, then something like (5) is indeed the strategy – the patterns of suppletion found with *good, better, best* are no different in nature from the Warlpiri pronouns composed of two such parts in (1).

Marantz thus suggests that everything that looks like a suppletive root may actually be a functional syntactic categorizing head. Embick and Halle (2005) argue that roots are subject to early insertion, while everything else is subject to late insertion – the mechanism that governs the Subset Principle for arrangements such as (4), stating "We note that Vocabulary Insertion only applies to abstract morphemes; Roots are not subject to insertion. A consequence of this view is that it is not possible for Roots to show suppletion" (pp. 5–6).

As we will see below, this claim is unsustainable. Languages like Hiaki have suppletion that simply cannot be analyzed in terms of light functional heads. Once verbs like 'arrive', 'lie down', and more are found to robustly show root suppletion that is conditioned in the context of plural number – the same way that Warlpiri pronouns are – one has to return to something like (5), although with less hokey features.

And perhaps with no features at all, except the very index that denotes this root itself. Suppose, therefore, that *bad* ~ *worse* does realize a feature – not a binary feature like [± participant] but rather a numeral that ranges into the thousands, one that provides a lookup pointer for the specific formative that a root like 'arrive' or 'bad' denotes. This is a kind of 'address' in our mental lexicon, in a dictionary of roots, such as 'Entry Number 553 in the list of Adjectival Roots of English':

(6)   a. Adj_{553} in the context of [+compar] ↔ worse
     b. Adj_{553} in the context of [+compar] ↔ bæd

The proposal that these kind of 'indices' govern the competition between roots, as part of the mental representation that leads to choosing the right suppletive allomorphs, actually comes from one of the highly relevant domains of understanding our lexicon: speech errors. When someone says the 'wrong word', by accident (those darn Freudian slips), there is actually a lot of speech planning and processing that is revealed. Consider the following slips of the tongue and their analysis, based on Pfau's (2009) study of speech errors. The phrase on the left is what was intended, while that on the right is what was actually produced:

(7) a. I saw him digging → I see him dugging
     b. Rosa only dated shrinks → Rosa only date shranks
     c. a maniac for weekends → a weekend for maniacs

To understand (7a), we see that the roots are all in the intended order but that the past tense is realized on the wrong root – on 'dig' instead of 'see'. The most straightforward way to analyze this error, therefore, is that the feature [± past] is independent of the root it attaches to and, during a transposition error, can move to a new host, leaving its former (and intended) host behind. In fact, we may view this as wholesale transposition between [+past] in one location and [−past] in the other. A similar pattern is found in (7b), where the [± past] originally destined for the root 'date' instead occurs on the root 'shrink'. Interestingly, in this case, the verbal base of the noun 'shrink' (denoting a psychologist) is first appropriately transformed to the past tense, then nominalized and pluralized.[1] Finally, in (7c), we observe the roots swapping on their own, leaving the number inflections in place. There, we can maintain the same kind of transposition that the other cases of speech errors have, except here, it's for elements like $Root_{719}$ (let's say, corresponding to *shrink/shrank/shrunk*) and $Root_{925}$ (corresponding to *date*).

The view of Distributed Morphology, therefore, very much bolstered by the kind of data found in speech errors, is that for the familiar syntactic trees we observe in linguistic theory, the leaves of the tree are morphemes (not words). Each morpheme corresponds to three separate, independent lists. There is the Formative List, determining syntactic behavior. There is the Exponent List, determining phonological form (including null Ø exponence). And there is the Encyclopedic List, determining semantic interpretation. Thus, the traditional lexicon is distributed across these three lists, rather than being bundled as one, and thereby allows allomorphy (same formative, same encyclopedic entry, different exponent in context) or allosemy (same formative, same exponent, different encyclopedic entry in context).

In a large-scale study of suppletive verbs from nearly 200 languages across the globe, in which suppletion is conditioned by number cross-linguistically, Veselinova (2006, pp. 222–224) compiles the following list. In boldface are verbs that are particularly ill-suited as candidates for 'light, functional items',

---

[1] Perhaps due to this spectacular chain of adjustments, this example was said to be one of the favorite speech errors collected by Victoria Fromkin, one of the foremost experts of slips of the tongue, in her longstanding notebook corpus of naturalistic annotations.

in the sense that Marantz (1997) proposed covered suppletive roots like *good, go,* or *person*, as these carry very specific lexical content:

(8) a. Motion, intransitive: go, fall, come, run, arrive, enter, start, get.up, return, rise, walk, **fall.in.water**, fly, go.about, **go.around .something.out.of.sight**, jump, move, stampede, swim, visit, walk
b. Motion, transitive: put, throw, take, give, drive.out, get, grasp, pick.up, pull.out, release, remove, take.out
c. Position: sit, lie, stand, hold, carry, store
d. Die/Injure: beat, **bite.off**, cut, die.of.old.age.or.hunger, injure, kill, break, hit
e. Stative: sleep, big, small, be.at, be lost, exist, long, short
f. Other: eat, belong.to, **bet**, **make.netbag**, make.noise, not.like, say

While the existence of suppletive verbal roots, whose suppletive form is conditioned by number, has been observed in linguistic theory, it was not until the publication of Harley's (2014) work on the Uto-Aztecan language Hiaki that the theory of Distributed Morphology – specifically, with the claim that roots did not undergo suppletion – underwent a significant change, in particular with an architecture that allowed roots with indices to have different allomorphs, depending on the context of number features surrounding them.

8.4 Going and Wending in Hiaki

Hiaki (also known as Yaqui) is an Uto-Aztecan language, probably most familiar to the non-specialist because of Carlos Castañeda's (1968) memoir about peyote and spirituality, *The Teaching of Don Juan: A Yaqui Way of Knowledge*. The history of the Yaqui, however, is less picturesque than this narrative alone portrays. Galeano (1997) writes "The Yaqui Indians of the Mexican state of Sonora were drowned in blood so that their lands, fertile and rich in minerals, could be sold without any unpleasantness … two-thirds of them died during the first year of slave labor" (p. 48). Many Yaquis fled to the United States and settled permanently in Arizona, in the beginning as squatters near Tucson but eventually, after struggles for economic and cultural survival and leadership, received Federal Tribal Recognition and land rights.

The pattern of verb suppletion in Hiaki described by Harley (2014) can be observed in pairs such as the following, in which the root 'walk' has wholly different realizations in singular and plural:

(9) a. Aapo **weye**
3sg walk.SG
'He/she/it is walking.'

b. Vempo **kate**
    3pl   walk.PL
    'They are walking.'

The example above is intransitive. For suppletive transitive verbs such as 'kill', these are conditioned by the number of the object, whereas the number of the subject makes no diference:

(10) a. Aapo / Vempo uka   koowi-ta **me'a**-k
          3sg / 3pl   the.SG pig-ACC kill.SG-PRF
          'He/They killed the pig.'
      b. Aapo / Vempo ume   koowi-m **sua**-k
          3sg / 3pl   the.PL pig-PL   kill.PL-PRF
          'He/They killed the pigs.'

The set of verbs undergoing these alternations observes a much broader pattern found throughout in North American languages, originally observed in Booker (1982). She writes "Cases of suppletion have traditionally been treated as irregularities of the grammar, as haphazard exceptions defying explanation. ... Yet, the fact that so many references are made to suppletion in Amerindian grammars leads one to suspect that further investigation might produce fruitful typological insights. This paper is an attempt to extract any patterns that would establish a degree of semantic systematicity among verbs which supplete for number" (p. 15). In Booker's study, a total of thirty-two languages from thirteen distinct genetic groupings (including Uto-Aztecan, though not Hiaki specifically) were found to have suppletive verbs marking what could be called *ergative* plurality – where the suppletive verb cross-references the number of the subject of an intransitive verb and the object of a transitive verb.

Booker's generalizations, among others, are that intransitives will supplete in languages when the transitives do not, but the reverse is not true. Furthermore, among the intransitives, locatives (verbs denoting position and motion) may have suppletive forms while nonlocatives do not, but not vice versa. Finally, the verb 'die' is unique in that it frequently tends to be the only suppletive form in the nonlocative nonstative intransitive category (though Booker draws attention to the euphemistic 'pass away' and to death conceived as a journey to the beyond); similarly, the verb 'kill' parallels 'die' in that it may occur as the sole representative of the nonlocative category. Hiaki's set of suppletive verbs fully adhere to these generalizations, and the list of suppletive verbs in Hiaki is provided below:

(11) Intransitive suppletive verbs:

Sg. Subj	Pl. Subj.	
weye	kaate	'go, walk'
vuite	tenne	'run'
weama	rehte	'walk around, wander'
siime	saka	'go, leave'
kivake	kiimu	'enter'
yepsa	yaha	'arrive'
weche	watte	'fall down'
kikte	hapte	'stand up'
yeesa	hooye	'sit down'
muuke	koko	'get up'
yehte	hoote	'die'

(12) Transitive suppletive verbs:

Sg. Obj	Pl. Obj.	
kivacha	kiima	'bring in'
me'a	sua	'kill'
kecha	ha'abwa	'stand (something) up'
yecha	hoa	'put down, place'

As Harley notes, these are typically verbs of motion, position, or appearance, according to the classification in Levin and Hovav (1995). As mentioned above, verb suppletion of this type always follows an ergative pattern (Veselinova, 2006) – agreement with the object number in transitive verbs, otherwise with the subject argument – even in otherwise nonergative languages.

The analyses of these singular–plural verb pairs is entirely parallel to that of *go~went* in English. However, recall that the English case is for a single verb, and one that had previously been dismissed (e.g., in Marantz [1997]) as a 'light functional item' (perhaps akin to what are called semilexical verbs in Corver and van Riemsdijk [2001]). We can tell that English *go* and *went* are the same verb in ellipsis contexts – consider *I went to the party, even though I wasn't supposed to* go to the party. Although historically the verb 'went' involved cobbling together a different allomorph (in fact, from the verb 'to wend', as in 'to wend one's way through the labyrinth'), these are now two allomorphs of the very same verb.

(13) a. English: Verb$_{551}$ in the context of [+past] ↔ went
     b. English: Verb$_{551}$ in the context of [−past] ↔ go

(14) a. Hiaki: Verb$_{322}$ in the context of [+singular] ↔ vuite
     b. Hiaki: Verb$_{322}$ in the context of [−singular] ↔ tenne

Under this kind of implementation, all roots are phonologyless indices and only receive the determination of their realization as one allomorph or another once the syntactic context is supplied. Thus, once these verbs are placed in the context of [±singular], it is decided which allomorph will be chosen for pronunciation.

Notice that, given the ergative pattern (in which the object is chosen instead of the subject in transitive verbs), it is the most local noun phrase (NP) to the verb that is used to determine this context. Assuming that in Hiaki the object and verb form a verb phrase (VP), to the exclusion of the subject, this falls out naturally – the object will always be the closest NP contextually to the verb, with transitive verbs, and hence lead to determination of number-sensitive allomorphy based on the object.

By considering another Uto-Aztecan language with number-sensitive suppletion, namely Northern Paiute (spoken in California, Nevada, and Oregon), we can learn more about the conditions under which an NP can trigger suppletion on a verb. As Toosarvandani (2016) shows, while Northern Paiute number-sensitive verbs supplete like those in Hiaki (i.e., according to the number of the direct object in a transitive verb like 'kill' and according to the number of the subject with an intransitive predicate like 'fall'),[2] there are two additional potential triggers that are surprising based on the ergative pattern otherwise found in Hiaki. Another trigger of this type of allomorphy can in fact be the external argument of an unergative verb, or even the applied object in an applicative (recall applicatives from Chapter 5). First, consider unergative verbs, whose subject is agentive and external to the verb phrase itself, but are still intransitive. The verbs meaning 'to talk' or 'to tell a lie' are suppletive in Northern Paiute:

(15) a. Su=nana yadu'a.
NOM=man talk.IPFV.SG
'The man is talking.'
b. Iwa-'yu naana abbika.
many-NOM men talk.IPFV.PL
'Many men are talking.'

(16) a. Su=mogo'ni isaya'e.
NOM=woman tell.lie.IPFV.SG
'The woman is telling a lie.'
b. Iwa-'yu momoko'ni isago'i.
many-NOM women tell.lie.IPFV.PL
'Many women are telling lies.'

---

[2] Indeed, while working on the related language Southern Paiute, Sapir (1930) observed "There are certain verb stems that are inherently limited in their reference to number, the singular-dual of the intransitive subject or transitive object being expressed by a stem which is etymologically distinct from that for the plural of the intransitive subject or transitive object" (pp. 241–242).

As Toosarvandani (2016) argues, neither verb in (15)–(16) is a motion or posture predicate, which are the semantic categories often associated with unaccusativity.[3] Even more convincingly, the passive construction can be used to show that *yadu'a* ~ *abbika* 'talk' and *isaya'e* ~ *isagoi* 'tell a lie' are unergative verbs, as these can appear with impersonal passives, whereas truly unaccusative verbs such as 'to fall' cannot occur in this passive construction:

(17)   a.   Na-yadu'a.
              PASS-talk.IPFV.SG
              'There is talking.'
        b.   *Na-w-i'i.
              PASS-fall.SG
              Intended: 'There was falling.'

As Toosarvandani (2016) argues, in Northern Paiute, the plural suppletive form is inserted as an allomorph if the closest determiner phrase (DP) to the verb has a plural ϕ-feature:

(18)   a.   *yadu'a* ↔ Verb$_{291}$ / D[ϕ:sg]
        b.   *abbika* ↔ Verb$_{291}$ / D[ϕ:pl]

Given a hierarchical phrase structure in which the direct object is always closer to the verb (as its direct sister of the verb within the VP) than an external argument (in the specifier of a higher projection), any time there is a direct object, this will be the DP that determines number-sensitive allomorphy. However, if there is no direct object at all, then the closest DP will indeed be the external agent, even in unergative verbs. (A similar formation is provided in Hale et al. [1991], who state for the case of suppletion triggers in Hopi, Papago – today referred to as Tohono O'odham – and Navajo: "the closest direct argument is found by counting the number of branch segments separating the verb from an NP" [p. 265].)

Interesting confirmation for the implementation in (18) comes from applicative benefactive constructions built on unergative verbs. In these cases, the verbal allomorphy varies with the number of the applied object, not the subject. Consider (19):

(19)   Su=nana   iwa-ggu   momoko'ni   abbiga-ggɨ-ti.
           NOM=man   many-ACC   women   talk.PL-APPL-TNS
           'This man is talking for many women.'

---

[3] Hale et al. (1991) also cast doubt on suppletion for intransitive verbs being limited to unaccusatives, based on the existence of number-sensitive allomorphy for the Hopi verb *tayati* ~ *cuyti* 'to laugh'.

This is entirely expected, as the applicative object is still closer to the verb than the external agent is (recall [43] in Chapter 5). In fact, the notion of relativized adjacency developed by Toosarvandani (2016) predicts that while the trigger for verb suppletion must indeed be the closest DP to the verb, it does not have to be strictly adjacent to the verb. For example, an adverb and prepositional phrase can intervene, as in (20):

(20) Nɨmmi kwaya nɨmmi tɨbongo o-tu mi'a.
1PL.EXCL far.away 1PL.EXCL downhill there-LOC go.PL.IPFV
'We, a long ways downhill we went.'

The Northern Paiute patterns thus provide convincing evidence that number-sensitive suppletion of the kind found in Hiaki and beyond is stated in terms of locality – but in terms of a kind of relativized locality, where the closest DP to the verb is the one whose number features matter for deciding which verbal allomorph is inserted, and this can even be an external argument or an applied object, depending on the configuration.

The phenomenon of number-sensitive verb allomorphy as found in the Uto-Aztecan languages such as Hiaki and North Paiute, described above, shows that once one looks beyond the Indo-European language family, suppletion is hardly 'marginal' (in Mel'čuk's [2003]'s words, quoted earlier). Indeed, the phenomenon requires a theory of linguistic structure in which verbal roots undergo the same kinds of allomorphic conditoning as functional items like suffixes or the Warlpiri agreement morphemes examined above and, once couched within a theory such as Distributed Morphology, require the mechanism of 'late' phonological insertion – namely, one in which the determination of verbal form needs to wait until the entire syntactic structure around it is built before examining the number features of the closest relevant DP.[4]

Since the theoretical consequences of our model of natural language are dramatically affected once we bring Uto-Aztecan languages into the canon, one might begin considering alternative accounts for number-sensitive suppletion, in which it is not the result of allomorphy conditioned by the local syntactic environment but rather some other grammatical phenomenon.

One such alternate explanation is offered by Thornton (2018), who argues that number-sensitive allomorphy of this type results from syntactic agreement (e.g., feature copying) – although it would have to be of an ergative pattern plus the kinds of modifications required to account for Northern Paiute. For example, 'omnivorous' number agreement, in the sense of Nevins (2011), involves the verbal agreement slot taking plural number from any of the arguments – but

---

[4] Although not widely discussed, Pranka's (1983) dissertation on the Uto-Aztecan language Papago (today referred to as Tohono O'Odham) explicitly argued that lexical insertion could not take place solely at the level of d-structure.

in the cases at hand, this is not what's happening. Instead, the presence of a singular object means that no further looking at the subject will take place. It is truly hard to think of cases of bona fide agreement in which the presence of a singular object or an applied object of an intransitive means that a plural subject will never be looked at – while at the same time, unergative subjects, if they are the only argument, can be looked at. In other words, shoehorning verbal suppletion into the category of agreement would require significant modifications to the existing typology of agreement and, moreover, would have to be limited to the list of roots that exhibit suppletion. As the list of suppletive verb roots is already a language-specific finite list (one which adheres to Booker's generalizations above), it would seem more natural to place allomorphy as a result of a listing like that in (18).[5]

Relevant data for the debate on whether suppletion can be reduced to agreement comes from Hale et al.'s (1991) discussion of Navajo. In this language, there is verbal suppletion for singular, dual, or plural subjects of intransitive verbs such as 'to walk'. However, in comitative constructions, one can find that the verbal agreement itself must be first-person singular, while the verb root exhibits the dual allomorph:

(21)   Shí ashkii bi-ł   yi-sh-'ash.
         I   boy   him-with PROG-1SG-walk.DUAL
         'I am walking with the boy.'

Even in the absence of a specific account of how the verbal suppletion is sensitive to the nature of a dual NP argument that is syntactically split across a subject NP and a separate postpositional phrase (see McNally [1993] and Baker et al. [2013] for relevant proposals as to the structure of comitatives), it is clear from (21) that the actual verbal agreement prefix and the suppletive root itself can go their separate ways, thereby rendering impossible any theory that attempts to reduce suppletion to agreement.

8.5 When Suppletion Is Based on Morphosyntactic Features

A second, distinct line of argumentation that attempts to dismiss the phenomenon of root suppletion as a phenomenon of late-determined allomorphy is one that suggests that, instead, the two apparent allomorphs are in fact not

---

[5] Camargo-Souza (2020), however, includes cases of 'additive' agreement conditioning number-suppletion in the Panoan language Yawanawa, where the combination of features on both subject *and* object can trigger verbal allomorphy. In this kind of 'smashing features together' approach, it is Vocabulary Insertion that can be sensitive to a combination of features from both subject and object. Again, this is a phenomenon not regularly found outside of cases such as Georgi's (2012) work on first-person inclusive portmanteaux in languages like Ikpeng that combine features of 1+2 arguments – a well-circumscribed exception.

even the same root to begin with. The logic goes, since it is known that English verbs like *go* and *went* were historically different but are now synchronically two allomorphs of the same root, it is valid to ask whether the Hiaki pairs are indeed cases of one single verb with two allomorphs or simply two wholly different roots with significant overlap in meaning. If they are different roots to begin with, there might no allomorphy to discuss.

Thus, Corbett (2000) reminds us to "think of English verbs like *scatter*: in the intransitive use, one person cannot scatter, and two or three can hardly do so. Ten clearly can. Equally in the transitive use, one cannot scatter two seeds, nor perhaps three, but it is hard to say what the lower limit would be. Thus, so-called plural verbs often require 'multiple participants' and do not show a strict singular-plural contrast as may be found with nominal number" (p. 248). Similarly, Borer (2014) urges us to "consider the English verbs *murder* and *massacre* side by side to see how extremely similar Content can give rise to distinct expectations concerning the number of object participants. But would we be justified in assuming that *murder* and *massacre* constitute alternative realizations of the same root, conditioned grammatically?" (p. 351).

However, Harley (2014) demonstrates that ellipsis involves 'filling in' with the same lexical verb. Thus, in (22), if the linguistic material after *the slug was* is elided, it will be filled in with 'massacred' and not with 'kill'.[6] Similarly, (23) is simply infelicitous, as a single sheepdog cannot stampede.

(22)   The cockroaches weren't massacred but the slug was _. (massacred /*killed)

(23)   #First the cows all stampeded, and then my trusty sheepdog did _. (#stampede)

We may now turn to Hiaki suppletive pairs. Consider *vuite~ tenni*, 'arrive'. In a fragment answer pair (of question and answer, with the given information, namely, the verb, elided), if the verb were unelided, it would be the plural allomorph:

(24)   a.   A: Havee vuiti-vae?
             A: Who   run.SG-PROSP?
             'Who is going to run?'
        b.   B: Jose intok Marcos (tenni-vae).
             B: Jose and   Marcos (run.PL-PROSP)
             'Jose and Marcos.'

---

[6] The relevant judgment here involves speakers for whom *massacre* is limited to plural objects. In my own judgments, *massacre* has a 'manner' reading, neutral as to the number of the object, and compatible with a brutal treatment of a singular object. For the former group of speakers, (22) should be impossible, as (23) is for me.

However, unlike the 'stampede' cases above, (24) creates no such problem. By hypothesis, this is because, unlike 'run away' vs. 'stampede', the two verbs *vuite~ tenni*, 'arrive' are the same – much like *go* and *went* (consider *I went to the party, even though I wasn't supposed to ~~go to the party~~*). Consider (25) as well, with transitive objects:

(25) Itepo ume toto'i-m hiva sua-k, kaa uka kowita
 We the.PL chicken-PL just kill.PL-PRF, not the.ACC.SG pig.ACC.SG
 (mea-k).
 (kill.SG-PRF)
 'We only killed the chickens, not the pig.'

Another argument that the suppletive pair are two avatars of the *same root*, as opposed to being semantically similar pairs, is based on idiomatic expressions. Idiomatic expressions, such as *a bucket list* (meaning the list of things one wants to do before one dies), are not substitutable by synonymous equivalents – if I tell you that skydiving is on my 'pail enumeration', this won't register at all as having the metaphorical or idiomatic listed meaning. This is presumably because idiomatic expressions require specific allosemic (i.e., contextual) lookup on the Encyclopedic List of the lexicon – the place where we know to interpret 'bucket' as 'life' in expressions such as *bucket list, kick the bucket*. This Encyclopedic listing is specific to Root$_{46}$ 'bucket', but not found with Root $_{47}$ 'pail',

With this background in mind, consider Hiaki suppletive verb pairs that participate in idiomatic expressions. In this case, the idiomatic expressions work across both singular and plural allomorphs of the same root. Thus, for the Root$_{900}$ 'sit', with *yehte~hoote*, both of these participate in the idiom *amae yehte~hoote*, 'to change one's mind, stand down from commitment':

(26) a. Tevan pahko-vae-n, ta ama-e yehte-k.
 Steven fiesta-PROSP-P.IMPF but there-OBL sit.SG-PRF
 'Steven was going to hold a fiesta, but he changed his mind.'
 b. Ne-mak weeri-me pahko-vae-n, ta kaa ama
 1SG-with relate-S.REL fiesta-PROSP-P.IMPF but not there
 yuma-kai, vena ama-e hoote-k.
 arrive-PPL, then there-OBL sit.PL-PRF
 'My relatives were going to hold a fiesta, but they couldn't manage it, so they changed their minds.'

The phenomena of ellipsis and idiomatic expressions demonstrate that the Hiaki suppletive verb pairs literally are the same root and are not distinct but similar roots akin to *run* vs. *stampede*. Instead, like *go* ~ *went* and as shown in (18) for Uto-Aztecan, we are dealing with a single root whose morphological form is determined depending on the syntactic environment it is placed in: it is conditioned by the number of the closest DP.

An appeal to the verbal semantics of collective or pluractional events (e.g., that *run* vs. *stampede* define different kinds of 'events', one being necessarily a plural event) is insufficient to replace allomorphy as an explanation of number-sensitive verbal suppletion. Indeed, in Maxakalí, which has similar ergative suppletion patterns (Silva & Nevins, 2020), it can be clearly shown that it is the grammatical number of the closest NP argument, not the number of events, that determines allomorphy. Consider the following pair:

(27) Ũn   puxet   mõxupa patix.
    woman one   run.SG two
    'One woman ran twice.'

(28) Un   tix   mõnũpa pxet.
    woman two   run.PL one
    'Two women ran once.'

A different kind of argument against the 'semantically related, two-root' alternative for number-sensitive root allomorphy can be found in the pattern of three-way suppletion in the Muskogean language Creek, as noted by Johnson (2021) (also anticipated in Booker's [1982] discussion of three-way suppletion systems). In this language (and indeed, many others, including Navajo, as mentioned above), there are distinct number-sensitive allomorphs for singular, dual, and plural NP subjects (Martin, 2011, pp. 199–200), as shown in the table below. Note that the suffix *itá* is an infinitive, and *-k* is a middle voice suffix:

(29) SG   DL   PL
    lit-k-itá   tokoł-k-itá pifa:t-k-itá 'to run'
    ley-k-itá   ka:-k-itá   apo:-k-itá   'to sit'
    ał-íta   wilak-itá   foll-itá   'to go about'

It stretches the imagination to say these are 'triplets' of related verbs – especially since they require precise numbers of participants, unlike *scatter* or *stampede*.

One last argument against the idea that number-sensitive allomorphy can be reduced to verbal semantics comes from the phenomenon of Hopi constructed duals. Consider the following pattern, in which the dual number is 'constructed' by a nonsingular subject and a nonplural verb:

(30) a. Nu' hohonaqa.
        1.SG play.SG
        'I am playing.'
    b. Itam hohonaqa.
        1.PL play.SG
        'We two are playing.'
    c. Itam hohonaqa-ya.
        1.PL play-PL
        'We are playing.'

The analysis of these patterns in Harbour (2020) is that duals are composed of two features: [−singular] and [−augmented]. The verbs show a two-way contrast for [−augmented], while the noun phrases show a two-way contrast for [−singular]. Now look at (31), with a suppletive singular-verb pair. Crucially, the 'singular' verb is still used when there is a dual subject to be constructed:

(31) a. mi?   maana paki.
        that.SG girl.SG enter.SG
        'That girl entered.'
     b. mima   maana-t paki.
        those.PL girl-PL enter.SG
        'Those two girls entered.'
     c. mima   maman-t yiŋʸa.
        those.PL pl-girl-PL enter.PL
        'Those (many) girls entered.'

Consider the verbal form in (31a–b): One cannot say that *paki* is for semantically singular subjects! Rather, it's formally sensitive to a specific morphosyntactic feature that is part of duals (as well as singulars): [−augmented]. The verbal suppletion is conditioned by a formal morphosyntactic feature, unlike the false analogies with *scatter* or *massacre*. In short, number-sensitive verbal suppletion is a kind of allomorphy based on morphosyntactic features in the local clause structure of the verb in question. By now, the theory of suppletion has actively changed, such that verbal roots undergo late insertion in just the same way as functional material like affixes.

8.6 Suppletion beyond Uto-Aztecan Verbs

In fact, even outside of the verbal domain, there is a great deal of nominal suppletion with singular–plural pairs. One clear set of examples comes from Archi (see Moskal [2013] for an overview), in which many such nouns cannot plausibly be called 'functional items', such as those meaning 'corner of a sack' and 'pier of a bridge':

(32) *Number-driven root suppletion in absolutive forms of nouns in Archi*

	Singular	Plural
'man'	bošór	kɬelé
'shepherd'	úɬdu	ɬ:ʷat
'corner of a sack'	bič'ní	boždó
'woman'	ɬ:onnól	χom
'cow'	χˤon	buc:'i
'pier of a bridge'	biq'ˤní	boʁdó

It should therefore be clear that Harley's arguments that root-suppletion of nonfunctional items demonstrates the need for late insertion of roots (and therefore abstract, phonologyless indices) transfer over directly to nouns as well.

Perhaps all along you may have been wondering why the kinds of root suppletion in question are limited to number distinctions – and indeed, this emphasis on number distinctions has arguably led to the explorations of alternatives such as verbal semantic differences of the kind discussed for *scatter* and *stampede* above. But in fact, root suppletion can be conditioned by features other than number, and one of the more striking such cases involves root suppletion that is determined by the person features of a possessor argument in kinship terms (Baerman, 2014). In particular, the languages of New Guinea show extensive suppletion patterns as determined by the *person* of the possessor. Thus, consider the three patterns below, which contrast cases of suppletion for one specific person feature alongside a regular set of affixal possessors:

(33)   Kamasau: *maternal grandparent* is suppletive with 1sg possessor:

	maternal grandparent	mother's brother
1sg	koku	wau
2sg	nu-qo	nu-wau
3sg	ku-qo	ku-wau

(34)   Vitu: *mother* and *father* are suppletive with 2sg possessor:

	father	mother
1sg	tama-gu	titina-gu
2sg	ka-mama	ka-titi
3sg	tama-na	titina-na

(35)   Kaluli: *daughter* is suppletive with 3sg possessor:

	daughter	sister
1sg	n-a:la:	n-ado
2sg	g-a:la:	g-ado
3sg	ida:	ado

The attempts to explain away number-sensitive suppletion in terms of lexical and semantic properties of collectives and pluractionality won't generalize to cases of person-sensitive suppletion; it seems inevitable that we have *roots* such as 'maternal grandparent' that undergo late-insertion, based on the properties they acquire through the course of a morphosyntactic derivation, as inalienably possessed kinship terms.[7]

---

[7] One last phenomenon demonstrating the intersection between suppletion and kinship can be found in the Amazonian language Tupari (Singerman, 2018), where suppletion is found in both auxiliaries and lexical verbs, and the two follow the same grammatical lines, clearly showing they are not a case of verbs with semantics based on collectivity or pluractionality. Thus, the the

To conclude, root suppletion is inevitable: it can be conditioned by allomorphic factors like tense, comparatives, number, or person, and can be implemented by late insertion mechanisms similar to those used for functional nodes. Harley's (2014) evidence from Hiaki changed the theory, and there is no going back to a divide between lexical and functional nodes for allomorphy.

In fact, with the theoretical tool of root suppletion in hand, even previously recalcitrant cases of inflectional conditioning can receive new light. Thus, the famously 'defective' nouns in Russian, such as the word *kochergá* 'fireplace poker' lack a form for the genitive plural, a fact so well-ingrained into the linguistic consciousness of native speakers that it formed the basis for a short story by the literary master Mikhail Zoshchenko about office workers who decided to requisition four instead of five fireplace pokers so as to avoid having to write out the genitive plural form for this noun (as is required in the nominal complement of numerals five and up). What makes nouns like *kochergá* 'fireplace poker' and *mechtá* 'dream' defective is that fact that in all twelve case-number combinations in Russian, the stress falls on the ending and not on the root – earning them the name 'nonrhizotonic'. Thus, in all forms with overt suffixes (e.g., *mechtí, mechtú, mechtáx, mechtámi*), stress stays off the root, but as the genitive plural form for these feminine nouns has no suffix, this would force a rhizotonic form such as *mécht. Once root suppletion as a post-syntactic mechanism based on the morphological context of these

---

main verb 'go' suppletes whether used as a verb of motion or as a diachronically related auxiliary verb (without the semantics of a verb of motion, akin to 'I'm going to stay' in English), although in Tupari, these verbs and auxiliaries supplete according to the external argument, perhaps for reasons having to do with its placement higher in the clause. Like in Creek and Navajo, there is three-way suppletion, although for singular, plural, and paucal (where paucal is a number category like dual, that refers to a small quantity of referents, akin to English 'a couple'). Now, what is particularly striking is the fact that for politeness reasons, all in-laws in Tupari must be referred to in the paucal – even when they refer to a single individual (this in itself is perhaps familiar from cases such as French *vous*, a plural form used to politely refer to single addressees) – and that this, too, triggers number-sensitive suppletion, as can be seen on auxiliary versions of 'go' and the habitual, which show nonsingular allomorphs. Thus, consider the following minimal pair, in which the first example refers to the speaker's daughter and the second to the speaker's daughter-in-law:

(i) Saletxi-t tobeko kot'oy-a **tero'e**-a te-**'eka**-a.
 Salete-TOP beans want-FV AUX.GO.SG-FV 3-AUX.HABIT.SG.-FV
 'Salete [=the speaker's daughter] has been wanting beans.'

(ii) Roza-t tobeko kot'oy-a te-**oro'e**-a te-**aka**-a.
 Roza-TOP beans want-FV 3-AUX.GO.PAUC-FV 3-AUX.HABIT.PL.-FV
 'Roza [=the speaker's daughter-in-law] has been wanting beans.'

The suppletion found on the auxiliary verbs 'go' and the habitual auxiliaries in (i)–(ii) supplete purely for the formal reason that in-laws are formally treated with paucal NPs. The verbal event itself is not any more collective or pluractional when referring to a daughter-in-law than when referring to a daughter, but the allomorphy rules simply see the paucal features on the local NP, and that is enough to trigger suppletion.

items is admitted into the theory, these can be modeled as nouns that have a nonrhizotonic allomorph but no rhizotonic allomorph:

(36)   √dream144 ↔ /mecht [-nonrhizotonic]
        √dream144 ↔ (no elsewhere item)

This short exemplification of defective nouns as a case of root allomorphy – very specific allomorphy, in fact, whereby the pattern involves the total absence of a given allomorph – is only enabled once roots are theoretically given the same treatment as functional items, allowing crucial progress to be made in longstanding morphological problems.

8.7   Uncountable Mass Events in Chechen

It was crucial to the discussion above, particularly in Section 8.5, that cases of root suppletion such as those found in Hiaki (and also Maxakalí) were not based on verbal semantics that depended on collective or plural verbal events. This is not to say, however, that no language has verbal morphology reflecting this kind of semantics. In fact, in the Chechen language, an extremely theoretically interesting connection can be found between the verbal ablaut (vowel-changing morphology) used to derive new verbal categories and the specific semantics of those verbs.

Chechen is part of the Vainakh language family that includes Tsova-Tush, which we have already encountered in Chapter 3. The war-torn Chechen republic has been influenced by a centuries-old set of conflicts beginning with the Russian involvement in the Caucasus since the sixteenth century and the spread of Islam at approximately the same time. Traditionally, the Vainakh peoples, like many other peoples of the North Caucasus, practiced a complex cosmology that included tree worship, as they believed that trees were the abodes of spirits. Vainakh peoples developed many rituals to serve particular kinds of trees, and the pear tree held a special place in the faith of Vainakhs.

Cross-linguistically, pluractionality is often expressed by reduplication, as described by Newman (1990) for Hausa, for example. According to Yu (2003), about twenty percent of the Chechen verbal lexicon indicates pluractionality by means of vocalic ablaut. These stem-vowel alternations prototypically signify the repetition of an event, for example, *saca/sieca* 'to stop once/many times' or *laaca/liica* 'to catch once/many times'. Phonologically, the stem vowel of a pluractional verb is generally the high, front counterpart of the theme vowel in a nonpluractional verb.

In Chechen, the difference between pluractional readings that indicate 'Xed many times' are demonstrably orthogonal to allomorphy for the number of the object, as can be shown in the following four-way contrast for the verb 'chase'.

Note that the allomorphy for the singular or plural object 'cows' triggers true number-sensitive root suppletion with a wholly different verb stem, whereas pluractional semantics are expressed by the phonological modification of the main root vowel as described above:

(37) a. as xyyrana jiatt dxa-liallira.
 I in.the.morning cow AGR-chase.SG.OBJ
 'I chased a cow in the morning.'
 b. as hoora xyyrana jiatt dxa-lwellura.
 I every morning cow AGR-chase-SG.OBJ-PLURACT
 'I chased a cow every morning.'
 c. as xyyrana bezhnash dxa-liakhkira.
 I in.the.morning cattle.PL AGR-chase-PL.OBJ
 'I chased cows in the morning.'
 d. as hoora xyyrana bezhnash dxa-likhkira.
 I every morning cattle.PL AGR-chase-PL.OBJ-PLURACT
 'I chased cows every morning.'

As the example above shows for the verb 'catch', pluractionality yields a frequentative reading, one that denotes the occurrence of the event over multiple occasions (e.g., every morning). Another such example can be found with the verb 'drink':

(38) a. adama takhan duqqa'a chai melira.
 Adam.ERG today many tea drink
 'Adam drank a lot of tea today.'
 b. adama takhan duqqa'a chai miilira.
 Adam.ERG today many tea drink-PLURACT
 'Adam drank a lot of tea over and over again today.'

The precise reading of the pluractional morpheme depends on the semantics of the root verbs. Thus, for verb roots such as *ghoattu/ghyttu* 'to get out of bed', the pluractional version typically refers to distribution across multiple participants (i.e., many different people getting out of bed at once), rather than to a repetitive or frequentative event. On the other hand, for verb roots such as *xowzhu/xiizha* 'to ache', the pluractional version refers to a durative event that lasts for a longer run-time than prototypically expected (i.e., aching for a while).[8]

Now, how can one account for these three different, though related, types of readings of pluractional verbs in Chechen? Yu (2003) suggests that the

---

[8] Kuhn and Aristodemo (2017) demonstrate that French Sign Language (LSF) has two pluractional morphemes: one involving repetition of the same sign with the same hand to indicate distribution over time, and another with alternation of the sign between the two hands to indicate distribution over participants.

semantics of the plural operator that expresses plural verbal events does not just map a singular entity into another garden-variety plural entity but rather specifically maps a singular entity into a mass event, similar to mass nouns like *rice, furniture, feedback, mail* or perhaps the coerced massified versions in English found with the suffix *-age* in constructions such as *I had serious acheage going on this morning* or *Adam's tea-drinkage was overboard today*. The terminology mass (as opposed to count) specifically refers to the fact that mass nouns are uncountable (e.g., *five furnitures, *six feedbacks, *seven acheages).

What's the evidence that this is truly a kind of 'mass event'? In the pluractional verb examples we have seen so far, one might have noticed, the number of event iterations is always left unspecified. This, as it turns out, is not accidental. Chechen prohibits the use of a pluractional verb when the exact number of repetitions is specified, as illustrated by the ungrammaticality of (39b):

(39)   a.   adama   takhan yttaza   chai melira.
             Adam.ERG today ten.times tea drink
             'Adam drank tea ten times today.'
    b.   *adama   takhan yttaza   chai miilira.
             Adam.ERG today ten.times tea drink-PLURACT
             'Adam drank tea ten times over again today.'

As Yu points out, there is no reason to think that pluractional verbs should be incompatible with the explicit mention of the number of iterations. However, as noted by Xrakovskij (1997), this incompatibility is observed cross-linguistically, a phenomenon found in English as well in frequentative verbal aspects:

(40)   John used to go fishing with his father (*four times).

Yu's suggestion is that the semantic operator responsible for verbal pluractionality in Chechen must yield an atelic event – an activity without a delimited endpoint. That is, verbal pluralization transforms a telic event (e.g., drinking a cup of tea, chasing a cow) into an atelic event – an activity repeated multiple times without a specific numeral quantity delimiting how many times it happened. When the verbal semantics are already that of a stative event (e.g., aching), the pluralization will yield a more prolonged situation than the canonical run-time of such an event. Finally, when the verbal semantics are of a 'semelfactive' action (e.g., an instantaneous event, such as waking up) and involve a plurality of subjects (e.g., family members), the massified event will be distributive, namely involving all of them waking up.[9]

---

[9] The specific implementation that Yu (2003) adopts in terms of event pluralization as a mass event finds a parallel in terms of the fact that in general in Chechen, there is an incompatibility between numeral marking and pluralization:

To summarize, Chechen demonstrates a clear case of verbal pluractionality, distinct from (and indeed, orthogonal to) root suppletion, though interestingly it has both. Root suppletion is a case of allomorphy determined by number features in the DP argument closest to the verb, as in (18), whereas pluractionality involves the semantic operation of turning a count event into a mass event. A mass event is the uncountably frequentative, distributive, or durative verbal equivalent of a mass noun. In the next and final section of this chapter, we turn to a deeper understanding of what exactly mass nouns are semantically, as informed by Dëne Sųłiné, a language with an underrepresented profile in mainstream linguistic theory, prior to recent work.

8.8 Mass and Count in Dëne Sųłiné

A highly influential proposal for the differences in noun phrase syntax and semantics, known as the Nominal Mapping Parameter, was advanced in Chierchia (1998) in a comparison of language types represented by Germanic vs. those represented by Mandarin Chinese. In the latter, Chierchia claimed that the extension of *all nouns* is mass, not count – even for nouns like *zhuozi* 'table', and as a result, a classifier is required in order to combine such nouns with numerals:

(41)   a.   *yi   zhuozi
                 one table
       b.   yi   zhang   zhuozi
                 one CL   table

Now, it is certainly interesting to propose a parametrization of the syntax–semantics mapping cross-linguistically within the domain of formal semantics, which for so long took cross-linguistic variation to be a matter of syntax and morphology, but not in the denotation of nouns. By claiming that Mandarin Chinese is a language in which all nouns are mass as deriving from more formal

---

(i)   a.   qwo   twop
                 three gun
                 'three guns'
       b.   *qwo tuepash
                 three gun-PL
                 'three guns'
       c.   massuo tuepash
                 all   gun-PL
                 'all guns'

This phenomenon of complementarity between numerals and pluralization is cross-linguistically recurrent, as found in languages such as Hungarian, Finnish, and Turkish; see Farkas and de Swart (2010) and Martí (2020) for discussion.

properties of how arguments and predicates are mapped, the idea is that (41b) requires the English equivalent of 'one piece of tablehood' to say "one table," even though *table* does not strike us as a typical granular/liquid/homogenous mass noun. For Chierchia, mass nouns cannot be pluralized because they are already plural.

According to Chierchia, the four properties of requiring classifiers for all nouns, the lack of plural marking on nouns, the generalized use of bare nouns for singular or plural reference, and the semantic property of all nouns being mass are all inherently related. Chierchia (1998) explicitly says about languages that lack plural marking and allow classifierless nouns in subject position, "Insofar as I know, languages of this sort are indeed unattested" (p. 358). Chierchia's position is the formalization of a long-standing tradition, starting from Greenberg (1972) and Sanches and Slobin (1973), that assumes that number inflection and numeral classifiers are in complementary distribution, both across languages and within a single language.

However, Wilhelm (2008) presents a thorough study of bare nouns in the Athapaskan language Dëne Sųłiné, spoken in the region of Cold Lake, Alberta, Canada. In this language, there is no singular–plural marking on nouns, nor any classifiers. What makes a noun a mass noun is not its lack of number-marking or requirement of a classifier but rather a semantic property known as *nonatomicity*. Atomicity of a noun means that it has minimal parts. Thus, if we choose something that satisfies the predicate *table*, smaller subparts of this thing do not satisfy the predicate *table*. In other words, "a table" picks out the minimal representative of tablehood. For nonatomic nouns such as *water*, whatever we call water has endless smaller subparts that will still be called *water*. This nonatomicity property is, in fact, what made the massified events (such as a blur of nonstop tea-drinkage) in Chechen noncountable: They did not have atomic parts to count up.

Thus, bare nouns in Dëne Sųłiné need not be interpreted as mass or as plural, though they can be, as in (42d–f):

(42) a. k'ásba nághiłnígh.
       chicken PERF-1SG.SUBJ-buy
       'I bought a chicken.'
   b. yeh hoghį?á.
       house LOC-PERF-SG round
       'There used to be a house there.'
   c. łį dëneyuaze the?áł.
       dog boy-DIM PERF-bite/chew
       'The dog bit the little boy.'
   d. dzé héłnágh.
       gum PERF-swallow
       'He swallowed the chewing gum.'

e. sas jíe   gheldel.
     bear berries PERF-consume.PL
     'The bear ate all the berries.'
  f. dzółxéł senádé.
     ball with IMPF-PL-play
     'They are playing with a ball/with balls.'

How, then, is plurality expressed? By overt use of numerals and quantifiers with the noun phrase, or via verbal morphology that expresses pluractionality (like Chechen) or suppletion for plural objects (like Hiaki):

(43) a. Larry ʔı̨łághe ʔejëre nághéłnígh.
        Larry one   bovine PERF-buy
        'Larry bought one cow.'
     b. Larry ʔejëre nádághéłnígh.
        Larry bovine DISTR-PERF-buy
        'Larry bought several cows/cattle.'

A similar pattern of verbal suppletion to disambiguate the number properties of bare nouns can be found in Maxakalí (Silva & Nevins, 2020):

(44) a. ixõg topaha.
        bird fly.SG
        'A/the bird flew.'
     b. ixõg kopuk.
        bird fly.PL
        '(The) birds flew.'
     c. tik te xapup putex.
        man ERG pig   kill.SG
        'The man killed the pig.'
     d. tik te xapup kix.
        man ERG pig   kill.PL
        'The man killed the pigs.'

As (43a) shows, in Dëne Sųłiné numerals combine directly with nouns, with no intermediation by classifiers. But not with mass nouns, as in (45a); these will require a measure or container:

(45) a. *sǫłághe bér
        five   meat
        'five meat'
     b. sǫłághe nedádhi bér
        five   pound   meat
        'five pounds of meat'

To summarize, in Dëne Sųłiné, count and mass nouns are not distinguished by their number-marking properties or by requiring a classifier but rather by the semantic property of atomicity, which for nonatomic mass nouns requires a measure or container.

What really makes Mandarin different may be not that 'all nouns are mass', but rather a much more restricted semantic parameter: the semantics of numerals themselves (see Krifka [1995] for an early version of this proposal). This idea is further developed by Sudo (2016) for Japanese, another numeral classifier language (where, indeed, numerals such as *sen* 'thousand' do not require classifers!). Indeed, as Wilhelm (2008) points out, one line of evidence that in classifier languages it is the numerals, not the nouns, that are 'deficient' (in the sense of requiring a classifier) is the fact that in such languages, classifiers form a constituent with the numerals rather than the nouns in terms of word order restrictions and prosody. Thus, the true cross-linguistic variation to be further explored is in the semantics of numerals, and in the properties that underlie nonatomicity in different types of nouns (including events such as the massified ones of Chechen, above). The grammatical encoding of number – whether it be through verbal suppletion, verbal pluractionality, numerals plus classifiers, or plural marking itself – is one of the most varied areas of all cross-linguistic variation, and our syntax–semantics models cannot restrict themselves to limited samples of a handful of nonminoritized languages if our aim is to develop non-brittle theories and truly challenge the view that English is as 'equally' representative of the human language faculty as any other language we choose to start from.

Further Reading

Additional discussion of pluractionality in Chechen and beyond may be found in Wood (2007). For evidence, even internal to Mandarin Chinese, that the language maintains a mass-count distinction independently of being a numeral classifier language, see Cheng and Sybesma (1999). Finally, while Sudo's (2016) idea is that numeral classifier languages like Japanese (or indeed Ch'ol, from Chapter 3; cf. Bale & Coon [2014]) employ classifiers to semantically support numerals that cannot stand alone, it is also conceivable that all languages have numeral classifiers but that they may be simply phonologically null (see Wągiel [2018] for a such proposal, as applied to Czech).

9 Conclusion

Towards Healthy Futures in the Language Sciences

> Prejudice is a burden that confuses the past, threatens the future, and renders the present inaccessible.
> – Maya Angelou

9.1 The Argument So Far

I have been the one to assemble these pages, but they tell a story that belongs to us all. Countless languages and language varieties are minoritized, marginalized, stigmatized, and even oppressed, for reasons that have nothing to do with their complexity, expressivity, cultural richness, or inherent scientific interest. The preceding chapters are but a few pieces of a jigsaw that I have collected and assembled, but the picture is one we as a field and as a species are continuing each day to build together. Within the two years I have spent writing this book, for example, the reality of the situation of the Uyghurs in China has drastically worsened by alarming proportions. Minoritization and oppression rages large for other peoples across the globe. A UNESCO report by Brenzinger et al. (2003) details that roughly ninety-seven percent of the world's people account for four percent of the world's languages, and thus that three percent of the world's population speak ninety-six percent of the world's languages.

Writing this book has been carried out with the goal of resonance with other concentric and overlapping circles of struggle against minoritization, whether politically and economically or within the canons of the academy itself. Even as academics that are part of larger, external institutional structures, we often unconsciously internalize biases that perpetuate the treatment of minoritized, indigenous, or signed languages as afterthoughts or addenda in our teaching as well.

Concern with language loss (endangered languages) is by now a well-known concern among linguists and the public at large, but the case of minoritized languages is partially distinct from endangered languages. There are minoritized languages that are not endangered per se but which continue to be underrepresented in the scientific canon. Take signed languages, which are not endangered but are rarely if ever included beyond cursory mention in phonology textbooks, or languages such as Zazaki Kurdish, which most of the general public does not know is an Indo-European language. More recently, scholars such as Tamburelli and Tosco (2021) have drawn attention to *contested* languages, such as Kashubian or Piedmontese in Europe – languages that are considered regional 'dialects' and hence of low sociolinguistic status and are thus increasingly marginalized sociopolitically as well as academically. As Hale (1992) points out, language loss and devalorization today is "part of a much larger process of loss of cultural and intellectual diversity, in which politically dominant languages and cultures simply overwhelm indigenous local languages and cultures" (p. 1). Part of this being overwhelmed, devalorized, and lost is reflected in the scientific community as well, where these cultures and languages are ignored, undervalued, or left aside in the formation of our shared understanding of the diversity and limits of human nature.

Speaker linguists (and signer linguists) are arguably fundamental to this continued effort for representative contributions to psychology and the language sciences. Basque, for example, is now one of the most well-represented languages studied in neurolinguistics, merely due to the presence of generations of highly trained speaker linguists, valorization of the importance of the language to scientific diversity, a few key players in laboratory leadership roles, and last but not least, government incentives for the study of minoritized languages. This last point is a policy issue. Large-scale thematic funding incentives in public science organizations such as the AHRC in England, CNPq in Brazil, the DfG in Germany, and the NSF in the United States (four of the largest global funders for language science research) should be providing incentives for the creation of large-scale laboratories for the neurolinguistic study of minoritized languages across these three continents.

I imagine that one cannot help but read the preceding fourteen or so case studies without feeling a twinge of activism, in terms of raising awareness about the need for greater inclusion of languages such as Ch'ol in Mexico, Kaingang in Brazil, or Xhosa in South Africa in today's cutting edge conferences, as staples of textbooks about irrefutable contributions to the completeness of linguistic theory and, indeed, to some of its more compelling moments of evolution as a scientific pursuit. Rice (2021) is one of many recent prominent voices calling for increased activism in our roles as linguists in securing continued rights, recognition, and representativity of languages of some of the world's *First Nations* – the communities that have been here (wherever 'here' is) for centuries before incursions of imperial, colonial, and globalizing waves completely upended local population dynamics.

9.2 On Unattested Chapters in This Version of This Book

Inspired by Borges' short story, 'The Library of Babel', I am aware that there are many parallel combinatorial possibilities that the universe might have reshuffled to yield a minimally different version of this same book with different case studies chosen instead. The choice of case studies that I have highlighted within this book has been designed to cover a typologically broad range of languages (from essentially every continent), phenomena across grammatical levels (syntax, morphology, semantics, phonology), and case studies that have, like an uncomfortable grain of sand inside an oyster shell, ended up truly generating a pearl through continued development and dialogue between previously unfamiliar linguistic facts and the limits and predictions of extant theories that have changed as a result. However, there are many other case studies one could have chosen as well. One extremely important case in the history of linguistic theory has been the importance of Berber syllabification for phonological theory (Dell & Elmedlaoui, 1985), where its syllabic consonants (italicized in words such as t*l*.bžt 'step-onto.2sg.perf' and t*r*.kst 'hide.2sg.perf') teach us that the syllabification algorithm in language works in a very particular way, by scanning an entire word first for its highest peaks and then proceeding successively downwards in the sonority hierarchy of consonants. Another case study to which I have not devoted a chapter, though I easily could have, involves the contribution of what are historically called creole languages (the results of forcibly imposed language contact), such as Haitian Creole, to understanding the 'factative effect' (Déchaine, 1991), whereby in a language without overt tense marking, the specificity of objects and inherent aspect of a predicate (such as 'sell a book' vs. 'like cats') leads to a default interpretation of tense as past or present. Ideally, books such as the present one can be but one set of collected case studies for extended efforts to continually reinforce and canonize the contribution of minoritized languages as recognized cornerstones of the development and evolution of linguistic theory.

Not every case of a confrontation between a minoritized language and extant theoretical models of linguistic structure has been covered in the preceding pages. The ones that have not made an appearance are of a few types, however. There are cases that I have not covered which, even though they represent genuine transformative moments between empirical discoveries and theory, have simply been beyond my scope as the person writing this book – but surely someone else, writing a parallel version of the same book, should and could describe them with their due presentation. Indeed, like almost everyone, I must admit that I inevitably have inherent limitations due to the lens and filter through which I view things, as much as I may yearn for panorama. The second set are cases that I contend that, challenging a theory alone without presenting a transformative solution that yields a change in that theory, do not qualify, though some day, of course, they might. The third set are ones that are extremely close to changing the theory right now and in a few years' time may indeed yield large-scale revisions to specific aspects of specific models.

In the preceding pages, we have seen in close-up detail that, by confrontation with novel empirical patterns from understudied and often undervalued languages, some of linguistic theory's major 'heroes' have been proven wrong in specific ways: Kaplan, Jakobson, Marantz, Chierchia, and Chomsky, to name a few, in terms of very specific theoretical postulates or aspects of the theory of possible human language structures. Crucially, all of these cases involved discrete aspects of theoretical claims about human language – for example, structures predicted to be impossible that turned out to actually exist. This is the way all science works: Specific theories – and not people – are what fall and are then reconstructed. It is important to point out, however, that there are also instances in which minoritized languages haven't (yet) changed linguistic theory.

The OVS word order of the South American language Hixkaryana (Derbyshire, 1977) has definitely changed inventories of language typology but hasn't really had a transformative effect on syntactic theory itself, as its direct impact on modeling is underconstrained by the data, and in fact can be analyzed in a range of ways (see, for example Kalin [2014]) without yet forcing specific changes to the theory of syntactic structure. In other words, Hixkaryana has not 'changed the theory' but has rather required reconsidering existing components of the word-order transformations that are generally available and an understanding of how they combine in this particular language. Alternatively, consider the claim that the Pirahã language lacks sentential recursion, made in Everett (2005). While the claim was based on a minoritized language (and indeed, to this day, the Pirahã people face a grim reality of minoritization, common throughout the Brazilian Amazon at present), it hasn't changed linguistic theory (at least not yet), as neither the evidence nor the proposed theoretical change were convincing enough to make any real difference. (In fact, work such as Rodrigues et al. [2018] and Sauerland [2018] cast serious empirical doubts on the claims about Pirahã lacking recursion). In all of the cases discussed above, linguistic theory has changed in dialogue with minoritized languages when specific aspects or cornerstones of the theory are rethought, reassembled, or removed. Everett's (2005) article was not concerned with any details of any specific linguistic theory or with framing specific theoretical ingredients that could be replaced as alternatives but was rather an attempt to obliterate the entire edifice itself, with all its results, models, and details – on the basis of either inconsistent or insufficient quantities and qualities of data. Productive dialogue between unfamiliar empirical patterns and linguistic theory requires attempts at mutual integration where the pieces do not fit, as opposed to outright nihilism with respect to the latter.

Conclusion: Towards Healthy Futures in the Language Sciences 167

Turning to a different case, the prosodic patterns of the Australian language Arrernte, as described by Breen and Pensalfini (1999) – who originally posited VC syllabification, but made clear that alternative analyses, if possible, were to be preferred – involve stress and reduplication, in which onset consonants contribute to syllable weight. In fact, the contribution of onset consonants to weight patterns including stress had been convincingly and clearly already argued for by Pirahã (Everett & Everett, 1984), in which voiceless onsets attract stress, and for English stress patterns by Davis (1988), in which obstruents attract secondary stress. In Topintzi and Nevins (2017), it was argued that the distribution of word-initial consonants, loanword phonology, and musicological evidence all point to CV syllabification for this language, with moraic onsets. In fact, Tabain (2004) looked for acoustic evidence of planned coarticulation and reduced variability in the production of CV vs. VC sequences in English and Arrernte but found that "It might be noted (contrary to our hypothesis) on the rare occasion results are significant for the Aboriginal data, it is the VC context which shows more variability than the CV context" (p. 185). Tabain (2009) then looked at articulatory kinematics, but the results showed no differences between patterns of English and Arrernte jaw movement. As Breen and Pensalfini (1999) stated, "Clearly, the more restrictive version of Universal Grammar, if tenable, is the best, so if there is a viable alternative to VC(C) syllabification for Arrernte, it should be preferred" (p. 10). Arrernte has thus far not changed the theory but has rather provided further evidence for an existing conjecture – moraic onsets. Nonetheless, for all of the three cases just mentioned, we must leave open the possibility that future investigations will in fact potentially lead to changes in linguistic theory. What seems crucial is the convergence from both directions of research: top-down (theoretical predictions) and bottom-up (empirically driven) and their constant interplay back and forth. Both components are equally important: seriously strong empirical evidence and well-formulated theoretical modifications. In sum, it is uncontroversial that studying these languages has been and will be interesting. But it is a far cry to say that they have, as of yet, yielded any significant changes in the nuts and bolts of linguistic theory in the sense that they have caused revisions to specific models of language structure.

Other cases of thorough study of minoritized languages forcing the revision of specific postulates within highly articulated, cross-linguistically accountable models of human language are no doubt waiting in the wings as I write this. A number of important efforts to intensively study minoritized language varieties are now underway, especially from what is called microcomparative work. There are rich results coming forth from microcomparative work of traditionally nonstandard and undervalued dialects of Europe (Andriani et al., 2022; de Mareüil et al., 2019; Barbiers et al., 2005), as well as their recontextualization in diaspora and heritage contexts (see Polinsky [2018]) for an overview), where one-way bilingualism, an operative force amongst minoritized languages, holds as well. Moreover, continued scientific attention to languages as spoken in diaspora and refugee contexts, and languages that have directly resulted from historical conditions of enslavement, will bear importance in establishing their grammatical validity, their neuropsychological processing, and their onward social and historical trajectories.

Increased focus on minoritized, heritage, refugee, and stigmatized dialects becomes especially urgent for policy, educational, and health-related decisions (for further discussion, see Hudley, Garraffa, and Nevins' (2022) podcast, in which bilingualism – often asymmetric bilingualism (or bidialectalism) – has direct communicative consequences for the people involved. In one example, Hudley et al. (2018) provide compelling arguments that speech–language pathologists in the United States have a pressing need for sociolinguistic and grammatical training with respect to African-American English for equitable assessment and treatment; the same conclusions and reasoning can doubtless be replicated in dozens of nations in which stigma and stereotypes about specific languages or language varieties exist. This is all the more important for the future of the language sciences, as it is currently the case that virtually no linguistic theory – either from formal linguistics or sociolinguistics – is present in the school curriculum of any of the world's to-be-citizens. As a result, some of the most fundamental discoveries that have been made about the biological and social nature of language are unknown to the general public, and given this lack of awareness, questions of language policy, educational inclusiveness, and critical thinking in terms of media reports on scientific results often operate in a thoroughly uninformed state. These concerns form part of a larger picture that will have to change.

9.3 The Value of Inclusivity, and Rethinking Aspects of Our Discipline

Consider search engines and everyday language automation tools. Bender (2019) observes that even the field of natural language processing research often treats English as a 'default proxy' for all languages, even though upon reflection, this practice (staying within one's linguistic comfort zone and privileging one particular language) is detrimental to any long-term goals of the field of NLP, alongside continuing to perpetuate inequalities in science and technology. Healthy futures ahead for minoritized languages include the commitment of us as language scientists to be as inclusive as possible in our teaching and in public engagement, resisting the comfort zone in which we simply take English as a stand-in representative of all human languages, when in fact many other languages provide equally compelling starting places for describing what we currently understand about the limits and possibilities of the language faculty. As Sanders et al. (2020) point out, "no matter how aware we might be of our language-based biases, if we do nothing to challenge or disrupt them, we will pass them on to our students, and the cycle will continue" (p. 3).

What would benefit linguistic theory (and the fields that indirectly depend on it) most directly in terms of the continued protagonism of minoritized languages within the canon, within the everyday nuts and bolts of the theoretical lynchpins, and within everyday classroom exemplification would obviously be more people who speak minoritized languages working within the fields of the language sciences. This has happened in increasing strides over the past four decades, but there haven't been enough conversations about the topic or the whys and hows of there being minority (and perhaps minoritized) numbers of speakers of minoritized languages within the field. Some important initial steps have been taken, such as the Linguistic Society of America's (2019) statement on race. However, our field lags behind that of *many* adjacent social sciences, in part, perhaps, because of the perception that linguistics is universalizing, colorblind, and humanist, and hence 'of course we're not a racist or biased field'. There are, however, by now quantitative statistics on representativity in higher academia (including, for example, the absence of linguistics programs at Historically Black Colleges and Universities) that reveal significant areas of shortcomings in diversifying the profession. Our everyday example sentences in linguistics, the empirical staple of the field, skewedly reflect a dominant white culture, far more than it does of minoritized races and ethnicities, often forgetting that "Who we hire, who we cite, and who we signal is a part of our field to our students and early career researchers has a large impact on its makeup. The shape of the world our example sentences convey to readers – students and active researchers alike – implicitly and sometimes explicitly sends powerful signals about who is welcome in our field and who is less so" (Kotek et al., 2021, p. 645).

Examples of unconscious perpetuation of racism aren't just about hiring, promotion, or graduate student recruitment and can even be found in the portrayal of conversations and canonical examples of populations in supposedly 'neutral' second-language learning textbooks (Anya, 2016), where 'only grammar is the concern' but, nonetheless, white supremacy, the native speaker construct, and other forms of normativity intrude; see Kubota (2002) on how 'a nice field like TESOL' is rife with everyday microaggressions against non-white scholars and students. Is it any wonder that students of color do not continue in the language sciences beyond, say French or Portuguese language-learning classes that already flunk any measure of inclusivity? Smitherman (2017) identifies one of the gravest areas of linguistic miseducation right in the language arts classrooms. These are uncomfortable truths to suddenly confront in the 2020s, but as Hudley et al. (2020b, p. e221) penetratingly observe, we currently face a discipline-wide failure to recognize that there is racism happening within linguistics as a field. This presumed colorblindness of academic subfields is now being widely revisited (Crenshaw et al., 2019) across disciplines, and we often forget or dismiss it as maybe an issue in other departments but not in 'ours', due to "the deeply entrenched societal ideology that positions racism as intentional and individual, rather than structural and often below the level of awareness of those who enact it" (Hill, 2008), as discussed by Hudley et al. (2020b, p. e212).

Numerous factors have led to the situation in which people whose identities are minoritized do not identify with the field of linguistics. Leonard (2020) calls attention to the fact that Native Americans continue to be the least represented within the discipline, in contrast to the extensive presence of Native American languages in linguistic scholarship. In part, this comes from what Hudley et al. (2020b) have diagnosed as narrow definitions of prestige, reward, and investment in research evaluation and "the constant policing of what counts as linguistics" (p. e221). The report in Silbiger and Stubler (2019) shows that unprofessional peer reviews within the publication process have disproportionately harmed underrepresented groups across STEM fields of academia. Gutiérrez et al. (2012) provide a range of case studies demonstrating the difficulties across every aspect of academia that women with minoritized identities face in careers, and Kilomba (2021) provides a particularly compelling personal narrative of the constant, daily, everyday uphill struggle that she faces as a Black woman in academia.

At the time of writing, there are not very many Kurdish, Maxakalí, Black ASL, or Hiaki-speaking linguists, and we should ask ourselves what might happen if this is to ever change significantly. In some places, such as Brazil, quota-based doctoral funding and admissions for indigenous, Deaf, and African-descent students have led to greater inclusivity in linguistics programs, and for me, it is an honor to be part of the supervision team for the first three Deaf doctoral students to be admitted to the linguistics program at the Federal University of Rio de Janeiro (while being aware that this kind of inclusivity ought to have started long ago). These changes in student populations must always be accompanied by changes in curriculum as well, a point carefully made by Baniwa (2013). As Kotek et al. (2021) observe, many aspects of the way the field is currently practiced affect "the kinds of research questions that are welcome, and the kinds of answers that we expect and ultimately adopt. Limiting access to the field inevitably leads to a reduced richness of ideas, research topics, approaches, and types of data collected, and more generally it limits the reach and breadth of our field. It is thus in everyone's interest to increase our field's inclusivity" (p. 654). How would the field of linguistics as it is practiced and structured as an academic discipline have to transform in order for more people from various racial groups to actively want to study, teach, and learn linguistics (Hudley et al., 2020a)? How can people from racially minoritized groups be empowered rather than isolated in linguistics? How can we signal that Black Minds Matter? How can we reverse the trend of countless talented, valuable, intelligent young people of color who decide to 'opt out' of postgraduate careers in academia (Beasley, 2011)? Relatedly, how can we overcome the difficulties in finding outlets for community-oriented scholarship (Montoya, 2020)?

9.4 When Minoritized Languages Change Linguists' Daily Work

In parallel, minoritized languages might require changes in linguists' daily work. Two colleagues of mine, who I hold extreme respect for as language activists, have deliberately left academia in order to leverage their linguistics training specifically by giving more time to serve community needs. I quote from Gabriella Hodge's remarks in Hodge, Jones, and Nevins, 2022 podcast, for example:

> I was tempted by academia for a while last year, but the job market and other factors such as audism and the difficulty of doing community engagement/social impact work makes it unattractive to me now. I don't want to spend my life teaching sign linguistics 101 to hearing nonsigning students who may never have anything to do with Deaf people beyond their degree. I feel my skills should be directed instead towards Deaf people. If you look at how energies from within and outside Deaf communities are directed, most of it is directed for hearing people: sign language classes, interpreter training, university courses, etcetera. These are important of course, but there also needs to be more focus on what Deaf people need and want. Currently, it is skewed.

We live in an age where content is abundantly available, be it from online videos, social media, e-books, or numerous other fora. Practical training and problem-solving should become more of a priority. Students in linguistics aren't taught even the basics of legal issues, safety and medical issues, or educational issues. As important as it is for people outside of linguistics to have basic knowledge of the discoveries of the field to avoid perilous language myths and their policy consequences, I contend that a healthier future for our field requires that students trained in the language sciences have required basic coverage and practical exercises in speech pathology and reading difficulties, legislational issues, scientific communication to the greater public, and/or native language pedagogy. As Kerry Jones observes in her interview in Hodge et al.'s podcast (2022) about work with the highly minoritized and endangered Khoesan populations of South Africa (see Jones, 2019),

> If the languages are protected in our constitution, they must show that an effort is being made to do so. The red tape with university finance departments is far too slow and complicated for urgent work. The academic system is littered with red tape and bureaucracy that hinders work that urgently needs to be done. I've had to go independent

to be able to do meaningful work. I do collaborate with universities, but I have to be practical in order to be more efficient and ethical in the way that I operate. The academic system gives very little real attention to ethics and fair exchange when it comes to this kind of work.

These are people who are leaving academia for the right reasons: They have seen that they can be more efficient outside of it in accomplishing goals of urgency and meaningfulness to the linguistic communities they work with. Field method courses must undergo reflexive steps towards decolonizing their traditions of approaching language data, as these courses often provide minimal time for students to learn about the epistemologies of their speaker-collaborators and indigenous research methodologies (Tsikewa, 2021) or the historical trauma that indigenous collaborators may experience in working on/with their own languages. Language archival data that we record with high-quality devices and metadata should be more focused on providing means that the speakers of these languages themselves can access in a meaningful way (Seyfeddinipur et al., 2019). As Rice (2006) emphasizes, truly collaborative research with indigenous communities must focus on relationships, reciprocity, respect, and responsibility.

For each of the studies I report in this book in which minoritized languages have directly benefitted theoretical linguistics, we might ask, how can theoretical linguists benefit these language communities in return? As Nora England makes clear within her contribution in Hale (1992), citing the words of Cojtií Cuxil (1990), "It is difficult in Guatemala for linguists to define themselves as neutral or apolitical, since they work on languages that are sentenced to death and officially demoted. The linguist who works on Mayan languages has the option of activism in favor of a new linguistic order in which equality in the rights of all the languages is made concrete" (p. 31; Cojtií Cuxil, p. 19). Projects related to indigenous participation and protagonism are underway across many countries as we speak, although not necessarily in the high-prestige institutions that are traditionally the centers of linguistic theory. In parallel, minoritized languages might require changes in linguists' daily work. Academic environments and funding agencies must continue to change and refocus to become more inclusive of minoritized linguists and the needs and priorities of historically colonized communities of speakers, as there currently is too "little 'bread and butter' for the speakers of these languages that linguists build their studies and careers on (DeGraff, 2020, p. e302). In a 2022 hiring interview in which I participated, the candidate remarked that he had not included his native speaker consultant as a coauthor on the high-prestige journal article for the sole reason that his doctoral advisors warned him about the importance of having singly authored publications for hiring and promotion. Among important voices envisioning a more equitable, symmetric role between linguists and the communities in which they make their careers, Czaykowksa-Higgins (2009) recognizes the importance of fieldwork and community-based language research that is done for the language communities, where the linguist may have the role of a consultant for an agenda defined by the community, and not solely by the values dictated in the system of academic hiring, promotion, and tenure.

Gerdts (1998) enumerates ways that linguists can serve communities, including training teachers and helping teach the language, serving as mediators between speakers and universities, acting as advocates for native language programs at universities, and serving as expert witnesses on matters involving language, including place names for land claims, ethnobiology for land use studies, and labels and translations for museum exhibits. Being able to secure land rights for the traditional communities that inhabited it regions long before colonial invasions, through means of linguistic arguments in the legal arena, is one of the highest ambitions we might all yearn towards, as is guaranteeing accurate subtitling and descriptions in documentaries, museum exhibits, and even the development of educational materials as seemingly easy as a coloring book with linguistically informed categories and vocabulary. Actions like these have the potential to benefit very young people in linguistically minoritized communities in relatively straightforward ways, so that our daily interactional work is not just limited to an audience of the eighteen to twenty-five-year-olds in university classrooms. The past years have witnessed a great development of collaborative linguistic fieldwork and models of empowerment for native speakers in the community (Yamada, 2007), along with a growth in the number of responsibilities that linguists can take on outside of the linguistic classroom and linguistic journal model that is routinely considered the core of the profession, such as working in language centers and developing community-oriented exhibitions (Truscott, 2014) or contributing to national census-type indices of linguistic diversity with accurate resources about the linguistic landscapes in indigenous communities (Galucio et al., 2018).

While I have relied in the introductory chapter on the importance of language scientists and the social sciences more generally in stepping outside of our comfort zone in terms of the languages that are spoken within our university classroom, I contend that our discipline will have healthier futures once we step more outside of the classroom itself. Minoritization of languagues, and indeed minoritization of people's very identities, forms part of a very large and often tragically repetitive historical pattern. But we as language scientists, psychologists, educators, health professionals, legal and judicial resources, or policymakers needn't replicate these same lines in our empirical bases for the most accurate theories possible and the most accurate application of linguistic expertise to real-world concerns as well.

Paraphrasing Saussure (1916), the task of the linguist is to denounce and dispel the myriad of absurd ideas, fictions, and prejudices that arise in the domain of language. I believe that the field has had a modicum of success over the past three decades or so and that minoritized languages have become protagonists within this narrative. You all can provide the forthcoming episodes, and I am excited at the prospects of keeping in touch and hear about your efforts, be they within academic channels or without them.

Bibliography

Abbott, Edwin A. 1884. *Flatland: A Romance of Many Dimensions*. London: Seeley & Co.
Alok, Deepak, and Mark Baker. 2018. On the mechanics (syntax) of indexical shift: Evidence from allocutive agreement in Magahi. Ms., New Brunswick: Rutgers University.
Alsina, Alex, and Sam Mchombo. 1990. The syntax of applicatives in Chichewa: Problems for a theta-theoretic asymmetry. *Natural Language and Linguistic Theory* 8:493–506.
Anagnostopoulou, Elena,. 2003. *The Syntax of Ditransitives*. Berlin: Mouton de Gruyter.
Anand, Pranav. 2006. De de se. Unpublished doctoral Dissertation, Cambridge, MA: MIT.
Anand, Pranav, and Andrew Nevins. 2004. Shifty operators in changing contexts. In *Proceedings of SALT 14* 20–37.
Anderson, Stephen R. 1976. Nasal consonants and the internal structure of segments. *Language* 52:326–344.
Anderson, Stephen R. 1977. On mechanisms by which languages become ergative. In Charles N. Li, ed. *Mechanisms of Syntactic Change*. Austin: University of Texas Press, pp. 1–23.
Andriani, Luigi, Jan Casalicchio, Franceso Ciconte, Roberta D'Alessandro, Alberto Frasson, Brechje Van Osch, Luana Sorgini, and Silvia Terenghi. 2022. Documenting Italo-Romance minority languages in the Americas: Problems and tentative solutions. In Matt Coler and Andrew Nevins, eds., *Contemporary Research in Minority and Diaspora Languages of Europe*. Berlin: Language Science Press, ch. 2.
Anya, Uju. 2016. *Racialized Identities in Second Language Learning: Speaking Blackness in Brazil*. New York: Routledge.
Apontes, Selmo. 2018. Descrição gramatical do oro waram, variante wari' norte. Doctoral dissertation, Belo Horizonte: Federal University of Minas Gerais.
Arregi, Karlos, and Andrew Nevins. 2012. *Morphotactics: Basque Auxiliaries and the Structure of Spellout*. Dordrecht: Springer.
Austin, Peter, and Joan Bresnan. 1996. Non-configurationality in Australian Aboriginal languages. *Natural Language and Linguistic Theory* 14:215–268.
Baerman, Matthew. 2014. Suppletive kin term paradigms in the languages of New Guinea. *Linguistic Typology* 18:413–448.
Baertsch, Karen, and Stuart Davis. 2003. The split margin approach to syllable structure. *ZAS Papers in Linguistics* 32:1–14.

Baker, Mark. 1988. Theta theory and the syntax of applicatives in Chichewa. *Natural Language and Linguistic Theory* 6:353–389.
Baker, Mark, Ken Safir, and Justine Sikuku. 2013. Complex anaphora in Lubukusu. In Ọlanike Ọla Orie and Karen W. Sanders, eds., *Selected Proceedings of the 43rd Annual Conference on African Linguistics*. Somerville, MA: Cascadilla Press, pp. 196–206.
Baker, Mark C. 1991. On the relation of serialization to verb extensions. In *Serial Verbs: Grammatical, Comparative and Cognitive Approaches*. Amsterdam/Philadelphia: John Benjamins.
   1996. *The Polysynthesis Parameter*. New York/Oxford: Oxford University Press.
   2014. On dependent ergative case (in Shipibo) and its derivation by phase. *Linguistic Inquiry* 45.3:341–379.
Baker, Mark C., and Chris Collins. 2006. Linkers and the Internal Structure of vP. *Natural Language and Linguistic Theory* 24:307–354.
Bale, Alan, and Jessica Coon. 2014. Classifiers are for numerals, not for nouns: Consequences for the mass/count distinction. *Linguistic Inquiry* 45:695–707.
Baniwa, Gersem. 2013. Lei das Cotas e os povos indígenas: mais um desafio para a diversidade. *Cadernos de Pensamento Crítico Latino-Americano*, 34:18–21.
Barbiers, Sief, Hans Bennis, Magda Devos, Gunther de Vogelaer, and Margreet van der Ham. 2005. *Syntactic Atlas of the Dutch Dialects (SAND), Volume 1*. Amsterdam: Amsterdam University Press.
Battison, Robbin. 1974. Phonological deletion in American Sign Language. *Sign Language Studies* 5:1–19.
   1978. *Lexical Borrowing in American Sign Language*. Silver Spring: Linstok Press.
Battison, Robbin, Harry Markowicz, and James Woodward. 1973. A good rule of thumb: Variable phonology in American Sign Language. In Ralph W. Fasold and Roger W. Shuy, eds., *New Ways of Analyzing Variation II*. Washington, DC: Georgetown University Press, pp. 291–302.
Baynton, Douglas C. 1996. *Forbidden Signs: American Culture and the Campaign against Sign Language*. Chicago: University of Chicago Press.
Beasley, Maya. 2011. *Opting Out: Losing the Potential of America's Young Black Elite*. Chicago: University of Chicago Press.
Beck, Sigrid, Sveta Krasikova, Daniel Fleischer, Remus Gergel, Stefan Hofstetter, Christiane Savelsberg, John Vanderelst, and Elisabeth Villalta. 2009. Crosslinguistic variation in comparison constructions. *Linguistic Variation Yearbook* 9:1–66.
Bender, Emily. 2019. English isn't generic for language, despite what NLP papers might lead you to believe. *Symposium on Data Science & Statistics*, Bellevue, WA, May 30.
Bhatia, Archna, Elabbas Benmamoun, and Maria Polinsky. 2009. Closest conjunct agreement in head final languages. *Linguistic Variation Yearbook* 9:67–88.
Bhatt, Rajesh, and Martin Walkow. 2013. Locating agreement in grammar: An argument from agreement in conjunctions. *Natural Language and Linguistic Theory* 31: 951–1013.
Blevins, Juliette. 1993. The nature of constraints on the nondominant hand in ASL. In Geoffrey R. Coulter, ed., *Current Issues in ASL Phonology*. New York: Academic Press, pp. 43–62.
Bobaljik, Jonathan David. 2012. *Universals in Comparative Morphology: Suppletion, Superlatives, and the Structure of Words*. Cambridge, MA: MIT Press.

Bock, K., and Carol Miller. 1991. Broken agreement. *Cognitive Psychology* 23:45–93.

Booker, Karen. 1982. Number suppletion in North American Indian languages. *Kansas Working Papers in Linguistics* 7:15–29.

Booth, Katie. 2021. *The Invention of Miracles: Language, Power, and Alexander Graham Bell's Quest to End Deafness*. New York: Simon and Schuster.

Borer, Hagit. 2014. Wherefore roots? *Theoretical Linguistics* 40:343–359.

Bošković, Željko. 2009. Unifying first and last conjunct agreement. *Natural Language and Linguistic Theory* 27:455–496.

Boyes-Braem, P. 1973. The Acquisition of Handshape in American Sign Language. Ms., La Jolla, CA: The Salk Institute.

Breen, Gavan, and Rob Pensalfini. 1999. Arrernte: A language with no syllable onsets. *Linguistic Inquiry* 30:1–25.

Brennan, Mary. 1992. The Visual World of BSL: An Introduction. In David Brien, ed., *Dictionary of British Sign Language/English*. London: Faber & Faber, pp. 1–133.

Brentari, Diane. 1998. *A Prosodic Model of Sign Language Phonology*. Cambridge, MA: MIT Press.

Brentari, Diane, and John A. Goldsmith. 1993. Secondary licensing and the nondominant hand in ASL phonology. In Geoffrey Coulter, ed., *Phonetics and Phonology 3: Current Issues in ASL Phonology*. San Diego, Academic Press, pp. 19–41.

Brentari, Diane, and Carol Padden. 2001. Native and foreign vocabulary in American Sign Language: A lexicon with multiple origins. In Diane Brentari, ed., *Foreign Vocabulary in Sign languages: A Cross-Linguistic Investigation of Word Formation*. Mahwah, NJ: Lawrence Erlbaum Associates, pp. 87–119.

Brenzinger, Matthias, Arienne M. Dwyer, Tjeerd de Graaf, Colette Grinevald, Michael Krauss, Osahito Miyaoka, Nicholas Ostler, Osamu Sakiyama, María E. Villalón, Akira Y. Yamamoto, and Ofelia Zepeda. 2003. Language vitality and endangerment. Document submitted to the International Expert Meeting on UNESCO Programme Safeguarding of Endangered Languages, Paris, March 10–12. www.unesco.org/culture/ich/doc/src/00120-EN.pdf.

Bresnan, Joan, and Lioba Moshi. 1990. Object asymmetries in comparative Bantu syntax. *Linguistic Inquiry* 21:147–185.

Camargo-Souza, Livia. 2020. Locality domains for number-based suppletion: Evidence from Yawanawa. Ms., New Brunswick: Rutgers University.

Carochi, Horacio. 1645. *Arte de la lengua mexicana*. Mexico City: Juan Ruyz.

Carstens, Vicki. 1991. The morphology and syntax of determiner phrases in Kiswahili. Doctoral dissertation, Los Angeles: University of California Los Angeles.

2019. Noun class, gender, and the workings of Agree: Evidence from agreement with conjoined subjects in Xhosa. Ms., Storrs: University of Connecticut.

Cheek, Adrianne, Kearsy Cormier, Ann Repp, and Richard P. Meier. 2001. Prelinguistic gesture predicts mastery and error in the production of early signs. *Language* 77.2:292–293.

Cheng, Lisa, and Rint Sybesma. 1999. Bare and not-so-bare nouns and the structure of NP. *Linguistic Inquiry* 30:509–542.

Chierchia, Gennaro. 1998. Reference to kinds across languages. *Natural Language Semantics* 6:339–405.

Choi, Incheol, Richard E. Nisbett, and Ara Norenzayan. 1999. Causal attribution across cultures: Variation and universality. *Psychological Bulletin* 125:1:47–61.

Chomsky, Noam. 1957. *Syntactic Structures*. The Hague: Mouton.
    1975. *Reflections on Language*. New York: Pantheon.
    1977. On wh-movement. In Peter W. Culicover, Thomas Wasow, and Adrian Akmajian, eds., *Formal Syntax*, New York: Academic Press, pp. 71–132.
Chomsky, Noam, and Morris Halle. 1968. *The Sound Pattern of English*. New York: Harper and Row.
Cinque, Guglielmo. 1999. *Adverbs and Functional Heads*. New York: Oxford University Press.
Clements, George N. 1975. The logophoric pronoun in Ewe: Its role in discourse. *Journal of West African Languages* 10:141–177.
Cojtí Cuxil, Demetrio. 1990. Lingüística e idiomas Mayas en Guatemala. In Nora C. England and Stephen R. Elliot, eds., *Lecturas sobre la lingüística Maya*. Guatemala City: Centro de Investigaciones Regionales de Mesoamerica, pp. 1–25.
Comrie, Bernard. 1973. The ergative: Variations on a theme. *Lingua* 32:239–253.
Connell, Bruce. 1994. The structure of labial-velar stops. *Journal of Phonetics* 22: 441–476.
Coon, Jessica. 2010. Rethinking split ergativity in Chol. *International Journal of American Linguistics* 76:207–253.
    2020. The linguistics of *Arrival*: Heptapods, field linguistics, and Universal Grammar. In Jeffrey Punske, Amy Fountain, and Nathan Sanders, eds., *Language Invention for Linguistics Pedagogy*. Oxford: Oxford University Press.
Corbett, Greville G. 1983. *Hierarchies, Targets and Controllers: Agreement Patterns in Slavic*. London: Croom Helm.
    2000. *Number*. Cambridge: Cambridge University Press.
Corbett, Greville G., and Alfred D. Mtenje. 1987. Gender agreement in Chichewa. *Studies in African Linguistics* 18:1–38.
Corver, Norbert, and Henk van Riemsdijk. 2001. *Semi-Lexical Categories: The Content of Function Words and the Function of Content Words*. Berlin: Mouton de Gruyter.
Crasborn, Onno. 1995. Articulatory symmetry in two-handed signs. Master's thesis, Nijmegen: University of Nijmegen.
    2011. The other hand in sign language phonology. In Marc van Oostendorp, Colin Ewen and Elizabeth Hume, eds., *The Blackwell Companion to Phonology*, pp. 223–240.
Crenshaw, Kimberlé Williams, Luke Charles Harris, Daniel Martinez HoSang, and George Lipsitz. 2019. *Seeing Race Again: Countering Colorblindness across the Disciplines*. Oakland: University of California Press.
Croneberg, C. 1965. Sign language dialects. In William C. Stokoe, Dorothy C. Casterline and Carl G. Croneberg, eds., *A Dictionary of American Sign Language on Linguistic Principles*. Silver Springs, MD: Linstok Press, pp. 313–319.
Cuervo, Cristina. 2003. Datives at large. Doctoral dissertation, Cambridge, MA: MIT.
Czaykowksa-Higgins, Ewa. 2009. Research models, community engagement, and linguistic fieldwork: Reflections on working within Canadian Indigenous communities. *Language Documentation & Conservation* 3.1:15–50.
Dahl, Östen. 1990. Standard Average European as an exotic language. In Johannes Bechert, Giuliano Bernini, and Claude Buridant, eds., *Toward a Typology of European Languages*. Berlin: De Gruyter Mouton, pp. 3–8.
Davis, Stuart. 1988. Syllable onsets as a factor in stress rules. *Phonology* 5:1–19.

Deal, Amy Rose. 2020. *A Theory of Indexical Shift*. Cambridge, MA: MIT Press.
Déchaine, Rose-Marie. 1991. Bare sentences. In *Proceedings of SALT 1* 31–50.
DeGraff, Michel. 2020. Toward racial justice in linguistics: The case of Creole studies (Response to Charity Hudley et al.). *Language* 96.4:e292–e306.
Dell, François, and Mohamed Elmedlaoui. 1985. Syllabic Consonants and Syllabification in Imdlawn Tashlhiyt Berber. *Journal of African Languages and Linguistics* 7.2:105–130.
Derbyshire, Desmond C. 1977. Word order universals and the existence of OVS languages. *Linguistic Inquiry* 8.3:590–599.
Dixon, Robert M. W. 1979. Ergativity. *Language* 55:59–138.
  1994. *Ergativity*. Cambridge: Cambridge University Press.
Dresher, B. Elan. 2009. *The Contrastive Hierarchy in Phonology*. Cambridge: Cambridge University Press.
Eccarius, Petra, and Diane Brentari. 2007. Symmetry and dominance: A cross-linguistic study of signs and classifier constructions. *Lingua* 117:1169–1201.
Edwards, Terra, and Diane Brentari. 2020. Feeling phonology: The conventionalization of phonology in Protactile communities in the United States. *Language* 96.4:819–840.
Embick, David, and Morris Halle. 2005. On the status of stems in morphological theory. In Twan Geerts, Ivo van Ginneken and Haike Jacobs, eds., *Romance Languages and Linguistic Theory 2003*. Amsterdam: John Benjamins, pp. 59–88.
Emonds, Joseph Embley, and Jan Terje Faarlund. 2014. *English: The Language of the Vikings*. Olomouc: Palacký University.
England, Nora C. 2007. The influence of Mayan-speaking linguists on the state of Mayan linguistics. In Peter K. Austin and Andrew Simpson, eds., *Linguistiche Berichte Sonderheft 14: Endangered Languages*. Hamburg: Helmut Buske Verlag, pp. 93–111.
Etxepare, Ricardo, and Aritz Irurtzun. 2021. Gravettian hand stencils as sign language formatives. *Philosophical Transactions of the Royal Society B* 376:20200205.
Everett, Dan, and Keren Everett. 1984. On the relevance of syllable onsets to stress placement. *Linguistic Inquiry* 15:1–25.
Everett, Daniel. 2005. Cultural Constraints on Grammar and Cognition in Pirahã. *Current Anthropology*. 46.4:640–641.
Farkas, Donka, and Henriëtte de Swart. 2010. The semantics and pragmatics of plurals. *Semantics and Pragmatics* 3.6:1–54.
Foley, William, and Robert Van Valin. 1984. *Functional Syntax and Universal Grammar*. Cambridge: Cambridge University Press.
Foppolo, Francesca, and Adrian Staub. 2020. The puzzle of number agreement with disjunction. *Cognition* 198:104–161.
Frishberg, Nancy. 1975. Arbitrariness and iconicity: Historical change in American Sign Language. *Language* 51.3:696–719.
Galeano, Eduardo. 1997. *Open Veins of Latin America: Five Centuries of the Pillage of a Continent*. New York: NYU Press.
Galucio, Ana Vilacy, Denny Moore, and Hein van der Voort. 2018. O patrimônio linguístico do Brasil: novas perspectivas e abordagens no planejamento e gestão de uma política da diversidade linguística. *Revista do Patrimônio Histórico e Artístico Nacional* 38:194–219.

Gary, Judith, and Edward Keenan. 1977. On collapsing grammatical relations in universal grammar. In Peter Cole and Jerrold Sadock, eds., *Grammatical Relations (Syntax and Semantics 8)*. New York: Academic Press, pp. 149–188.

Georgi, Doreen. 2012. A relativized probing approach to person encoding in local scenarios. *Linguistic Variation* 12, 153–210.

Geraci, Carlo. 2014. Spatial syntax in your hands. In *Proceedings of NELS 44*, 123–134.

Gerdts, Donna. 1998. Beyond expertise: The role of the linguist in language revitalization programs. In Nicholas Ostler, ed., *Endangered Languages: What Role for the Specialist? Proceedings of Second Foundation for Endangered Languages Conference*. Bath, England: Foundation for Endangered Languages, pp. 13–22.

Gold, Jana Willer, Boban Arsenijević, Mia Batinić, Michael Becker, Nermina Čordalija, Marijana Kresić, Nedžad Leko, Franc Lanko Marušič, Tanja Milićev, Nataša Milićević, Ivana Mitić, Anita Peti-Stantić, Branimir Stanković, Tina Šuligoj, Jelena Tušek, and Andrew Nevins. 2018. When linearity prevails over hierarchy in syntax. *Proceedings of the National Academy of Sciences* 115.3:495–500.

Greenberg, Joseph. 1963. Some universals of grammar with particular reference to the meaning of elements. In Joseph Greenberg, ed., *Universals of Language*. Cambridge, MA: MIT Press, pp. 73–113.

Greenberg, Joseph. 1972. Numerical classifiers and substantival number: Problems in the genesis of a linguistic type. *Stanford Working Papers on Language Universals* 9:1–39.

Gu, Shengyun. 2018. The feature system of handshapes and phonological processes in Shanghai Sign Language. Doctoral dissertation, Shanghai: East China Normal University.

Gutiérrez Sánchez, Pedro. 2014. Las clases de verbos intransitivos y el alineamiento agentivo en el Chol de Tila, Chiapas. Master's thesis, Mexico City: CIESAS.

Gutiérrez, Gabriella y Muhs, Yolanda Flores Niemann, Carmen G. González, and Angela P. Harris. 2012. *Presumed Incompetent: The Intersections of Race and Class for Women in Academia*. Logan: Utah State University Press.

Hale, Ken. 1983. Warlpiri and the grammar of nonconfigurational languages. *Natural Language and Linguistic Theory* 1:5–47.

1992. On endangered languages and the safeguarding of diversity. *Language* 68.1:1–3.

Hale, Kenneth. 1973. Person marking in Warlbiri. In Stephen Anderson and Paul Kiparsky, eds., *A Festschrift for Morris Halle*. New York: Holt, Rinehart and Winston, pp. 308–344.

Hale, Kenneth L. 1967. Review of *Hidatsa Syntax* by G. H. Matthews. *International Journal of American Linguistics* 33.4:329–341.

Hale, Kenneth, Laverne Masayesva Jeanne, and Paula M. Pranka. 1991. On suppletion, selection, and agreement. In Carol Georgopoulos and Roberta Ishihara, eds., *Interdisciplinary Approaches to Language: Essays in Honor of S.-Y. Kuroda*. Dordrecht: Kluwer Academic Publishers, pp. 255–271.

Halle, Morris. 1997. Impoverishment and fission. In Benjamin Bruening, Yoonjung Kang, and Martha McGinnis, eds., *PF: Papers at the Interface*. Cambridge, MA: MIT Working Papers in Linguistics, pp. 425–450.

Harbour, Daniel. 2020. Frankenduals: Their typology, structure, and significance. *Language* 96:60–93.

Harley, Heidi. 2009. A morphosyntactic account of the 'Latinate' ban on dative shift in English. Talk delivered at UCSC, May 15. Available at: https://dingo.sbs.arizona.edu/~hharley/PDFs/2009-05-15UCSCExhibitHandout.pdf.

2014. On the identity of roots. *Theoretical Linguistics* 40:225–276.

Heim, Irene, and Angelika Kratzer. 1998. *Semantics in Generative Grammar*. Oxford: Blackwell Publishers.

Henderson, Brent. 2018. Bantu applicatives and Chimiini instrumentals. In Augustine Agwuele and Adams Bodomo, eds., *The Routledge Handbook of African Linguistics*. Abingdon: Routledge, pp. 262–280.

Henrich, Joseph, Steven J. Heine, and Ara Norenzayan. 2010. The weirdest people in the world? *Behavioral and Brain Sciences* 33:61–83.

Herbert, Robert K. 1986. *Language Universals, Markedness Theory, and Natural Phonetic Processes*. Berlin: Mouton de Gruyter.

Hickok, Gregory, Mark Kritchevsky, Ursula Bellugi, and Edward S. Klima. 1996. The role of the left frontal operculum in sign language aphasia. *Neurocase* 2:373–380.

Hill, Jane H. 2008. *The Everyday Language of White Racism*. Malden, MA: Wiley-Blackwell.

Hill, Joseph C. 2021. Black ASL. www.josephchill.com/black-asl.

Hockett, Charles. 1960. The origin of speech. *Scientific American* 203:88–97.

Hodge, Gabriella, Kerry Jones, and Andrew Nevins. 2022. Refocusing the priorities of academic linguists: a discussion. Podcast in preparation.

Holisky, Dee Ann. 1987. The case of the intransitive subject in Tsova-Tush (Batsbi). *Lingua* 71:103–132.

Hudley, Anne H. Charity, Maria Garraffa, and Andrew Nevins. 2022. Refocusing the priorities of academic linguists: a discussion. Podcast in preparation.

Hudley, Anne H. Charity, Christine Mallinson, and Mary Bucholtz. 2020a. From theory to action: Working collectively toward a more antiracist linguistics (Response to commentators). *Language* 96.4:e307–e319.

2020b. Toward racial justice in linguistics: interdisciplinary insights into theorizing race in the discipline and diversifying the profession. *Language* 96.4:e200–e235.

Hudley, Anne H. Charity, Christine Mallinson, Kenay Sudler, and Mackenzie Fama. 2018. The sociolinguistically trained speech-language pathologist: Using knowledge of African American English to aid and empower African American clientele. *Perspectives of the ASHA Special Interest Groups* 3.1:118–131.

van der Hulst, Harry. 1996. Acquisitional evidence for the phonological composition of handshape. In Charlotte Koster and Frank Wijnen, eds., *Proceedings of Gala*. Munich: Lincom Europa, pp. 39–56.

Humboldt, Wilhelm von. 1836. *Über die Verschiedenheit des menschlichen Sprachbaues*. Berlin: Die Druckerei der Königlichen Akademie der Wissenschaften.

Hyman, Larry M. 1976. Phonologization. In Alphonse Juilland, ed., *Linguistic Studies offered to Joseph Greenberg*. Saratoga, CA: Anma Libri, pp. 407–418.

Iverson, Gregory K., and Joseph C. Salmons. 2007. Domains and directionality in the evolution of German final fortition. *Phonology* 24.1:121–145.

Jakobson, Roman. 1941. *Child Language, Aphasia and Phonological Universals*. The Hague; Mouton (originally published as *Kindersprache, Aphasie und allgemeine Lautgesetze*).

1962. Why "mama" and "papa"? In Roman Jakobson, ed., *Phonological Studies (Selected Writings, Vol. 2)*. The Hague: Mouton, pp. 538–545.

Jelinek, Eloise. 1984. Empty categories, case, and configurationality. *Natural Language and Linguistic Theory* 2:39–76.

Jeong, Youngmi. 2007. *Applicatives: Structure and Interpretation from a Minimalist Perspective*. Amsterdam: John Benjamins.

Jespersen, Otto. 1913/1961. *A Modern English Grammar on Historical Principles*. Copenhagen: Munksgaard/London: George Allen & Unwin.

Johannessen, Janne Bondi. 1998. *Coordination*. New York: Oxford University Press.

Johnson, Charlene A. 2014. Articulation of deaf and hearing spaces using deaf space design guidelines. Master's thesis, Albuquerque: University of New Mexico.

Johnson, Kimberly. 2021. Suppletion in a three-way number system: Evidence from Creek. *Linguistic Inquiry*. Available at: https://doi.org/10.1162/ling_a_00429

Johnston, Trevor, and Adam C. Schembri. 1999. On defining lexeme in a signed language. *Sign Language & Linguistics* 2:115–185.

Johnston, Trevor, and Adam C. Schembri. 1999. *Australian Sign Language (Auslan): An Introduction to Sign Language Linguistics*. Cambridge: Cambridge University Press.

Jones, Kerry. 2019. Contemporary Khoesan languages of South Africa. *Critical Arts* 33:55–73.

Kalin, Laura. 2014. The syntax of OVS word order in Hixkaryana. *Natural Language and Linguistic Theory* 32:1089–1104.

Kaplan, David. 1977. Demonstratives. In Joseph Almog, John Perry and Howard Wettstein, eds., *Themes from Kaplan (1989)*. Oxford: Oxford University Press, pp. 481–564.

Kasbarian, J.-M. 1997. Langue minorée et langue minoritaire. In Marie-Louise Moreau, ed., *Sociolinguistique, concepts de base*. Bruxelles: Mardaga, pp. 185–188.

Kayambazinthu, Edrinnie. 1998. The language planning situation in Malawi. *Journal of Multilingual and Multicultural Development* 19.5:369–439.

Kayne, Richard S. 1994. *The Antisymmetry of Syntax*. Cambridge, MA: MIT Press.

Kelso, J. A., Dan L. Southard, and David Goodman. 1979. On the nature of human interlimb coordination. *Science* 203:1029–1031.

Kenstowicz, Michael. 2004. *Studies in Zazaki Grammar*. Cambridge, MA: MIT Working Papers on Endangered and Less Familiar Languages.

Keyser, Samuel Jay. 2011. Reversals in Poe and Stevens. *Wallace Stevens Journal* 35:224–239.

Keyser, Samuel Jay, and Kenneth Noble Stevens. 2006. Enhancement and overlap in the speech chain. *Language* 82:33–63.

Kilomba, Grada. 2021. *Plantation Memories: Episodes of Everyday Racism*. Toronto: Between the Lines.

Kimenyi, Alexandre. 1980. A Relational Grammar of Kinyarwanda. Doctoral dissertation, Berkeley, CA: University of California.

Kiparsky, Paul. 1982. Word formation and the Lexicon. In Frances Ingemann, ed., *Mid-America Linguistics Conference*. Lawrence: University of Kansas, pp. 3–29.

1995. Indo-European origins of Germanic syntax. In Ian Roberts and Adrian Battye, eds., *Clause Structure and Language Change, 1995*. Oxford: Oxford University Press, pp. 140–169.

Klima, Edward, and Ursula Bellugi. 1979. *The Signs of Language*. Cambridge, MA: Harvard University Press.

van der Kooij, Els. 2002. Phonological categories in Sign Language of the Netherlands: Phonetic implementation and iconic motivation. Doctoral dissertation, Leiden: University of Leiden.

Kotek, Hadas, Rikker Dockum, Sarah Babinski, and Christopher Geissler. 2021. Gender bias and stereotypes in linguistic example sentences. *Language* 97.4:653–677.

Krifka, Manfred. 1995. Common nouns: A contrastive analysis of English and Chinese. In *The Generic Book*. Chicago: University of Chicago Press, pp. 398–411.

2007. Functional similarities between bimanual coordination and topic/comment structure. *Interdisciplinary Studies on Information Structure* 8:61–96.

Kroeber, A. L. 1958. Sign Language Inquiry. *International Journal of American Linguistics* 24.1:1–19.

Kubota, Ryuko. 2002. The author responds: (Un)raveling racism in a nice field like TESOL. *TESOL Quarterly* 36.1:84–92.

Kuhn, Jeremy, and Valentina Aristodemo. 2017. Pluractionality, iconicity, and scope in French Sign Language. *Semantics and Pragmatics* 10.6:1–49.

Kurlansky, Mark. 1999. *The Basque History of the World*. New York: Walker and Company.

Kusters, Annelies. 2015. *Deaf Space in Adamorobe: An Ethnographic Study of a Village in Ghana*. Washington, DC: Gallaudet University Press.

Labov, William. 1963. The social motivation of a sound change. *Word* 19.3:273–309.

1966. *The Social Stratification of (r) in New York City Department Stores*. Washington, DC: Center for Applied Linguistics.

Ladefoged, Peter. 1975. *A Course in Phonetics*. New York: Harcourt Brace Jovanovich, Inc.

Laka, Itziar. 2006. Deriving split ergativity in the progressive. In Alana Johns, Diana Massam, and Juvenal Ndayiragije, eds., *Ergativity: Emerging Issues*. Dordrecht: Springer, pp. 173–196.

Lakoff, George. 1987. *Women, Fire, and Dangerous Things*. Chicago: University of Chicago Press.

Lane, Harlan., Penny Boyes-Braem, and Ursula Bellugi. 1976. Preliminaries to a Distinctive Feature Analysis of Handshapes in American Sign Language. *Cognitive Psychology* 8:263–289.

Laughren, Mary. 1982. Warlpiri Kinship Structure. In Jeffrey Heath, Francesca Merlan, and Alan Rumsey, eds., *Languages of Kinship in Aboriginal Australia*. Sydney: Oceania Linguistics Monographs, pp. 77–85.

Legate, Julie Anne. 2001. The configurational structure of a nonconfigurational language. *Linguistic Variation Yearbook* 1:63–99.

Léglise, Isabelle, and Sophie Alby. 2006. Minorization and the process of (de)minoritization: The case of Kali'na in French Guiana. *International Journal of the Sociology of Language* 182:67–85.

Leonard, Wesley Y. 2020. Insights from Native American Studies for theorizing race and racism in linguistics (Response to Charity Hudley, Mallinson, and Bucholtz). *Language* 96:e281–e291.

Lepic, Ryan, Carl Börstell, Gal Belsitzman, and Wendy Sandler. 2016. Taking meaning in hand: Iconic motivations in two-handed signs. *Sign Language & Linguistics* 19:37–81.

Levin, Beth. 1983. On the nature of ergativity. Doctoral dissertation, Cambridge, MA: MIT.

Levin, Beth, and Malka Rappaport Hovav. 1995. *Unaccusativity: At the Syntax-Lexical Semantics Interface*. Cambridge, MA: MIT Press.

Liddell, Scott K. 2003. *Grammar, Gesture and Meaning in American Sign Language*. Cambridge/New York: Cambridge University Press.

Liljencrants, Johan, and Björn Lindblom. 1972. Numerical simulation of vowel quality systems: The role of perceptual contrast. *Language* 48:839–862.

Lillo-Martin, Diane, and Edward S. Klima. 1990. Pointing out differences: ASL pronouns in syntactic theory. In Susan D. Fischer and Patricia Siple, eds., *Theoretical Issues in Sign Language Research*. Chicago: University of Chicago Press, pp. 191–210.

Lima, Suzi. 2018. New perspectives on the count-mass distinction: Understudied languages and psycholinguistics. *Language and Linguistics Compass* 12:e12303.

Linguistic Society of America. 2019. LSA statement on race. Online: www.linguisticsociety.org/content/lsa-statement-race, approved May 4, 2019.

Longobardi, Giuseppe, and Cristina Guardiano. 2009. Evidence for syntax as a signal of historical relatedness. *Lingua* 119:1679–1706.

Lucas, Ceil, R. Bayley, and C. Valli. 2001. *Sociolinguistic Variation in American Sign Language*. Washington, DC: Gallaudet University Press.

Lucas, Ceil, Amber Goeke, Rebecca Briesacher, and Robert Bayley. 2007. Phonological Variation in American Sign Language: 2 Hands or 1? Paper presented at NWAV 36, University of Pennsylvania, October 11. Available at: https://www.ling.upenn.edu/NWAV/abstracts/nwav36_lucas_goeke_briesacher_bayley.pdf.

Lupyan, Gary, and Rick Dale. 2010. Language structure is partly determined by social structure. *PLOS ONE* 5.1:e8559.

MacNeilage, Peter F., Lesley J. Rogers, and Giorgio Vallortigara. 2009. Origins of the left and right brain. *Scientific American* 301:60–67.

Maier, Emar. 2014. Language shifts in free indirect discourse. *Journal of Literary Semantics* 43:143–167.

Major, Travis, and Connor Mayer. 2019. What indexical shift sounds like: Uyghur intonation and interpreting speech reports. In *Proceedings of NELS 49* 255–264.

Mallery, Garrick. 1886. *Sign Language among North American Indians Compared with That among Other Peoples and Deaf-Mutes*. New York: Madison & Adams Press.

Mantovan, Lara. 2020. Exploring the effects of phrase-final lengthening in Italian Sign Language (LIS) noun phrases. *Revista Linguíftica* 16:250–273.

Marantz, Alec. 1991. Case and licensing. In Eric Reuland, ed., *Arguments and Case*. Amsterdam: Benjamins, pp. 11–30.

   1993. Implications of asymmetries in double object constructions. In Sam A. Mchombo, ed., *Theoretical Aspects of Bantu Grammar*. Stanford: CSLI Publications, pp. 113–150.

   1997. No escape from syntax: Don't try morphological analysis in the privacy of your own lexicon. In Alexis Dimitriadis, Laura Siegel, Clarissa Surek-Clark, and Alexander Williams, eds., *Proceedings of the 21st Annual Penn Linguistics*

Colloquium. Vol. 4.2 of *U. Penn Working Papers in Linguistics*. Philadelphia: Penn Linguistics Club, University of Pennsylvania, pp. 201–225.

Marentette, Paula., and Rachel I. Mayberry. 2000. Principles for an Emerging Phonological System: A Case Study of Early ASL Acquisition. In Charlene Chamberlain, Jill P. Morford, and Rachel I. Mayberry, eds., *Language Acquisition by Eye*. Mahwah, NJ: Lawrence Erlbaum Associates, pp. 71–90.

de Mareüil, Philippe Boula, Gilles Adda, Lori Lamel, Albert Rilliard, and Frédéric Vernier. 2019. A speaking atlas of minority languages of France: Collection and analyses of dialectal data. In Sasha Calhoun, Paola Escudero, Marija Tabain, and Paul Warren, eds., *19th International Congress of Phonetic Sciences, Melbourne*. Canberra: Australasian Speech Science and Technology Association, Inc.

Marten, Lutz, and Maarten Mous. 2017. Valency and expectation in Bantu applicatives. *Linguistics Vanguard* 3.1:1–15.

Martí, Luisa. 2020. Numerals and the theory of number. *Semantics and Pragmatics* 13.3:1–57.

Martin, Jack B. 2011. *A Grammar of Creek (Muskogee)*. Lincoln, NE: University of Nebraska Press.

Martinet, André. 1957. Arbitraire linguistique et double articulation. *Cahiers Ferdinand de Saussure* 15:105–116.

Marušič, Franc, and Andrew Nevins. 2020. Distributed agreement in participial sandwiched configurations. In Peter W. Smith, Johannes Mursell, and Katharina Hartmann, eds., *Agree to Agree: Agreement in the Minimalist Programme*. Berlin: Language Science Press, pp. 179–198.

Marušič, Franc, Andrew Nevins, and William Badecker. 2015. The grammars of conjunction agreement in Slovenian. *Syntax* 18:39–77.

Marušič, Franc, Andrew Nevins, and Amanda Saksida. 2007. Last-conjunct agreement in Slovenian. In Robert Compton, Magda Goledzinowska, and Ulyana Savchenko, eds., *Formal Approaches to Slavic Linguistics 15, (The Toronto Meeting)*. Ann Arbor, MI: Michigan Slavic Publications, pp. 210–227.

Matthews, G. H. 1965. *Hidatsa Syntax*. The Hague: Mouton.

Matthewson, Lisa. 2013. Strategies of quantification in St'át'imcets and the rest of the world. In Kook-Hee Gil, Stephen Harlow, and George Tsoulas, eds., *Cross-Linguistic Studies of Quantification*. Oxford: Oxford University Press, pp. 15–38.

McCarthy, John J., and Alan Prince. 1993. Prosodic morphology: Constraint interaction and satisfaction. Amherst: University of Massachusetts Amherst Linguistics Department Faculty Publication Series 14.

McCaskill, Carolyn, Ceil Lucas, Robert Bayley, and Joseph C. Hill. 2011. *The Hidden Treasure of Black ASL: Its History and Structure*. Washington, DC: Gallaudet University Press.

McGinnis, Martha. 2001. Phases and the syntax of applicatives. In Min-Joo Kim and Uri Strauss, eds., *Proceedings of NELS 31*. Amherst, MA: GLSA Publications, pp. 333–349.

Mchombo, Sam. 2004. *The Syntax of Chichewa*. Cambridge: Cambridge University Press.

McNally, Louise. 1993. Comitative coordination: A case study in group formation. *Natural Language and Linguistic Theory* 11:347–379.

Meinhof, Carl. 1906. *Grundzüge einer vergleichenden Grammatik der Bantusprachen*. Berlin: Dietrich Reimer.

Mel'čuk, Igor. 2003. Suppletion. In William J. Frawley, ed., *International Encyclopedia of Linguistics* 2nd ed. Oxford/New York: Oxford University Press.

Mitchley, Hazel. 2015. Agreement and coordination in Xitsonga, Sesotho, and IsiXhosa: An optimality theoretic perspective. Master's thesis, Makhanda, South Africa: Rhodes University.

Miyagawa, Shigeru, and Takae Tsujioka. 2004. Argument structure and ditransitive verbs in Japanese. *Journal of East Asian Linguistics* 13:1–38.

Montoya, Ignacio L. 2020. Enabling excellence and racial justice in universities by addressing structural obstacles to work by and with people from racially minoritized communities: Response to Charity Hudley et al. *Language* 96:e236–e246.

Moosally, Michelle. 1998. Noun phrase coordination: Ndebele agreement patterns and crosslinguistic variation. Doctoral dissertation, Austin: University of Texas.

Moskal, Beata. 2013. On some suppletion patterns in nouns and pronouns. Paper presented at PhonoLAM, Meertens Instituut, Amsterdam, September 6th. http://homepages.uconn.edu/~bam09006/Downloads_files/PhonoLAM_On some suppletion patterns in nouns and pronouns.pdf.

Msaka, Peter Kondwani. 2019. Nominal classification in Bantu revisited: The perspective from Chichewa. Doctoral dissertation, Stellenbosch, South Africa: Stellenbosch University.

Murdock, George Peter. 1959. Cross-language parallels in parental kin terms. *Anthropological Linguistics* 1.9:1–5.

Murphy, Andrew, and Zorica Puškar. 2017. Closest conjunct agreement is an illusion. *Natural Language and Linguistic Theory* 36:1207–1261.

Napoli, Donna Jo, and Rachel Sutton-Spence. 2010. Limitations on simultaneity in sign language. *Language* 86:647–662.

Napoli, Donna Jo, and Jeff Wu. 2003. Morpheme structure constraints on two-handed signs in American Sign Language: Notions of symmetry. *Sign Language & Linguistics* 6:123–205.

Nevins, Andrew. 2011. Multiple agree with clitics: Person complementarity vs. omnivorous number. *Natural Language & Linguistic Theory* 29:939–971.

Newman, Paul. 1990. *Nominal and Verbal Plurality in Chadic*. Dordrecht: Foris.

Nicodemus, Brenda, and Caroline Smith. 2005. Prosody and utterance boundaries in ASL interpretation. *Proceedings of the Annual Meeting of the Berkeley Linguistics Society* 32.1:275–285.

Nowak, Martin A., Karen M. Page, and Karl Sigmund. 2000. Fairness versus reason in the Ultimatum Game. *Science* 289:1773–1775.

Noyer, Rolf. 1992. Features, positions and affixes in autonomous morphological structure. Doctoral dissertation, Cambridge, MA, MIT.

Ohala, John, and James Lorentz. 1977. The story of [w]: An exercise in the phonetic explanation for sound patterns. *Proceedings of the Annual Meeting of the Berkeley Linguistics Society* 3:577–599.

Olson, D. 1977. From utterance to text: The bias of language in speech and writing. *Harvard Educational Review* 47:257–281.

Ortega, Gerardo, and Gary Morgan. 2015. Phonological development in hearing learners of a sign language: The influence of phonological parameters, sign complexity, and iconicity. *Language Learning* 65:660–688.

Padden, Carol A., and David M Perlmutter. 1987. American Sign Language and the architecture of phonological theory. *Natural Language & Linguistic Theory* 5:335–375.

Padden, Carol A., and Tom Humphries. 1988. *Deaf in America.* Cambridge, MA: Harvard University Press.

Pesetsky, David. 1995. *Zero Syntax: Experiencers and Cascades.* Cambridge, MA: MIT Press.

Pettenati, Paola, Silvia Stefanini, and Virginia Volterra. 2010. Motoric characteristics of representational gestures produced by young children in a naming task. *Journal of Child Language* 37:887–911.

Pfau, Roland. 2009. *Grammar as Processor: A Distributed Morphology Account of Spontaneous Speech Errors.* Amsterdam: John Benjamins.

Plaster, Keith, and Maria Polinsky. 2007. Women are not dangerous things: Gender and categorization. *Harvard Working Papers in Linguistics* 12:115–158.

Player, David. 2021. How the white deaf people benefit from white privilege. Available at https://dplayer84.medium.com.

Polinsky, Maria. 2013. Applicative constructions. In Matthew S. Dryer and Martin Haspelmath, eds., *The World Atlas of Language Structures Online.* Leipzig: Max Planck Institute for Evolutionary Anthropology. URL https://wals.info/chapter/109.

2018. *Heritage Languages and Their Speakers.* Cambridge: Cambridge University Press.

Postal, Paul. 1963. Some syntactic rules in Mohawk. Doctoral dissertation, New Haven, CT: Yale University.

Pranka, Paula M. 1983. Syntax and Word Formation. Doctoral dissertation, Cambridge, MA: MIT.

Py, Bernard, and René Jeanneret. 1989. *Minorisation linguistique et interaction.* Genève: Droz.

Pylkkänen, Liina. 2008. *Introducing Arguments.* Cambridge, MA: MIT Press.

Quer, Josep. 2013. Attitude ascriptions in sign languages and role shift. *Proceedings of the 13th Meeting of the Texas Linguistics Society* 12–38.

Rezac, Milan, Pablo Albizu, and Ricardo Etxepare. 2014. The structural ergative of Basque and the theory of Case. *Natural Language and Linguistic Theory* 32:1273–1330.

Rice, Keren. 1986. Some remarks on direct and indirect speech in Slave (Northern Athapaskan). In Florian Coulmas, ed., *Direct and Indirect Speech.* Berlin: Mouton de Gruyter, pp. 47–76.

2006. Ethical issues in linguistic fieldwork: An overview. *Journal of Academic Ethics* 4:123–155.

2021. Can formal linguistics help language reclamation? Paper presented at the WCCFL 39, Tucson: University of Arizona. Available at: https://youtu.be/1gWAw0O-1vM.

Riedel, Kristina. 2009. The syntax of object marking in Sambaa: A comparative Bantu perspective. Doctoral dissertation, Leiden: Leiden University.

Riehl, Anastasia. 2008. The phonology and phonetics of nasal obstruent sequences. Doctoral dissertation, Ithaca, NY: Cornell University.

Rizzi, Luigi. 1982. *Issues in Italian Syntax.* Dordrecht: Foris.

1997. The fine structure of the left periphery. In Liliane Haegeman, ed., *Elements of Grammar*. Dordrecht: Kluwer, pp. 281–337.

Rodrigues, Cilene, Raiane Salles, and Filomena Sandalo. 2018. Word order in control: Evidence for self-embedding in Pirahã. In Luiz Amaral, Marcus Maia, Andrew Nevins, and Tom Roeper, eds., *Recursion across Domains*. Cambridge: Cambridge University Press, pp. 111–126.

Ross, Lee D., Teresa M. Amabile, and Julia L. Steinmetz. 1977. Social roles, social control, and biases in social-perception processes. *Journal of Personality and Social Psychology* 35:485–494.

Sagey, Elizabeth. 1986. The representation of features and relations in nonlinear phonology. Doctoral dissertation, Cambridge, MA: MIT.

Salanova, Andrés. 2007. Nominalizations and aspect. Doctoral dissertation, Cambridge, MA: MIT.

Samek-Lodovici, Vieri. 2015. *The Interaction of Focus and Givenness in Italian Clause Structure*. Oxford: Oxford University Press.

Sanches, Mary, and Linda Slobin. 1973. Numeral classifiers and plural marking: An implicational universal. *Stanford Working Papers on Language Universals* 11:1–22.

Sanders, Nathan, and Donna Jo Napoli. 2016. A cross-linguistic preference for torso stability in the lexicon: Evidence from 24 sign languages. *Sign Language & Linguistics* 19:197–231.

Sanders, Nathan, Pocholo Umbal, and Lex Konnelly. 2020. Methods for increasing equity, diversity, and inclusion in linguistics pedagogy. In Angelica Hernández and M. Emma Butterworth, eds., *Proceedings of the 2020 Annual Conference of the Canadian Linguistic Association*. Online: https://cla-acl.artsci.utoronto.ca/wp-content/uploads/actes-2020/Sanders_Umbal_Konnelly_CLA-ACL2020.pdf.

Sandler, Wendy. 1989. *Phonological Representation of the Sign*. Dordrecht: Foris.

2012. Visual prosody. In Roland Pfau, Markus Steinbach, and Bencie Woll, eds., *Sign Language: An International Handbook*. Berlin: De Gruyter Mouton, pp. 55–76.

Sandler, Wendy, and Diane Lillo-Martin. 2006. *Sign Language and Linguistic Universals*. Cambridge: Cambridge University Press.

Sapir, Edward. 1930. Southern Paiute, a Shoshonean language. *Proceedings of the American Academy of Arts and Sciences* 65:1–296.

Sauerland, Uli. 2018. False speech reports in Pirahã: A comprehension experiment. In Luiz Amaral, Marcus Maia, Andrew Nevins, and Tom Roeper, eds., *Recursion across Domains*. Cambridge: Cambridge University Press, pp. 21–34.

Saussure, Ferdinand de. 1916. *Cours de linguistique générale*. Paris: Ch. Bally et A. Sechehaye with the collaboration of A. Riedlinger.

Schembri, Adam, David McKee, Rachel McKee, Sara Pivac, Trevor Johnston, and Della Goswell. 2009. Phonological variation and change in Australian and New Zealand Sign Languages: The location variable. *Language Variation and Change* 21:193–231.

Schlenker, Philippe. 1999. Propositional attitudes and indexicality: A cross-categorial approach. Doctoral dissertation, Cambridge, MA: MIT.

Segall, Marshall H., Donald T. Campbell, and Melville J. Herskovits. 1966. *The Influence of Culture on Visual Perception*. Indianapolis, IN: Bobbs-Merrill.

Seki, Lucy, and Andrew Nevins. 2018. Strategies of embedding and the complementizer layer in Kamaiurá. In Alessandro Boechat and Andrew Nevins, eds., *O apelo das árvores*. Campinas: Editora Pontes, pp. 417–444.

Sells, Peter. 1987. Aspects of logophoricity. *Linguistic Inquiry* 18:445–479.

Seyfeddinipur, Mandana, Manfred Krifka, Felix Ameka, Susan Kung, Lissant Bolton, Miyuki Monroig, Jonathan Blumtritt, Ayu'Nwi Ngwabe Neba, Brian Carpenter, and Sebastian Nordhoff. 2019. Public access to research data in language documentation: Challenges and possible strategies. *Language Documentation and Conservation* 13:545–563.

Shklovsky, Kirill, and Yasutada Sudo. 2014. The syntax of monsters. *Linguistic Inquiry* 45:381–402.

Siedlecki, Theodore, and John D. Bonvillian. 1993a. Location, handshape & movement: Young children's acquisition of the formational aspects of American Sign Language. *Sign Language Studies* 78:31–52.

Siedlecki, Theodore, and John D. Bonvillian. 1993b. Phonological deletion revisited: Errors in young children's two-handed signs. *Sign Language Studies* 80:223–242.

Sigurðsson, Halldór Ármann. 1991. Icelandic case-marked PRO and the licensing of lexical arguments. *Natural Language and Linguistic Theory* 9:327–363.

Silbiger, Nyssa J., and Amber D. Stubler. 2019. Unprofessional peer reviews disproportionately harm underrepresented groups in STEM. *PeerJ* 7:e8247.

da Silva, Mário Coelho, and Andrew Nevins. 2020. Maxakalí has suppletion, numerals and associatives but no plurals. *Linguistic Variation* 20.2:271–287.

Simango, Silvester Ron. 2019. English prepositions in isiXhosa spaces: Evidence from code-switching. In Raymond Hickey, ed., *English in Multilingual South Africa: The Linguistics of Contact and Change*. Cambridge: Cambridge University Press, pp. 310–328.

Simpson, Jane, and Gillian Wigglesworth. 2019. Language diversity in Indigenous Australia in the 21st century. *Current Issues in Language Planning* 20.1:67–80.

Singerman, Adam. 2018. The Morphosyntax of Tuparí, a Tupían language of the Brazilian Amazon. Doctoral dissertation, Chicago: The University of Chicago.

Siple, Patricia. 1978. Visual constraints for sign language communication. *Sign Language Studies* 19:95–110.

Skilton, Amalia. 2021. Tone, stress, and their interactions in Cushillococha Ticuna. Ms., Austin: University of Texas.

Smith, Henry. 1997. "Dative sickness" in Germanic. *Natural Language and Linguistic Theory* 12:675–736.

Smitherman, Geneva. 2017. Raciolinguistics, "mis-education," and language arts teaching in the 21st century. *Language Arts Journal of Michigan* 32.2:Article 3.

Snyder, William, and Karin Stromswold. 1997. The structure and acquisition of English dative constructions. *Linguistic Inquiry* 28:281–317.

Soltan, Usama. 2007. On agree and postcyclic merge in syntactic derivations: First conjunct agreement in standard Arabic. In Elabbas Benmamoun, ed., *Perspectives on Arabic Linguistics: Papers from the Annual Symposium on Arabic Linguistics*. Volume XIX: Urbana, IL, April 2005, 191–213.

Sotto-Santiago, Sylk. 2019. Time to reconsider the word minority in academic medicine. *Journal of Best Practices in Health Professions Diversity* 12.1:72–78.

Speas, Margaret. 2000. Person and point of view in Navajo. In Eloise Jelinek, Andrew Carnie, and Mary Willie, eds., *Papers in Honor of Ken Hale*. Cambridge, MA: MIT Working Papers in Linguistics.

Stampe, David. 1969. The acquisition of phonetic representation. In *Papers from the Fifth Regional Meeting of the Chicago Linguistic Society*, 443–451.

Steriade, Donca. 1993. Closure, release, and nasal contours. In Marie K. Huffman and Rena A. Krakow eds., *Nasals, Nasalization, and the Velum*. San Diego, CA: Academic Press, pp. 401–470.

Stewart, Dafina-Lazarus. 2013. Racially minoritized students at U.S. four-year institutions. *The Journal of Negro Education* 82.2:184–197.

Stewart, Jesse, and Martin Kohlberger. 2017. Earbuds: A method for analyzing nasality in the field. *Language Documentation and Conservation* 11:49–80.

Stoianov, Diane, and Andrew Nevins. 2017. The phonology of handshape distribution in Maxakalí sign. In Geoff Lindsey and Andrew Nevins, eds., *Sonic Signatures*. Amsterdam/Philadelphia: John Benjamins Publishing Company, pp. 231–262.

Stokoe, William C. 1960. *Sign Language Structure: An Outline of the Visual Communication Systems of the American Deaf*. New York: Buffalo University, reprinted in *The Journal of Deaf Studies and Deaf Education* 10.1:3–37.

Stokoe, William C., Dorothy C. Casterline and Carl G. Croneberg. 1965. *A Dictionary of American Sign Language on Linguistic Principles*. Washington, DC: Gallaudet College Press.

Sudo, Yasutada. 2012. On the semantics of phi features on pronouns. Doctoral dissertation, Cambridge, MA: MIT.

2016. The semantic role of classifiers in Japanese. In Susan Rothstein and Jurģis Šķilters, eds., *Number: Cognitive, Semantic and Crosslinguistic Approaches*. Vol. 11 of *Baltic International Yearbook of Cognition, Logic and Communication*. Kansas: New Prairie Press, pp. 1–15.

Sundaresan, Sandhya. 2011. A plea for syntax and a return to first principles: Monstrous agreement in Tamil. In Neil Ashton, Anca Chereches, and David Lutz, eds., *Proceedings of SALT 21*:674–693.

2012. Context and (co)reference in the syntax and its interfaces. Doctoral dissertation, Tromsø: University of Tromsø.

Suomi, Kari. 1983. Palatal vowel harmony: A perceptually motivated phenomenon? *Nordic Journal of Linguistics* 6:1–35.

Tabain, Marija. 2004. VC vs. CV syllables: A comparison of Aboriginal languages with English. *Journal of the International Phonetic Association* 34:175–200.

2009. A preliminary study of jaw movement in Arrernte consonant production. *Journal of the International Phonetic Association* 39:33–51.

Tabak, John. 2006. *Significant Gestures: A History of American Sign Language*. Westport, CT: Praeger.

Tamburelli, Marco, and Mauro Tosco. 2021. *Contested Languages: The Hidden Multilingualism of Europe*. Amsterdam: John Benjamins.

Tanaka, Yu. 2017. Phonotactically-driven rendaku in surnames: A linguistic study using social media. In Aaron Kaplan et al., eds., *Proceedings of the West Coast Conference on Formal Linguistics 35*. Somerville, MA: Cascadilla Press, pp. 519–528.

Telles, Edward. 2004. *Race in Another America*. Princeton, NJ: Princeton University Press.

Thornton, Abigail. 2018. Plural verbs, participant number, and agree. In William. G. Bennett et al. eds., *Proceedings of the West Coast Conference on Formal Linguistics 35*. Somerville, MA: Cascadilla Press, pp. 391–398.

Tkachman, Oksana, Gracellia Purnomo, and Bryan Gick. 2021. Repetition preferences in two-handed balanced signs: Vestigial locomotor central pattern generators shape sign language phonetics and phonology. *Frontiers in Communication* 5:612973.

Toosarvandani, Maziar. 2016. Vocabulary insertion and locality: Verb suppletion in Northern Paiute. In Christopher Hammerly and Brandon Prickett, eds., *Proceedings of NELS 46*. CreateSpace Independent Publishing Platform, pp. 247–257.

Topintzi, Nina, and Andrew Nevins. 2017. Moraic onsets in Arrernte. *Phonology* 34:615–650.

Truscott, Adriano. 2014. When is a linguist not a linguist: The multifarious activities and expectations for a linguist in an Australian language centre. *Language Documentation and Conservation* 8:384–408.

Tsikewa, Adrienne. 2021. Reimagining the current praxis of field linguistics training: Decolonial considerations. *Language* 97.4:e293–e319.

Veselinova, Ljuba. 2006. *Suppletion in Verb Paradigms: Bits and Pieces of a Puzzle*. Amsterdam: John Benjamins.

Voegelin, Charles F. 1958. Sign language analysis, on one level or two? *International Journal of American Linguistics* 24.1:71–77.

van der Wal, Jenneke. 2022. A featural typology of Bantu agreement. Oxford: Oxford University Press.

Weisser, Philipp. 2017. Why is there no such thing as closest conjunct case? In Andrew Lamont and Katerina Tetzloff, eds., *Proceedings of NELS 47*. CreateSpace Independent Publishing Platform, pp. 219–233.

West, La Mont. 1960. The sign language, an analysis. Doctoral dissertation, Bloomington: University of Indiana.

Westbury, John. 1983. Enlargement of the supraglottal cavity and its relation to stop consonant voicing. *Journal of the Acoustical Society of America* 73.4:1322–1336.

Wetzels, W. Leo, and Andrew Nevins. 2018. Prenasalized and postoralized consonants: The diverse functions of enhancement. *Language* 94:834–866.

Wilhelm, Andrea. 2008. Bare nouns and number in Dëne Sųłiné. *Natural Language Semantics* 16:39–68.

Wągiel, Marcin. 2018. Subatomic quantification. Doctoral dissertation, Czech Republic: Masaryk University.

Woo, Nancy. 1969. Prosody and phonology. Doctoral dissertation, Cambridge, MA: MIT.

Wood, Esther Jane. 2007. The semantic typology of pluractionality. Doctoral dissertation, Berkeley, University of California.

Woodward, James, and Susan DeSantis. 1977. Two to one it happens: Dynamic phonology in two sign languages. *Sign Language Studies* 17:329–346.

Woodward, James C., Jr. and J. Woodward. 1976. Black Southern Signing. *Language in Society* 5.2:211–218.

Woolford, Ellen. 1997. Four-way case systems: Ergative, nominative, objective, and accusative. *Natural Language and Linguistic Theory* 15:181–227.

Wray, Alison, and George W. Grace. 2007. The consequences of talking to strangers: Evolutionary corollaries of socio-cultural influences on linguistic form. *Lingua* 117:543–578.

Xavier, André Nogueira. 2014. Uma ou duas? Eis a questão!: Um estudo do parâmetro número de mãos na produção de sinais da Língua Brasileira de Sinais (Libras). Doctoral dissertation, Campinas, Brazil: UNICAMP.

Xrakovskij, Viktor. 1997. Semantic types of the plurality of situations and their natural classification. In Viktor Xrakovskij, ed., *Typology of Iterative Constructions*. Munich: Lincom Europa, pp. 3–64.

Yamada, Racquel-María. 2007. Collaborative linguistic fieldwork: Practical application of the empowerment model. *Language Documentation and Conservation* 1:257–282.

Yu, Alan C. L. 2003. Pluractionality in Chechen. *Natural Language Semantics* 11:289–321.

Zeller, Jochen. 2012. Object marking in isiZulu. *Southern African Linguistics and Applied Language Studies* 30:219–235.

Zimmer, June. 1989. Toward a description of register variation in American Sign Language. In Ceil Lucas, ed., *The Sociolinguistics of the Deaf Community*. New York: Academic Press, pp. 253–272.

Zoerner, Cyril Edward. 1995. Coordination: the syntax of & P. Doctoral dissertation, Irvine: University of California.

Index

absolutive, 27, 37, 40
agent role, 27, 28, 34, 38, 39
agreement attraction, 48, 49
allocutive agreement, 24
applicatives, 62, 146, 147
　asymmetric, 74, 78
　leapfrogging in, 67, 69, 70, 80
　recursive, 65
　suffixal, 63
　symmetric, 66, 67, 69, 70, 74
　syntax of, 65, 73, 79, 80
Arrernte, 167
assimilation of [+bimanual], 130–133
audism, 171

Basque, 26, 27, 30–33, 35–41
　gerundive forms, 33
　modal verbs, 34, 35
　perception verbs, 32–34
benefactive, 61–67, 69, 71–74, 78, 80
Berber, 165
Black ASL, 100, 101, 119, 122–125, 127, 128, 134
Bosnian/Croatian/Serbian, 46, 51, 53

causative, 69, 70
Ch'ol, 38–41
　genitive case, 39–41
Ch'ol, 38
Chaga, 64, 65, 69–71, 74, 78, 79
Chechen, 156–162
Chichewa, 62, 66, 67, 69–74, 78
circumoralized nasals, 92, 93, 95, 96
comitative, 149
conjunct agreement
　closest, 44, 46, 47, 54–56, 58, 60
　default, 47, 52, 54, 58, 59
　highest, 47–49, 52, 56, 58, 60
　in Arabic, 43
　resolution, 47, 48
　with objects, 59, 60
contested languages, 164

context parameters, 13, 15, 17, 18
　overwriting of, 15, 16, 19
contour tone, 94
Creek, 152, 155
CV syllables, 85

Dëne Sųłiné, 160, 162
Deaf Space, 101
diachronic change, 103, 105, 114, 115, 119, 121–123, 128, 130, 133
discourse buoys, 112, 127
Dispersion Theory, 96, 110, 111, 120, 134
ditransitives, 61, 69, 78
dual number, 53, 54, 139, 149, 152, 153, 155
　constructed, 152, 153
Dyirbal, 27, 28

earbuds, 88, 89
encumbrance, 118, 121
enhancement, 90–93, 95, 97
ergativity, 27, 28, 30, 31, 33, 34, 38, 41, 148
　and volitionality, 29, 30, 39, 41
　in suppletion, 145, 146
　split, 35–38, 40

fortition, 121
fundamental attribution error, 6

grammatical gender, 47, 53, 57
　agreement, 45, 49, 54, 55, 57, 59, 60
　and noun classes, 28, 57, 59

H_2, 102, 105, 107–109, 112, 115, 126, 132–134
Haitian Creole, 165
Hiaki, 138, 141, 143, 144, 146, 148, 150, 151, 155, 156, 161
Hindi–Urdu, 29–32, 37, 47
Hixkaryana, 166
Hopi, 147, 152
hypervoicing, 89, 91

193

Icelandic, 29–32
  dative sickness, 30
idiomatic expressions
  in Basque, 33, 35
  in Hiaki, 151
implicational universals, 85
index parameters, 16
indexical shift
  constraints on, 16
  implicational hierarchy of, 23
  obligatory, 21
indirect quotation, 12–14, 21, 24
inherent case, 30–32, 34
instrumentals, 62, 63, 65–67, 69, 71, 72, 74, 83

Kaingang, 92, 93, 95–97
Kamaiurá, 7
Kinyarwanda, 63, 64, 69, 70, 74

linearization of syntax, 45, 49, 55, 56, 58

Müller-Lyer illusion, 4
malefactive, 64, 65, 69, 70, 78, 80
markedness, 84
mass events, 158, 159
Maxakalí, 88–91, 93, 95–97, 152, 156, 161
minoritization, 8
monstrous operator, 2, 12, 18, 21, 22
morpheme structure conditions, 104, 108
mouthing, 101, 127

nasal shielding, 92, 97
nasal venting, 90, 91, 97
Navajo, 147, 149, 152, 155
Nez Perce, 23
'nonconfigurational' languages, 75, 77, 81, 83
nondominant hand, 108
  as a base location, 109, 110, 115
  as a classifier, 113
  representation of (*see also* H_2) 102, 107, 108, 132
nonmanual marking, 114, 121, 128, 135
Northern Paiute, 146–148
numeral classifier, 159–162

one-way bilingualism, 8, 167

perceptual decrowding, 120, 121
peripheralization of location, 105, 122
Pirahã, 166, 167
pluractionality, 116, 126, 152, 154, 156–159, 161, 162

postoralized nasals, 91–96
prenasalized consonants, 88–91, 94, 95
progressive aspect, 35–37, 39–41
Pronominal Argument Hypothesis, 77

reciprocalized semantics, 116, 117
roots
  as phonologyless indices, 141, 146, 154

Sambaa, 59
scrambling, 21, 23, 76
Sesotho, 58–60
Slave, 17–19, 23
slips of the hand, 105, 114, 130, 132, 133
Slovenian, 44–47, 53–56
speech errors, 142
structural case, 31, 32, 35, 36
sublexical structure, 99, 102, 103, 105
suppletion
  and defective nouns, 155, 156
  in kinship terms, 154
  number-sensitive, 146–148, 152–154, 157
  root, 138, 149, 153–156, 159
Symmetry Condition in ASL phonotactics, 105–108, 112–114, 121, 127, 134
syncretism, 54–56, 58

Tohono O'Odham (formerly Papago), 147, 148
transfer of possession, 61, 71–73, 78, 80, 81
Tsova-Tush, 29, 32, 39
Two-Step Agreement, 55, 56
Txapakura, 97

Ultimatum Game, 6
unaccusative predicates, 147
unconscious racism, 169
underspecification and the Subset Principle, 139–141
unmarked handshapes, 108, 110–112, 115, 119, 134
Uyghur, 19, 20, 22–24

Venda, 70
visual acuity, 119

Warlpiri, 75–79, 81–83, 138, 139, 141, 148
Weak Drop, 118, 119, 127–129
WEIRD populations, 3

Xhosa, 7, 56–60, 74

Zazaki, 2, 4, 6, 10–19, 21, 24
Zulu, 7, 58–60

For EU product safety concerns, contact us at Calle de José Abascal, 56–1°, 28003 Madrid, Spain or eugpsr@cambridge.org.

www.ingramcontent.com/pod-product-compliance
Ingram Content Group UK Ltd.
Pitfield, Milton Keynes, MK11 3LW, UK
UKHW020403120325
456051UK00006B/75